DAZZLED BY
DAYLIGHT

DAZZLED BY
DAYLIGHT

PETER CORNISH

DZOGCHEN BEARA

GARRANES PUBLICATIONS

First published in 2014 by
Garranes Publications
Garranes, Allihies, West Cork, Ireland

CreateSpace paperback	ISBN: 978 1 909483 576
Hardback	ISBN: 978 1 909483 545
eBook – mobi format	ISBN: 978 1 909483 552
eBook – ePub format	ISBN: 978 1 909483 569

Produced by Kazoo Independent Publishing Services
222 Beech Park, Lucan, Co. Dublin
www.kazoopublishing.com

Kazoo Independent Publishing Services is not the publisher of this work. All rights and responsibilities pertaining to this work remain with Garranes Publication.

Kazoo offers independent authors a full range of publishing services.
For further details visit www.kazoopublishing.com

Cover design by Red Rattle Design
Printed in the EU

Acknowledgements

I would like to thank all of the many people who have shared the dream and helped to bring it to fruition over the past forty years. It is thanks to you that there is now this jewel of peace and awareness on the far shore of the south-west of Ireland.

I would like also to thank those who have backed me in the recording of this little story, especially Patrick Naylor, who offered the visual aids that enabled me to write again, after decades, and thereby ignited this project. To my daughter Tara Sinclair, for her help and advice. To Kathleen Greco who worked tirelessly on editing the book while patiently deciphering my emails. And to Deirdre Gleeson who listened and laughed, and whose hard work kept me going. Thank you everyone. I love you and hope the result does you justice.

Contents

Book One

LEARNING TO DANCE

I

Salt Breeze of Freedom

We lingered between dreams in a grey summer town called Swansea. We were there because that's where the road from a past life had ended and a ship to the next one was waiting.

It was 1973 and we'd driven from Scotland in Harriet's old Renault 4. The small car was packed with essentials like a dustbin of dye plants and a Siamese cat, a spinning wheel and its sack full of tangled sheep fleeces. Top heavy, with two tea chests on the roof, we were thrown about while Harriet drove fast between juggernauts and a cross wind. I held my door shut because, like the bonnet, it was tied up with string.

On our way to the docks we stopped at a pub. The landlord said that we were underage and refused to serve us, although Harriet was twenty-four and I was already thirty. When I was younger that had happened a lot. I was never sure if it was my youthful looks or my childish behaviour. This time, perhaps it was our raggedy clothes or the long hair that was hiding our faces. Harriet started to argue, injustice being one of the few things that made her see red. As the publican escorted us to the door, she gave him one of her withering looks and snorted, 'Bizarre.'

We headed for the 'Innisfallen' which would shortly be sailing for Cork. Harriet hadn't heard of Cork until we decided to go there. The English were careful not to teach their children Irish geography, for fear that it might lead to history.

The ship began to vibrate as the sea boiled at its stern. Was I really going to Ireland at last? As a child, how many times had I dreamt of making this crossing? I felt the excitement catch in my throat as the cries of the seagulls were drowned by the siren. Was I finally leaving the old life behind? Would it be possible to get back to who I was, before integrity was traded for techniques of survival?

For centuries, people had been leaving Ireland in search of the future. Following the scent of material gain, our ancestors had succeeded and lost themselves in their rush down that road to success. Now we were going in the other direction. Chasing the grace that dies unmourned in the sickbed of mindless consumption; hoping to encounter ourselves in the silence of a land deprived of most of its people.

I leant on the rail to watch a beautiful gap widen between me and the past. They said that we'd love the easy freedom of Ireland, where they still used donkeys and carts and cut hay with a scythe. There were peat fires and long-handled pumps in the yard, and a humour that had all of the time in the world to concoct its unlikely story.

I watched the land fade and went below. I walked through the flashing nightmare of amusement machines and persons hurrying away from themselves. Why do we humans give off so much noise? I watched from a distance, too far from it all to be sickened or sucked into its vortex. How close we are to perfection. One glass door between us and the salt breeze of freedom, or a few steps downstairs to this hell of sugared distraction.

Harriet was tired and went off to look for a spare piece of deck. I climbed the steps to the night air, to dream and flip back through the pages. This crossing would serve as a 'bardo', or the space that is said to exist between two flickering facets of being. The space where we wander alone through the actions of our recent existence, while we're drawn like this ship on the tide to the next life.

I'd spend this night reviewing the years that had made me. Then I'd be ready for the new life to begin where the green fields of Ireland rise from the mists of the morning.

2

A Place Further In

My father taught us that every occurrence should be viewed as a lesson in our evolution. If we saw things like that, we'd benefit from both the good and the seemingly bad. Later, I realised the profundity of this simple doctrine, as it directed the flow of my life, but first, I needed to test it and its teacher.

Three small boys hurried down to breakfast while Dad was still shaving. He liked golden syrup on his porridge. The tin sat with its lid off, on a saucer, in the centre of the table. Aware of his aversion to touching anything sticky, we smeared syrup all over the green and gold label. Concentrating on his face as he reached for the tin, we whooped with delight at his theatrical grimace. Was Dad living up to his theory? Was he learning patience from his three little masters?

Washed ashore from those early years there remains the usual jetsam. Like lying in a pram, gazing at a perfect sky, with meaningless sounds from beyond. Now and again, a face would peer in to breathe at me. That's my earliest memory, I think. It's how it all started and nothing has changed. Life has been rather like that ever since. Half-interested strangers, wandering into my picture, making peculiar noises and wondering whether to poke me.

My mother read to me, my favourite story about Ferdinand

the Bull. He refused to go to the bullring to fight like the others. Instead he sat, all day, under a cork tree sniffing the flowers. Ferdinand the Bull was my hero.

Apart from that, it's all bikes and frog spawn, sticklebacks and snowballs, and leaping out of bed for the next adventure. There was day one of only one term at my first school. It was a convent that took a few small boys in order to terrorise them into never going near a girl in the future. I was called before the Mother Superior who sailed down on me like a malevolent albatross. She was vast and frightening. The starched white wings and canopies of her headdress circled above her. Pointing and threatening, they turned me to stone. And the big bold girls in the playground were equally scary. They were noisy and different and infinitely senior. They crowded my privacy with the menace of secret demands that they never made. They were the first girls that I'd encountered and I prayed that they'd be the last.

God lived beyond the forbidden corridor, in the dark swirling incense, guarded by his sister, the albatross. I never met him because he was very old and probably ill. At the end of that term he answered my prayers by arranging for my parents to move, and for me to be placed in a boys' school.

Here, there were people of the same age as me, who also wore short trousers and lifted the seat. There was a Dickensian classroom with a Dickensian master who lived on a perch near the ceiling. From a high wooden stool, behind a towering lectern, he read aloud for hours on end. He followed the lines with a long red nose that dripped like a tap. At the end of each page he'd look up to peer at his pupils. A dewdrop of snot would gather and glisten and finally splash into the book. Instantly, he'd turn the page with a flourish and slam his fist down to glue it, in an act of triumphant revenge.

This was the sixth year, and I wondered, would they go on getting better like this? My life expanded into the derelict school, in which we were the only class. There were corridors of empty rooms and wild gardens full of mysterious doorways. The whole contrivance was suspended in space, between a tree-fringed lake and a sweetshop. I decided that God was all right for delivering me from the aliens and letting me romp in his heaven.

Looking for ways to economise, my parents had decided to dispense with their car. So it was by train that, in the spring of 1950, I went for my interview at a preparatory school in Somerset. It was one hundred and forty miles from all that I knew, and I was seven years old.

In the May sunshine we walked up a leafy drive. My mother left me outside a friendly old building, surrounded by trees, on a path that was bordered by wallflowers. I breathed in their scent until it filled me and the world. There was no sound, except for the humming of bees, and the distant murmur of my mother and someone deciding my future.

I stood there, unexpectedly and utterly relaxed. Everything seemed to slow down and silently fizz with the ease of its own perfection. The warmth and its scent poured into me, until there was no room for the formation of meaning. I was alert and alone in the splendour. If words existed, they wouldn't have dared to enter this place. I seemed to have drifted into a different dimension; a realm where nothing matters and everything is always all right. It was my first intimation that there's a secret that lives further in. And the scent of wallflowers, warmed by May sunshine, has taken me there ever since.

Meanwhile, I was about to receive the first indication of something that would have a strong impact on the rest of my life. Eventually, it would usher me out of the pure land and make me a restless and rebellious youth.

We were walking down the hill past the church. My mother asked me to read what was written on a noticeboard at the church gate. I stared. The letters were too blurred for me to make out, although they were bright blue and bold. Trying not to show her concern, my mother read, 'The Kingdom of Heaven is Within.' Later, I couldn't help laughing at the thought that it was those words that informed me that I was half blind. As a teenager, I wondered if it was a message to tell me that there was no point in studying this external stuff, that I should look for answers inside.

At the time, however, neither this news nor its subliminal message made any impact at all. Except that I became the proud possessor of a pair of gold-rimmed spectacles. Unaware of the confusion to come, I was happy to be different and to look so very grown-up.

That September, I started at Thone as a boarder. It would be thirteen weeks before I'd see my family again; ten years until I'd be home for my birthday. Nevertheless, I found my way through by enjoying it all. I was good at my lessons and popular, so who cared about washing in icy water and suffering from permanent hunger? Who cared about the cold new formality that had something to do with becoming a man?

For all of my life I'd been Peter, and Peter was my guide and best friend. Now they changed me to someone called Cornish, who had to write home once a week and leave the letters unsealed to be censored. And they told us to give up 'Dear Mummy and Daddy', and start writing to 'Mother and Father'.

On Sundays, there was the long walk to church. We were kept in a crocodile by a sadistic Scotsman who hacked at our shins with his cane. He was no worse than homesickness or hunger. You just had to get used to them and, when it hurt, remind yourself how lucky you were, and that the bad was for your own good. And nothing was actually bad. Just when the winter term had lasted forever, it came to an end with the thrill of a train journey home. Home. I could hardly believe it. Home for Christmas. Home on a *steam train* for *Christmas*.

My mother came running along the platform to meet me. Years later, she dispelled the delusion that I looked so grown-up in my short-trousered suit and my glasses.

'You looked adorable, heart-breaking and much less than eight,' she told me. 'The peak of your cap was over one ear. Your glasses were filthy and bent. One lens was over your forehead and the other one over your cheek. They were held together with sticky tape. Your long socks were around your ankles and your muddy shoes were on the wrong feet, with the laces undone.'

And home was so warm and full of food and the absolute absence of school bells. And 'Father' came home from the office, laughing and hiding secrets in bright-coloured wrapping, while 'Mother' was exactly as kind as she'd been when she was still 'Mum'. As always, she inhabited the background and kept inviting us in.

Back at school, the years rambled in and out of their seasons. Even with my glasses, I wasn't sure that I could see like the others. The specialist patted my head and assured me that, with the new glasses, I'd have the sight of an airline pilot. So it couldn't be because of my eyes that I let through five goals in five minutes. When they called me 'butterfingers', the boys must have been right. None of us knew how little I could actually see, and it caused me few problems, because I did well in most subjects, but Latin.

When I was nine, our English master burst a dam in the stream of my thinking. He put words to vague intimations that were shuffling around in the schoolwork.

An old, ink-stained table was raised on a dais at the front of a dimly lit classroom. Beyond open windows, chestnut trees creaked in the warm afternoon. Pencils of sunlight dissected the darkness to spot-light the stage where the master was speaking.

'You see, all things have an edge to define them. Somewhere they stop and the next thing begins. This table, this chair and this book. This lesson, this day and the world. Everything you can think of has an edge or an ending. Can you think of one thing that does not?' Twenty-four small boys kept silent. They were forced to attention by the suggestion that we might be going somewhere less boring than grammar.

'Well?' He'd allowed the silence just enough time to underline his words twice. Then he said slowly, 'What about space, or the universe? Does space have an end? Think about that. Does it? Look up there, it must end somewhere, everything does. So if it has an end, where and what is that end, and what lies beyond it, and where does *that* end?' A cuckoo called from Gypsy Wood and a car door slammed in the distance. The master's words continued.

'So we cannot imagine its end, nor imagine it endless. Whichever option we choose, we have a dilemma. It doesn't make sense. It's beyond us. Although it's there, every day of our lives, our reason can't reason it out. We're baffled by something as simple as the space that we live in. So what do we do? We slap on a name like infinity. If we say infinity often enough, we start to take it for granted, but nothing is solved. We've merely tethered the truth to a label. Then, turning our eyes back to earth in relief, we ignore what's written in every day's sky: a startling reminder of mind's limitation, this encounter with proof that the truth is beyond the reach of our thinking. If you think about this, you'll begin to open your minds, and that is the start of true education.'

The sun still filtered through the chestnut trees. Scents of the summer drifted into the darkness to flirt with specks of luminous dust. The afternoon ambled in the direction of after-school games, and everything followed its normal routine. Everything except that, through this simple instruction, my life had changed, and a door had swayed open in the wall of the world that I was building around me.

I'd spent four happy years at that school. Academic success and my love of painting meant that failure at sports was no problem. I passed into 'Big School' and looked forward to entering that mysterious world that began by the cherry trees, at the end of the infirmary fence.

3

Rebellion

I was eleven years old. With the success of my first decade to support me, I might have been destined to sleep-walk into some bottomless profession. Now, all of this was to change. I was about to discover that those pretty cherry trees grew at the edge of a jungle.

My train arrived early on the first day of term. The old stone pile was deserted, so I walked alone in its grounds. Acres of rugby pitches stretched out to the horizon. Great white capital aitches sneered from every field. I wondered if they stood for 'Hero' or 'Hell' or, 'Ha-ha, we've got you now.' Here and there lurked the facilities that the English had devised to prepare their children for war; a gymnasium, rifle range and a cricket pavilion, a parade ground, armoury, tennis courts, running track, squash courts and more. I saw that the whole place was dedicated to the one thing at which I was useless. I had strayed into an adolescence to be wasted in the pursuit of an invisible ball.

As my heart sank, I took a deep breath. It was said that in 'Big School' you weren't always guarded so much. Maybe I could escape to roam in the unexplored world of the Somerset lanes. I consoled myself with the thought that, although this awful place might be a desert, it was a desert within an oasis.

In those first days I learnt that you were no longer judged by who you were, but by what you achieved in sport. If you failed, you were letting your side down, your house down, the school and your country beyond. Good at sport, and you were a hero. Good at lessons, you were a swot. I was placed on the wing of the worst team at rugby, which meant that the ball never got near me. I passed long hours alone in the outfield. Shivering and dreaming, I daubed mud on my knees and prayed for the final whistle.

Meanwhile, work was proving more difficult too. Larger classrooms meant that the blackboards were further away, and I was sure that the others could see them better than me. Almost sure. Except that again and again I was patted on the head by expensive consultants who assured me that, with these new glasses, my sight was as good as anyone else's. I wasn't sure what was going on. If my eyesight was all right, there must be something else wrong.

As the terms passed, I began to slip down through the grades. None of the staff realised that I couldn't see. They just considered me stupid and I settled for that. There was less stigma attached to being thick than to being short-sighted.

Seniority was everything. The first thing that you did, on returning to school, was to race to the notice board. Had you been promoted to a senior dormitory, and then made a prefect, maybe? Term after term I ran to that board only to turn away disappointed. As my friends passed me by, the initial anguish was fading. I began to find ways to subvert their primitive regime of jugular justice. Now, in class and outside, I was in the company of those of supposedly lesser intelligence.

I watched them and concluded that intelligence had nothing to do with it. These people, like me, had their own secret reasons for failure and, like me, they weren't sure what those reasons might be. Maybe it was psychological; maybe it was physical. Maybe life had already been tough. Perhaps, unlike some of us, they'd not had an idyllic beginning. As I saw them getting hurt and hiding their pain, I felt a growing contempt for the system that labelled them 'stupid'. I despaired of the brutality that never asked why, at 'lights out', they pulled the blankets over their heads when it was safe, at last, to cry.

Subjects like algebra and physics were worst. With formulae explained on an out-of-range board I'd dream through the lessons and get nought in the tests. The establishment used humiliation as an aid to shame you into pulling your socks up. Sometimes, I was made to stand up, to answer some especially easy question, sarcastically chosen for me. I'd discovered that silence provoked slightly less derision than a wrong answer. Standing before the class without speaking, I felt as though I'd crash-landed alone on the moon.

From all of this I learnt, first, that you should never judge anyone by their apparent achievement, and then that you should never judge anyone at all.

Whenever I could I escaped, beyond the school gates, to breathe the free air of unsupervised being. An industrial estate would have done, or anywhere else to get lost in. But what I found was a network of footpaths and animal trails that led to successions of sacred domains, each one a bit further into the magic. Like the stream in the fields at the foot of Rag Hill that slid through the day and my veins with willows to shade it from time. Like the wild iris pool where I once saw a snake in the water, as urgent as a dangerous whisper, come to entice me away from the seemingly real. Where I opened a door in the afternoon silence, and slipped into a world that was speechless and still.

In hours that I stole from timetables tightly configured to waste all your time, I picked at the knots of their training. In those long days of summer, I listened to the hum of the life-force at work in its garden. As the radiance increased and the afternoons stretched, I wondered why the world wasn't there on its knees. For in those natural retreats all worldly concerns soon come to a standstill. You pass through mental events like curtains of rain in suspension. The silence puts a finger to the lips of any attempt at a question. The bonds of requirement have loosened. You arrive at the place where thoughts relax into meaningless rhythms that dance with the incoming rustle of now. All that doesn't matter has faded away and nothing else matters at all. For one moment you've slipped from your tethers and nothing is left. Nothing is left but the love that belongs to those who no longer belong to the world.

And then the other life would come back, invading my pores like splinters of glass. I walked slowly towards the shouts and the whistle, sure of nothing but my footsteps beneath me, enriched by the secret that couldn't be spoken and entirely devoid of intent.

For some reason, I'd remained quite popular. Maybe it was because I was no threat, not being a part of the game. Or maybe it was because I hadn't the slightest inclination for anger or revenge. There was just this mischievous resolve to rock their pompous old boat, to expose their injustice, and have some fun in the process.

Challenges came from staff like 'the Pervert'. When giving a beating, he'd bend you over a chair on one side of his study and slowly reverse to the opposite wall. Then he'd run at you, holding the cane high over his head with both hands. Each stroke thrashed down so hard that sometimes it cut into your skin. We all dreaded this beating, which kept most of the other boys 'good'.

We were each given a little blue book of one hundred school rules. I decided that my education would be based on seeing how many rules I could break. I got beaten many times, and each beating only strengthened my resolve to put another tick in their book.

I was never bored when left to my own devices. Boredom came when I was forced to participate in something which I couldn't do. Like most of my lessons. Day after day, for interminable years, I gazed in the direction of a blackboard that I couldn't see. So, as an antidote, I developed the daydream and learnt how to practise it while remaining alert. This trick enabled me to avoid missiles from irritated teachers, like the wood-backed, blackboard duster.

It would come hurtling across continents towards me, while I hid deep in the rainforest, or hung floating in space, half of a light year from Saturn and Latin.

After a while, this curriculum of privileged misery had subjugated most of my friends. They'd been lured into the maze of the mad masquerade by the offer of various prizes. In the half-light that remained, once their spark had been smothered, they could no longer see what was happening to them. They were being churned out, like their fathers before them, on the conveyor-belts of tradition. In one hundred years everyone would be dead, but the system would have replicated itself to perfection.

I'd had enough of their gloom. I was constantly rescued from alienation by a slight sense of humour. My Irish grandfather had given me that, and it made me take myself and everything else with a large pinch of salt. I tried not to be distracted by the background drone of the lessons. Why were they boring us with all of this stuff, instead of revealing the secrets of the lanes and the stars?

When things got a bit tough, I would find a hidden location and build a new den. An alternative world of my own. It was a practice that would continue throughout my life, until I ended up building retreat dens for others.

From Rocky Ridge to Gypsy Wood, I built dens in the hedgerows and thickets. Usually I was caught and beaten and made to demolish them. Finally, on one of those shivering Sundays, in the after-lunch dusk of November, I discovered the ultimate refuge. There was a ruined and 'out-of-bounds' house in the woods, at a place they called Duckponds. Deep in the trees, a small lake surrounded an island covered with a grove of bamboo. You had to take off your socks and wade through a stretch of black water. Having cut a tunnel through the dense growth, from a concealed entrance behind an old willow, I carved out a circular clearing.

With a friend, sworn to secrecy, I wove the cut bamboos

through the growing stems to make walls and a roof. We spent all of our spare time in this hidden world, beyond the reach of the rules and the rulers. And it was always almost time to return to school. How could a Maths class last for a decade, when one stolen hour in a bamboo cave would race like the flash of a kingfisher flying downstream? The first intimations of the relative nature of time began to rustle like the wind in bamboo. Perhaps things weren't as sewn up as they were trying to teach us. Perhaps things like clocks were no more than a brazen attempt at control and consensus.

Years later I was to realise that, if you're somewhat awake, you really can learn from the continuous stream of instruction that comes without words. However if, like me, you're sound asleep and dreaming, progress comes more by way of a series of jolts. So, the next lesson I needed to learn in the hard way.

One misty Sunday, I clambered up the bank behind the guardian willow. Slipping on the mud, I fell on the pointed stump of a cut bamboo. It struck the left lens of my glasses, skidded off and buried itself in my scalp. I got back to school in a sticky red haze, my Sunday suit covered in blood. The doctor told me that I was lucky to still be alive. My schoolboy's toughened Triplex lens had saved my eye and maybe my life. I had fallen with such force that the stake would have thrust through my eye and into my brain.

Lying in hospital, I thought about being teased and called 'four-eyes'. How I'd wished that I didn't need glasses, and what a waste all that wishing away was. The glasses had been sitting on my nose, waiting to save my life. I wondered if it was like that with everything? Perhaps we just get dealt what we need, but fail to see it because we're so busy complaining. Perhaps the negative is not really negative, but is there to help us to grow. My father had started that thought. From that moment onwards I was happy with the sight that made me wear glasses. When things became difficult, I told myself that if I could see I'd be dead.

And that was the point of my bamboo retreat. It taught me that this precious life is a necklace of events, strung on a thread made of breathing. And its fragility is constantly increased by the way that we take it for granted.

Since the school had a policy of avoiding all of the relevant subjects, it certainly wasn't going to teach its boys about sex. However, in our first term, a prefect treated us to a sex lecture one night after 'lights out'. From then on we were left to dream about girls, as well as we could, especially those of us who had yet to meet one in person. They were shrouded in mystery, so high on their plinths in the sky that I had no idea of how I would ever make contact.

I began to devote myself, more and more, to the breaking of rules and taking the beatings. I'd walk into the Pervert's lair with my head held high in silent defiance. Various boys stood outside, in solidarity, counting the strokes. Holding back tears, I told myself that they could beat me as much as they liked, but I'd never be beaten.

The masters would ask who else was involved in a given misdemeanour, but they'd receive no answer. This was the one rule in our own book, and it could never be broken. We took extra lashes in order to protect other boys from a beating. It was under interrogation, with the housemaster tapping the cane on his palm, that they accidentally taught us the meaning of honour. As a side effect of the establishment's crimes, I learnt the satisfaction of taking the blame for another. This was the true team spirit that had no sides, but included us all. It had nothing to do with the insidious divide of the playing field. That 'team spirit' was no more than a device to train us to fight for the empire. I watched the boys chasing the ball and obeying the whistle. How uncivilised to put your team before anyone else's. How ignorant to think that there could be more than one team.

I lay in the grass out of sight, and miles from being told what to do. Life was perfect when everything but the natural world had subsided and you were escaping from cricket. I was in the team that they contemptuously labelled 'The Rabbits'. Sometimes our lot would go unsupervised because we didn't matter. This day was a day like that. We put on our flannels and strolled to the remotest pitch. Once there, we fiddled the scorebook for a game that we had no intention of playing.

I relaxed and inhaled the scent of July. I would have quite liked to play cricket. Why couldn't I do so? I *knew* that my eyes weren't as good as the consultants insisted. I *knew* it, whatever they said. I wished that I knew what the others could see, then I'd know about me.

My thoughts sailed lazily by, like a string of clouds in the Somerset sky. Can we ever know what anyone else sees? Or tastes, or is feeling, or hears? I watched two dragonflies drift from the stream, to clatter around me in clumsy embrace. We might merge our genes for the future, but no one can marry another one's mind. Afloat on the swell of a moment's release, I lay there, with nothing more urgent than dreaming.

'Hey, Cornish,' Rawlins was peering into my pram, 'we think we'd better play a couple of overs, before we go in.'

'Rawlins, see that cloud up there, what does it look like to you?' I asked.

'Like the games master coming to find out that we've cheated,' he snorted.

'No seriously, d'you think we all see the same world, or do we see things differently? I mean, look at that cricket bat.'

'Oh God, here we go. It's a bloody cricket bat. Of course we all see it the same.'

'But I'm not sure that we do,' I went on. 'For a start, I bet if you scored a century with it, you'd see it differently to me, if the Pervert had used it to beat me. But that's not the question. The real question is *how do we know?* Maybe I see this grass as green and you see it as red. How can I possibly know what you see?'

'You could get me to paint a picture.'

'That was my answer at first,' I replied. Rawlins sat down

beside me. He knew that the only way back to the cricket was via the end of my theory.

'You see green as red. I give you the paintbox and ask you to paint me a field. You want to paint the field red because that's the colour you see it. So which colour paint do you stick your brush in?'

'In the red,' he said.

'No you don't. You put your brush in the paint which you *see* as red, which is green. With this green paint you paint a lovely green field, which you see as red. So you have your red field, I have my green field, and neither of us is any the wiser. All that's happened is that we've both joined the conspiracy that a field is *called* green, whatever colour we see it. We agree to disagree without even knowing that we differ. I suspect that maybe it's always like that. In which case, reality is no more than a gentleman's agreement to pin down the truth with a title. I heard about that in an English lesson at prep school. Now I'm wondering, if we all see things differently, who is correct? Who sees things as they actually are?'

And as we ambled back to the cricket, I swore that I would find out. I wondered if we just make everything up as we go along, until we end up with a life. 'There must be an answer,' I said to the dragonflies and the unimpressed afternoon.

I'd accepted that my time at school was not to be highlighted by academic achievement or sporting success; rather, it would be defined by occasional thoughts, interspersed with corporal punishment. My childish reveries were enabled by my failure, which ignited in me the certainty that *they* had got it all wrong. This was what my English master had meant, when he said that everything's possible if we open our minds and refuse to believe blindly all that we're told. The experts assured me that I could see, but I didn't see what the other boys saw. At the time, this made me unique and confused. I was forced to puzzle about our perception. Later, I saw it as the nucleus of my self-education and the reason why, at an early age, I was already questioning the so-called 'real'.

I was aware that all of my thoughts had been thought for

aeons before me, and my eyes would prevent me from getting much from the books of previous thinkers. I wasn't going to come up with anything new, but I had to find out for myself.

Two subjects made little use of the blackboard. I still came top in English and Art, although top of the bottom class meant nothing at all. I loved the little that I was able to read, one word at a time, and I loved the smell of oil paints and the colourful world that I entered through the gates of the easel.

The high point of summer holidays was a trip to Cornwall where Grandpa Mac had a cottage called Downderry in honour of Ireland, or otherwise south to the Hampshire coast. At 'Woodlawn', in the New Forest, he lived with an uncle and aunt. The country was soft and the yellow clay at the entrance to fields made even the earth look like gold. There was a leaping Dalmatian called Hamlet who came to collect us from New Milton station in the old black Daimler that smelt of pipe smoke and leather warmed by the sun. There were clouds of Red Admirals, and an ancient tortoise on Grandpa Mac's lawn. He had a large, timbered house with mullioned windows and a fig tree that held up the sky. The dark interior glinted with copper warming-pans, clocks, and porcelain ladies who curtsied when you entered the room. Treasure glittered in the light of log fires and the scent of apple smoke clung to your dreams.

And wrapped around the old house was the Garden of Eden on Earth. It was our magical playground, hived off from a school-life that had ceased to exist, and where the only discipline in the whistle-free world was being called in for lunch or the beach.

The old-fashioned herbaceous border cascaded with colour. Haloed by butterflies drunk from the buddleia, it shimmered with excitement at being alive. There was a fishpond for my younger brother to fall in, the moment that we arrived, and the bewildering scent of mimosa. The sky-piercing spires of cypress trees were where the fairies slept in the daytime. They were tired from their night-rides on petals of roses that drifted down from the walls of the house. They knew that we boys were coming to visit their garden, so they left sweets for us in secret nests made of moss.

Grandpa Mac sat in the conservatory with the French windows open onto the lawn. He read reports of the cricket in the Times and puffed on his pipe. He looked as kind, as wise, and as slow as his tortoise, with whom he'd been there forever. And he'd stay like that, in his Trilby hat, until the whole world was all right.

Then, too soon, it was time for the train back to school. I failed to notice my mother trying not to show us her tears, because I was too busy hiding my own. She thought that I loved school because I'd started that way. I couldn't disillusion her. It would have broken her beautiful heart.

Dormitories stretched on either side of the headmaster's study, and above it rose the school tower with its clock. Proud and severe, it struck out the time of our lives. It brainwashed its students into accepting that there are twenty-four hours in a day, and thirty-odd years in a mortgage. It stood at the centre of all that was wrong, believing itself to be right. I knew that I had to conquer that clock and take my revenge for its lack of compassion.

There was a ladder in an 'out-of-bounds' hall, next to the headmaster's door. This led to a trapdoor fastened by a padlock. The rare quality of the upcoming adventure cried out to be shared, so I recruited four more boys who were confused by their failure.

It was two in the morning when one of them woke me. At the top of the ladder we unscrewed the clasp of the lock and climbed excitedly into the darkness. By torchlight, we climbed further ladders to the works of the clock. We found a small door that led outside to a ledge with a parapet. Five proud young princes surveyed their domain, from the castle that they'd taken in the silence of the Somerset night.

That tower became campaign headquarters for the nocturnal

activities of an elite group of barefoot boys in pyjamas. We had the run of the school, from the chapel to the kitchens. We climbed over the roofs to the pool for moonlight swims in the pee-soup that was suddenly inviting. One boy was intent on devising a way into the armoury, while another was studying the works of the clock.

Every few nights for all of that summer, we turned their battlefield into our playground, the boys who were no good, and I. We'd thrown off the chains of their judgement and, at least while they slept, we could fly.

Each morning, before breakfast and after our cold-water wash, the sixty boys of School House were lined up outside the library. We were brought to attention as the clock struck the first stroke of eight. On the last stroke we were marched off, in step, to the chapel, like the oppressed generations before us.

One morning the clock started to strike and we came to attention. When it reached nine, no one was sure if they'd miscounted the strokes. By eleven, the sniggers gave way to applause, as the solemn old clock struck on and on. We looked at one another, those of us on the inside. Our nights in the tower were over. We had put a small spanner in the spokes of tradition, for the boys who'd obeyed for a hundred years. And we smiled because each of us knew that, at last, we'd done something truly worthwhile with our lives.

I was always mindful of what that master had taught me when I was nine. Of how little we see and how much there is to be seen. I related this to my own experience of random events that seemed to defy explanation. Like predictions that I'd made which had somehow come true. These were never thoughtful forecasts of some future occurrence. Rather, they were spontaneous outbursts that arose without any thinking at all. If I thought for an instant, it wouldn't work.

Hearing a list of the Derby runners, one name had stood out so clearly that I involuntarily said it aloud. The horse won, and when I'd done this a few times, people took notice. Each time I'd absolutely no doubt that the horse would win. If however, I thought that I'd *try* to predict a winner, it invariably lost.

There were various other incidents, and the result was a thought which represented the next stage in my self-education. These predictions made no logical sense, yet were just too frequent to be coincidental. Where did they come from? There must exist a knowledge that's always available; a knowledge that's beyond temporal constraints; that's obscured by this process of thinking. I was sure that everyone had the same capacity for encountering stray fragments of information released from the storehouse of infinite knowing. I was a long way from understanding anything yet, but I was sure that I'd blundered through the next door.

While my mind was trying to inch open, my heart was flooded with the light of the lanes. With a couple of boys, I joined a natural history project. They were recording the movements of small mammals in the overgrown fields adjoining the woods. This entailed rising before dawn to check the aluminium traps that we'd set the previous day. Suddenly, it became legal to wander our world while the rest of its boys were still sleeping.

In awe we'd walk to the fields, where an early mist was wrapping the morning in silence and silver. The sky grew lighter as we knelt by the hedgerow not daring to whisper. Hidden and tingling, we witnessed the procession of upcoming day. No one would dare to sleep through the increasing magic, except for the arrogant ones they call 'human'. All else that was living was waiting and holding its breath.

First slowly, then quickly, and all at once, suddenly, the birds started to sing and the mist turned to rose. The day was on fire with the brilliance of being, and we were as young as its morning and in the front row. We moved round the fields through the gossamer dew, trying not to upset the perfection. One by one, we opened the traps, checking the tags, and releasing the exquisite small creatures.

Why did we need to map out the magic? What right did

we have to meddle with the balance of these ancient domains? Should we not sit and watch from a distance, or tiptoe through the fields of existence, aware that our eyes are too far from our feet? It was from those early days in the kingdom of voles that I developed the life-long habit of rising in time for the dawn.

And so, as the years passed, my childhood was enacted in the near distance. Always I wondered, who was this boy who followed me around, tethering his dreams to the stars? I lived in the space between him and the disturbance called 'people', which brushed past me now and again. And it was all a mysterious journey into whatever came next. I never had to deal with gremlins and phantoms, demons or the big bad wolf. It was everyday life that lurked, out of range of my sight, in the shadows; such an unlikely story that leapt out to surprise me, and then kept turning out fine.

One afternoon I sat in the library, towards the end of those days. I was supposed to be studying options for a career. The stuffed heads of various wild creatures, shot by old boys, eyed me from plaques on the walls. I watched sunlight struggle through the leaded panes of the past. They'd tried to stuff my head too, but I couldn't arouse the slightest interest in any of their schemes for my future. Besides, the exam results would rescue me from so restricting my life.

I gave up and reached for one of my favourite books. It was a large, leather-bound *Life of Vincent Van Gogh*. He, too, recognised the insubstantiality of all that surrounds us. He never jumped into their bucket. Here was a real man in whom I could believe, unlike all of these spendthrifts of possibilities' promise.

Again I read about his dream of gathering a group of free-thinking artists, living and working together. Now *that* inspired me. A stuffed antelope gave me a wink. There's my career option; that's what I'll tell them. I'll start an antidote to this school. A place where there's no competition and prizes are given for kindness. A place where we can find out who we actually are. Perhaps that's the point, that's what they've been trying to teach me. I'll find some land and invite people who respect the rights of the spider as much as the president's tiger and have no need to hang trophies on walls.

The art master wanted me to go to art college. I told him that my painting was the one thing that I didn't want anyone to infiltrate, to channel or change it. Secretly, the main reason was that I knew I'd not see the still-lifes or the models. I was so tired of pretending, and had no wish to start it all over again. And I'd have given the whole of this world and half of whatever comes next to have enrolled at a College of Art.

I decided, instead, that the place for me was a course in hotel management. I could do that for a while. It would get me out of school and might equip me to enact my new-found dream and even enable me to travel. And I wouldn't give a damn in a subject like that, whether I failed or succeeded.

My father wanted me to stay at school but, by sixteen, I'd had enough. I left in the summer of '59, not on the fine white stallion on which I'd raced to the start, but on my own feet and ready to go.

In all of that time I'd met no one that I didn't actually quite like. I felt that even staff like the Pervert were all right, in their way. Perhaps there was an advantage in being unable to see much. I wondered if they could see things too clearly to leave any room for doubt. Doubt about the substantiality of an object. Doubt about themselves and me, and everything that happens under the sun and beyond it. I thought, doubt is the first ingredient. Essential, until you are certain. And I'd already discovered that you've no right to be certain, until you've found where the end of the universe is.

4

Ephemeral Action

Back at home, an uncertain schoolboy wondered how he could travel to manhood without ever driving a car. I decided that I could probably handle one of those fashionable Italian scooters. My parents, who'd hitherto denied me nothing said, emphatically, 'No'. The disappointment made me cry at the loss of freedom and status. I bought two panniers for my push-bike and cycled off into the traffic. Staying at hostels throughout Southern England, I came slowly to terms with the realisation that life on the outside might also include a few problems. But as I pedalled my way past dreams that I'd never achieve, I began to celebrate the feel of the wind in my hair, and the simplicity that has no need for a motor. Some weeks later I returned, ready for anything, secure in the decision that my own energy would drive me to wherever I wanted to go.

In the autumn I started at college. Being shy, it took time to make friends. I was living in my parents' house at Wylde Green and catching a train to the city. My room had two windows framed by a Mermaid rose and a jasmine, in a tangle of flowering that flooded the house with their scent. I'd drawn a map of the world across a whole wall, to inspire me to dream my way round the planet. My current painting always stood on its easel next to the bed. It was drawn up close so that I could see it when I awoke, full of ideas from the night. In my spare time I rambled the great wild park and longed for a friend. If you couldn't really see their faces, you couldn't catch their eye. If you couldn't catch their eye, how could you ever catch girls?

My mother brought healthy novels from the library, insisting that reading broadens the mind. But those books were like everything else. It all seemed to stop short of something that was waiting to happen, but never quite did. Something was missing but I didn't know what. I'd jump on my bike and ride to the country. Alone in the natural world, I felt that the trees, the lakes and the very air of the hilltops were concealing the secret. If I spent enough time with them on my own, surely they'd allow me to find out.

Of course, there was a purpose to the harmless trash that my mother brought home. I was reading a Nevil Shute novel when a paragraph leapt at me from the page. As I read it, I could feel my skin tingling and the hairs on my neck standing up. I stared at the page in a dream and read it again and again. It was nothing. Just a few lines about Buddhist monks in Rangoon. I'd no idea of what Buddhism was, and no idea of what had just happened, but from that moment on, I resolved to find out.

On Wednesday afternoons we were taught biology, and after one of those classes my world was changed by a first hint at the secret for which I'd been searching. That day, the lecturer had obtained a number of frogs. We were each expected to vivisect one, and do something obscene with its still-beating heart. I had no problem with the insides of animals. To the disgust of my brothers, it was I who asked to help Mother disembowel the Christmas goose. But the goose was already dead.

I despaired at the thought of this carnage; at the lack of respect for those beings. Cutting them open while they were still breathing was one more example of the barbarity of the system. I said that I wouldn't do it. Could I not take the frogs to the pond, and we'd believe whatever the lecturer told us? He said that they sometimes got students like me, and it was all right to be squeamish. Realising that this otherwise affable man had been brainwashed, I agreed to sit out the class. But I couldn't leave it at that.

'Do you really think that I won't do it because I'm squeamish?' I asked. 'This is not about me; it's about these beautiful creatures. I believe there's no difference between what you're about to do, and me performing live experiments on you. At least if I did, I'd save you from torturing frogs.' I went to the canteen with a book, surprised at my new-found audacity.

'What are you reading that trash for?' Harvey enquired when their orgy was over.

'I don't know,' I replied, 'I keep asking myself the same question.'

'I'll lend you mine when I've finished,' he said. 'It's a real book. It's called Demian. It'll lead you towards a place that they kept secret at school.'

And there it was. 'A place that they kept secret at school' was the only place that I wanted to be. I'd been handed a key to the next shining door and, through it, I began to meet real people amongst the pages of a new world of books. There were *others* who knew that something was missing, and I could hardly bear the excitement.

I discovered the spoken-word section in the record shop. I saved up and bought *Molly Bloom's Soliloquy*, *Under Milk Wood* and Dylan Thomas reading poems by Auden and co. It was a start. I sat in my room every evening, entranced as they silenced the new rock 'n' roll and the homework.

This period of my life was like falling in love with someone who was struggling to break through from a different dimension. She stole my appetite, making me tremble as she flitted through the pages, leaving her scent but never quite achieving a form. I longed for her to step shyly into my world, to take my hand and be real.

Hudson's was Birmingham's one bookshop that offered more

than trivial novels, mechanics and football. Now I hung about
Hudson's as much as I dared without buying. It was here that the
muse came to life. She was called Sandra, and she was a siren of
the beat generation, sent to beckon me in. She had a pale moon face
with enormous eyes that were outlined in black. Her jet straight
hair was parted in the middle, and curved down to two points
at her chin. She drifted amongst phrases of hidden significance
that might have been ordinary when spoken by anyone else.
Occasionally, she emitted the first syllable of a chuckle that was
as unnerving as her black stockings, black corduroy coat and the
corduroy bag that hung from her shoulder and grazed on the
ground.

I couldn't take my eyes off Sandra from Hudson's. One day
I actually spoke and it sounded all right, so the next day I spoke
a bit more. Then we met at the Kardomah Cafe on New Street.
I was already in danger, before she told me that her father had
been Dylan Thomas's doctor.

At the jazz club I met Danny who played the trumpet. He was
the coolest guy on the planet. England's haircut was a 'short,
back and sides', and America's was the crew cut. If a boy's hair
touched his ears, it was considered outrageous. Hair was about to
become the symbol of our revolution: the rejection of Victorian
values that still ruled society and stifled our attempts to start
breathing.

Danny's long flaxen hair fell straight off his head and over
his ears, with an inverted 'v' for his face. He wore a baggy black
suit with trousers a foot too long for his legs. They ruffled in
folds above his exaggerated winkle-picker boots. His mouth
was occupied in rotation by a trumpet, a pipe and a bottle. From
amongst his various layers, he'd fish out something by Beckett,
and proclaim it to an unconvinced world. Samuel Beckett was
an honorary member of Danny Pawson and the Artesian Hall
Stompers, and Danny was one of his characters.

I began to skip college as I followed the trail that was opening
before me. The work was easy and I could keep up by attending

half of the lectures. Ought I to allow myself to go on being tutored in commerce and the anatomy of the pig? Or was my place on the edge of a seat in the deserted matinee picture house, with Brando and Tennessee Williams? Or finally taking my first girl to the flicks, only to find that she was with James Dean, and I was there to pass her the tissues. That girl was Christine Perfect, later of Fleetwood Mac.

Hoping to entice me to spend more time at home, my parents purchased their first television. But it was too late. I was proud that I was the only boy at school who'd grown up without one. I wasn't going to let it infiltrate my independence of thought at this stage.

Sometimes, the students got jobs as waiters at functions. We worked for little and relied on the tips. The girls were told to serve food while the boys took care of the wine. It was back-to-front thinking by the system as usual. One time like this was a banquet for The Worshipful Company of Masons. When they locked the doors to do whatever they do in secret, we pulled the corks from forty bottles of wine. Out of respect, we took a swig from each bottle, to ensure that the wine was all right. Then the guests, in evening dress, seated themselves at the tables. Standing behind a diner's chair, I couldn't see clearly the glass. It was somewhere out there, on the white cloth, beyond the far side of the plate. I'd learnt to aim my bottle in roughly the right direction, then feel for the glass with its neck. Locating it, if I poured slowly, I could see the first splash of red on the linen, and adjust my alignment. With white wine though, sometimes the table got nearly as much as the glass.

So being a waiter was usually fun, but not always. One Christmas Day I decided to work because the tips would be great. The meal, at Sutton Golf Club, was for a bevy of Birmingham businessmen and their Birmingham businessmen's wives. We were on our best behaviour because we needed those tips. The meal went well and we served the coffee but still the wallets remained stubbornly in their pockets.

Each of the staff had given up Christmas for this. Some waitress mothers had travelled many miles, leaving their children at home. I decided to act. I got three silver platters and ostentatiously placed them along the length of the table. There were banal comments from sleek diners, who'd turned pink and wet and were mopping their brows. I retired to the kitchen and waited. They were still stuffing chocolates into smug faces, to reward themselves for material success. After an appropriate interval I entered to find that no tips had appeared. They started to cheer and to clap me. They might as well have been throwing tomatoes. Then they started to sing.

'Little donkey, little donkey ...' they sang, as I cleared the last plates from the table. 'Little donkey, plodding onwards ...' as I brushed the crumbs from the table. 'Little donkey, had a he-a-vy day ...' as I turned in the doorway, fighting the urge to bend down, grab the fucking table and upturn it. Upturn it to shower coffee and contempt all over these men, their fetid wives and their tiny, self-satisfied lives.

It was a great lesson, only half of which I learnt at the time. I'd learnt a little of the humiliation of the slave, although it was easy for me whose only chains were my own. And I'd failed to learn that, before I could grow, I'd need to replace contempt with compassion.

In June, my parents went away for a week, so it was *our* turn for a banquet. We prepared the traditional thirteen-course menu, as we'd been taught. The table was set in the open French windows, and the scent of the flowers was as intoxicating as the wines that came with each course. As Scheherazade played with rays of the evening sun, we toasted our right to be free. 'I am young, I am young, I am me,' I thought. 'Like a stray note of music that breaks from the score, to dance for a while with its kind, before it flies off into space.'

Philippa folded and fed me slips of smoked salmon while someone threw rose petals over our heads. After all, we'd recently seen *Dolce Vita*, and we were just seventeen. She'd been keen on me, Philippa had, while I was in love with Sandra from Hudson's. Maybe she'd given up on me now, so we could have fun, and I'd get rid of my wretched virginity at last. She'd gone to such lengths to look beautiful in her mother's silk dress. Previously, I'd only seen her in her art-college gear. In that, she looked so bedraggled and ragged that they'd affectionately nicknamed her 'Philth'.

Entremets was various exotic fruits doused with kirsch, but the food had become little more than a trolley, on which to wheel in the wine. It was misguided to risk hijacking the flight of the spirit with chewing. At school, I'd learnt to treat the constant hunger with disdain, and to eat anything that wouldn't actually kill me. Bored by the boys' endless discussion of dinner, I'd become scornful of eating, except as a means of survival. In any case, excessive feeding, in a starving world, was almost as gross as talking about it while doing so. I'd been brought up *never* to mention food at the table. So I raised my glass, intent only on erasing the mental activity that ruins the feeling.

After coffee and liqueurs I walked in the garden with Philippa, waist-deep in arcades of flowers. Then we went up to my room. The last rays of sunlight shone through petals of the Mermaid that filled in the window. The warm scent ushered us to the bed. I'd never even kissed a girl yet.

As I stroked her brow, she looked so fragile and vulnerable. Not at all like those too-glossy pictures of film stars that I'd imagined stretched out on my sheet. She lay there and looked at me, and I looked at her incredible eyes. I realised that I'd never really seen a girl's face. I'd never been close enough until now. Now I could see what all of the fuss was about. I'd no idea that eyes had such depth, or that they moved like that. I'd always seen them as static, fixed in their whites, like in paintings. They seemed so alive, so shining with light that I wanted to join her inside them. I was shocked by her lashes. They flickered so nonchalantly across her dark eyes, as though it were the easiest thing in the world. I saw her hair a-curl on my pillow, and touched it to check it was real. She smiled at that, a quick, uncertain smile that made me shiver with warmth.

'You are so alive,' I said quietly. Far away, I heard a song thrush and a steam train stake claims on the silence of evening. She smiled again, and then, instead of kissing her, because I didn't know how to, I said clumsily, 'Can I make love to you?'

She looked at me for a long time before she spoke in a whisper, with a smile close to tears. 'If you tell me that you love me, you can.'

I gazed at her lying there, and all I could think of was how incredibly precious she was. Of course I loved her and I could have said it without lying, but not in the way that she wanted. Not with commitment and strings round tomorrow and the eventual upheaval. So I knew that now she'd be hurt, whatever I answered. I thought that she might want me to say it, even if it was a lie, but I couldn't deceive her. And I felt sorry, and sadly inadequate, as we lay there in silence and turned back to back.

Moving into my parents' attic, I persuaded myself that this was all right because I'd really left home at the age of seven. Besides, most of my peers were still at school, so it was quite cool to have my own key to a garret.

I'd found the *Third Programme* on the radio and listened, enthralled, to broadcasts between the classical concerts. Someone read 'Howl' and discussed it with Ginsberg. There was a Cocteau play and Jean-Paul Sartre and Camus. I was discovering an amazing new world behind the facade of the old one. Running out onto the shining field, I was dazzled by displays of the new significance that taught me to dance without moving. Looking around, I saw nothing but networks of possible openings. I'd found out that it's true that there *is* more to a life than just this.

During this period, my parents' tolerance was thoroughly tested. I didn't offer much to the family meals, which I rarely attended. When I did, I'd sit there trying not to let their small talk impinge on my state of suspension. Sometimes, I'd want to explode. 'Phenomena are in flux all around you, I'm almost too excited to swallow, and you sit there discussing the price of the *butter* ...'

I began to write poetry. I knew that it was awful, but so what? Then we arranged readings in an upstairs room at the Greyhound. Under pressure to contribute, I delivered my first embarrassing poems to the world. Fortunately, the world wasn't listening because it was drunk. Fifty years later, in an old cardboard box, I came across some lines that I'd written to Sandra.

'... in this garden of flickering instants, nothing is real. Everything is changing too fast to be pinned with a meaning. Tides roll in and out without ceasing. There's only a state of perpetual dissolution and regeneration. How could I impose my feelings upon such a fluid revolution?

And the main thing is that it doesn't matter. Nothing matters. Not even who I am. For who could I possibly be, when I'm changed by each person and place that befalls me? So then, how could this evanescent flurry of energy want to be free? Surely freedom is the absence of wanting; even this wanting to be.'

Sandra failed to respond, but that was just part of the sensation of tingling that was beckoning me into the urgent new dawn of the sixties.

Four of us arranged summer jobs at a hotel near Bath, in a village called Limpley Stoke. I took my paintbox, 'The Outsider' and a chef's hat. The hotel was floating in iridescent space, close to the banks of the Avon. I was to live on my own, in a seventeenth-century cottage, in a deep wooded lane by the river. My job was to help with cooking, and to take charge of the breakfasts. It was going to be hard to concentrate on anything other than the radiance of the landscape in June.

On the first morning, I gazed at a pan of boiling froth, into which I'd just broken twenty-one would-be poached eggs. With my glasses steamed up, I was fishing around with a wooden spoon, hoping to make contact with yellow. I was asking myself if I'd really found my vocation, when I was rescued by a kind old Irish cleaner. She arrived equipped with a perforated spoon and shoo'ed me away, saying that I'd more important things to be doing. Like the charcoal rashers that I'd left on the stove, and the long line of waiters waving dockets that I couldn't read.

That summer, anything could have happened without causing the least surprise. Situations arose and faded, leaving trails of graffiti, like laughter scribbled on sky. I was seventeen and head over heels in love with being alive. It seemed sacrilegious to do anything other than open and allow the magic to flow. I was thrilled into focus by the significance that fizzled in minor events, as I soared the thermals of freedom. Taking my paints, I sat for hours by the river, then drifted home, having forgotten to open the box.

Nothing was ordinary, while the extraordinary kept crashing through, into the so-called 'real'. One such event took place in the garden while I was painting amongst the roses. The lorry from Flowers brewery was climbing the steep drive to make its delivery. As it passed me, roaring and belching, the driver changed gear with a lurch. Before my eyes, a single barrel of beer dislodged itself from the load. It rolled down the hill, turned right, and buried itself in a ditch. After a while the lorry returned from its delivery and drove away towards Bath. It had dropped, at my feet, one hundred and forty-four pints. I strolled down the hill and did a little gardening, to keep our prize concealed until nightfall.

Later, after dinner, three of us rolled the barrel out of the gates, along the road and down a small track to the river. There was an ancient roofless cottage, unvisited and overgrown, in a coppice alongside the Avon. All of that summer we ran down to the river to drink and recite poems to the night-birds and stars. Sometimes Harvey brought his girl from the hotel and we swam naked in the slow dark water. Everything was new and enticing, as we re-wrote the world and promised to stay young until it exploded. By the shining river, I wrote my 'goodbye' to Sandra, inspired by a desire to transmit the extraordinary sensation of breathing.

'... I see people grow indignant over small issues. They huff and puff and submit, in flurries of participation. I find myself adrift in a world of irrelevant significance. Events dislodge themselves and dissolve in the void that conceives them. There must be more to space than space. It flexes as thoughts pass through it and erupts, here and there, in shell-bursts of ephemeral action.

'Sandra, I want to tell you of my discoveries before our time has run out. I'd like to kiss you but my mouth is too full of words. Perhaps I can fashion them into a bridge, to span this gulf, and meet you out there in the middle. But the same letters, in a different order, remind me that none of us meet. We only stumble into dream figures, dancing in a clearing of the wind. We strut about to stutter at our strangers, who hear no more than a slight rattling of bars. And to pass the time, we persuade ourselves that someone who looks cute, like you, might have once felt something similar.

'So, will we attempt to meet once more, or is our so-called "meeting" done? Did we only pass each other on the far sides of a foreign thought? Is everything already lost in the tossing of the waves between us all whose ways have crossed?

'In spite of everything, it seems to me that there's no need to go on shouting. No need to hide amongst the phrases that are but tombstones of moments that we missed while talking. The sadness surely comes from our temporary lack of silence and its clarity. If we could only stop demanding meaning, the whole ridiculous contraption might come sailing into view. It would bedazzle us, and blind our eyes with sight; these eyes of flesh that steal from us the ancient art of seeing.'

And then the leaves turned deeper green and it was time to leave the dream before its summer faded.

Now some of us began to display our attitude in our appearance. We wandered their suited cities with lengthening hair and scruffy clothing. The public became aware of this strange new phenomenon of 'will-o'-the-wisp' kids in navy corduroy and denim, sitting on their pavements. They labelled us 'beatniks' and said that beats were dirty.

We began to hitch to London. There were proper bookshops there, and London pubs and coffee bars with people who knew what we were saying. Sometimes an art college girl might come with us, but girls were still quite rare. More closely guarded than the boys, they had less freedom to rebel. However, there were a few in London. With crazy clothes and swirling, waist-length hair, they danced their strange mesmeric dance, those outcast angels of the jazz clubs. From a great distance, we fell in love with the bewitching beat-girls of the city called The Smoke.

On Friday nights, we slept on the embankment by the bridge at Charing Cross. We'd find some cardboard and lie down amongst the bushes by the river. When my visits started to extend from weekends into weeks, I looked for more permanent accommodation. I found the flat roof of an annexe to the bandstand that backed onto Villiers Street. I slept for many nights up there amongst the overhanging branches, and woke to watch the bowler hats beside me, bobbing by to business in the city. Sometimes, by the fires of the homeless, you'd feel the irrelevance of the endless fabrication; sitting on a kerb beside the Thames, cold and excited, wishing for nothing more urgent than morning.

On Saturdays we'd meet at a pub at Cambridge Circus and walk to the small basement at 51, Great Newport Street, and the all-night session at Ken Colyer's Jazz Club. Two kind old women sold tickets to the huddle of kids whose donkey jackets were pulled tight to keep out the wind. Below the narrow stair there was a long bare room, at the far end of which the band played while their heads grazed on the ceiling.

Ken Colyer, known as 'the Guvnor', was the real thing. He

never made money but he played all night while we danced, or lay listening on the floor. By four in the morning, half of the kids had crashed out where they lay, while a few still danced to the band that played whether anyone was conscious or not.

It was Easter '61, and we joined the 'Ban the Bomb' march when it rested for the night at Turnham Green. We got free food and a floor to sleep on, before the walk to Trafalgar Square. Then I hitched to Paris with John Klimczak, carrying sleeping bags and books in hempen sacks, having rejected anything as bourgeois as a rucksack. And it was Easter and I was in Paris. I was face to face with the paintings that had illuminated those empty years of schooling, and I was walking the shabby, shining streets of all my childhood heroes. Armed with a list for friends, in the Rue de Seine, we bought *Capricorn* and *Cancer*, *Ulysses* and other masterpieces banned in Britain. And we walked those famous pavements suspended by the love that knows of no need for another.

On our return to London, we went in search of a Dylan Thomas pub of Danny's. We found the Duke of York through an alley on Rathbone Street. It was run by the Mad Major, whose Great Dane occupied a chaise longue in the bar. The Major had a collection of neck-ties which hung along tier upon tier of strings, and covered every inch of each wall. Like most of our treasured pubs, it dispensed rough cider to students, poor artists and the unemployed, because cider was half the price and twice as strong as the beer.

High on Rilke and Rimbaud, how could I go back to college? Was not a precious moment of illumination wasted each time that the mind strayed into the wasteland of mundane education? For years I'd known that there must be another way; now I was close to where it might begin.

Uninclined to court a confrontation with events, I preferred to let things happen. It was all part of the dream in which I drifted. So, when I was warned that my lack of attendance at lectures might disqualify me from sitting the exams, I tried to look concerned, until it was agreed that I should pull my socks up. Having passed the first year's exams, I was sure that I could pass the next lot. Then I'd be qualified as a chef, and the final year would make a manager of me. I saw no point in that. They'd never give me a job when they saw my choice of attitude and clothing.

At the end of that summer term I sat the exams and passed them. Harvey, another friend and I, had secured jobs for the season in Davos. I was to work in the Hotel Meierhof, as the *garçon de buffet*, or slave. The pay was five pounds per week with no tips. It was nothing, and less than nothing in Switzerland, but the job was my passport to the mountains.

And before I knew it, there I was in the mountains. I'd woken the others in a panic. The train from Paris had stopped at Basel where we had to change. There were vinyl discs and their portable player. There were books and hats, bottles and us, scattered all over the carriage. We opened the door to hold the train and shovelled everything onto the platform.

Now we stood outside on the deck at the back of the mountain train from Zurich. The air was singing with the scent of the alpine flowers of the meadows. As we climbed towards Davos, apprehension was tapping my shoulder. Could I blackguard my way through this job without seeing it? I'd managed it so far but this one, in a foreign tongue, was different. My bad French was no use because they spoke Old Swiss. Could I manage without both speech and seeing? Would a *garçon de buffet* need to read illegible orders scribbled by flapping Italian waiters?

The others were working in a different hotel. Mine was smart, and I was soon settled into a room with fine views of the mountains. There were dockets all right, but I trained the Italians to call them out. I had to dispense the local wines, each into its relevant carafe. At first I got them wrong. Then, realising that my sense of taste was more reliable than my eyesight, I put it to work with each new order. Squatting behind the counter, out of sight and swigging, I still got it wrong, but it seemed to matter less.

We had to work from seven in the morning until ten at night, with a short break after lunch. Even so, sometimes I woke early and climbed the hill on the Strela side. I sat on a rock and watched fingers of mist pressed to the lips of the morning. They silenced that sacred hour, before the stirring of humans. High in my eyrie and perfectly still, I absorbed the grace that eradicates thought and grants you permission to be. 'Why be alone with the world,' I said, 'when, without it, you dance with the stars?' Far from the confusion of irrelevant action, up there, high above time and the people-line, there is infinite, decision-less space. There is nothing to prove and nothing to grasp at, nothing but the void and its flickering objects that dare you to defile them with need.

By the time that my weekly day off arrived, I was tired but determined to walk far up past the trees. Climbing higher, my lungs filled with the sparkling air and fatigue was shed like an overweight coat.

There's a point at which the clarity begins to shimmer. If you're still, you can hear it. The wide-open silence that is the sound of the mountains. Entering the moment, side-stepping the finite, you're in. You've slipped through a secret tear in the fabric and onto the terrace of eventual release.

You follow the looping of slopes that sweep to the sky. The natural perfection of geophysical motion that glides into life when time comes to rest. You've entered the realm of excitement that lowers the pulse rate. Paused in expanding space, you experience the tomorrow-less reception of all.

When humans are heard, everything freezes, and so we continuously miss all that is happening. We witness the world with its button on 'hold'. We've done that. We've frozen the movement like a sub-zero wind on the water. We've transformed reality from a miracle into a postcard.

But if you sit very still for a while, it all starts moving again. So, when our bodies move, they scare the natural world to a standstill. When our minds move, their motion makes everything solid. They pin it down, stick on our trademarks with a sigh of relief, and display it in the catalogue of absolute fact. But, with our bodies still, we allow the dance into being. Then, when our minds come to rest, we witness the scintillating flow of phenomena. In the stillness is revealed the constant fluorescing in and out of existence. The further from movement we stray, the closer we get to the innate movement of the seemingly static.

In those days, my uninformed mind had approached the first rudimentary glimpses of what I would later call meditation.

At the end of August I left the Meierhof, having arranged to meet Harvey in Zurich. He'd gone before me, to stay with relatives there. I spent a few days hitching in the hot sun with nights in ditches and hedges. It wasn't easy hitching in Switzerland, and less so when you looked like I did.

I met Harvey at the station and we took a tram by the lake to find somewhere to sleep. We came up with some rose-beds on the water's edge, still in the heart of the city. We waited for the evening sun to turn the lilac silk of the lake into velvet and went for a swim. Then we fed ourselves rye bread, salami and wine and sat by the shoreline, watching the lights of the steamers and stars.

In the morning, we took a boat for the day on the water. We rowed out into the centre and read Duino Elegies to the violet hills. We drank and we swam and we swam and we talked with the urgency of being alive at the start of it all. And we knew that there were no gods who'd ever been so brilliant, so young and so free.

Then we got a train to Schaffhausen, and a lift in the back of a straw-filled truck that took us to Turbingen with a disgruntled pig. Harvey's girl, Rosemarie, met us in Nuremburg and drove us home to real beds. I relaxed in the peace that came with the knowledge that I'd properly run up the aisles of eighteen, clanking my stick on their railings.

At a party in a candlelit cellar, Rosemarie came over and said, 'You should dance Peter. It's not good to be always alone.'

'But I'm never alone, and it's always good.'

'You were alone until I came over,' she said.

'I was dreaming in a room full of people. I don't have to dance, or even to talk. I can love you from here,' I claimed, with a mixture of honesty and brave self-defence. I wanted to tell her the other half of the truth. The aching half, which said that I was dying to dance with one of her beautiful friends, but I couldn't see how to make contact.

And it seemed that most of the best times, that year, had all been spent on my own. My journey had led me to the edge of the map of everyday things, and left me to find my way onwards. Perhaps I was too ready to think that no one else understood. Or perhaps I was merely protecting my 'self', as I tried to fly in the mysterious haze that sparkled with promise around me.

I reckoned that girls would take place when the time was right, even if the time was taking its time. So I thanked Rosemarie for her warmth as a stranger, who once took my hand at the end of a beautiful summer.

5

At the Party Alone

I returned to England and gave up my place at the college. I wanted to spend the winter in my attic, painting, writing and improving my French. There were times when I longed for a friend to share my secret despair at the void where my future should be. Then I'd wake, jump to my feet, bless my eyes for keeping me out of the rat race, and make plans to go a long way away when the spring came.

Now in the second year of the sixties, it seemed that something was stirring in Britain. Each time that we hitched to London there were a few more guys with long hair and a few more cool-looking girls. With our tongues too excited to be bothered with eating, we debated the world in the Partisan Caff. With each of us leaders of our empires of one, we stuck our proud flags in lands of the borderless future. We'd redress the balance, not with bullets or ballots, but by our crazy example. And we burnished our promise of change at jazz club nights on Eel Pie Island, while hitching south to the coast, or on the wall at St Ives.

I borrowed a new book from the library. It was *Seven Years in Tibet*. I was spellbound by every word of those stories of the ancient land and its wisdom. Perhaps it was beyond the Himalayas that I'd find the bit that was missing.

Then I met Norma. She was an art college girl. She came into the Kardomah Cafe, sat at my table and talked to a friend. The friend left and we stayed for a while. She was stunning looking, full of life, and I knew that I'd meet her again.

I found a job at an Exmouth hotel, where I could work for the season and save enough money to travel. I got off the train at the South Devon coast in May. The hotel was a rambling old pile that had fallen asleep one afternoon before the Great War. It snoozed by its fire of logs with its feet up, unaware of the passage of time, content in its threadbare enough-ness. I liked the garden and my small basement room, and I knew that this was about to become another radiant summer.

I was a station waiter with four tables to tend. The job was easy so long as you didn't take yourself or the customers seriously. When they were up the wall in the kitchen I simply stood back and let the others fight to go first.

After work sometimes, I'd cross the road and lie down for the night in the sand dunes. I loved to sleep under the stars, and wake to the sound of the surf and the taste of its salt, and the first light over the water.

On a day off, I caught a train up the river to Exeter. Wandering the town, I drifted away from my body and entered the ceaseless stream of perfection. I could see myself walking, although I could no longer feel the disturbance of action. I'd slipped into a state that was vividly awake but entirely detached from sensation. I watched from outside and above me, the exquisite movements of a unified dance, in which all phenomena were timelessly equal. I was divorced from identity and out of range of the effect of events.

That's how I remember a spiritual experience that inspired the rest of my life. Having seemed to exist for a while, outside my body, I received confirmation that there's more to us than this physical form, with its projected version of a universe to contain it. Decades later, I found the following description that I wrote at the time, as the ordinary state began to come back and stick like glue to perception. I wanted the clarity to continue forever, and that 'wanting' was wearing it out.

'... I'm in Exeter, sitting in the Old Ship Inn. The radiant serenity of the morning is slightly less bright, as I chase the state with my pencil. I'm neither happy nor sad, nor equally both, whatever those words care to mean. I'm cast off, adrift and slightly trembling, without the implication of movement.

'A particular place, a certain time, a chance glimpse through a side window; an inaudible click, and I'm out of my hands, suspended in immaculate space and ready to die or whatever. I am untouchable, for who is there to touch or be touched when gross physicality is subsumed in the subtle? How could there be any such thing as a meeting when everything is already met in this dance of diffusion and fusion? When superimposed upon one another, our forms glide in and out of manifestation?

'I feel so close to the source that I smell it, but I mustn't try to follow the scent. I must let it occur and let it drift by. You can never find your way here if you try. You can only open your fists and feel the stream as it brushes your fingers. The door is wide open but you have to stumble upon it. If you start fishing around for a meaning, the spell will be broken. Besides, in this place, each proposition is perfectly matched by its opposite. Conflicting philosophies collide like ghost ships that sink, leaving only ghost ripples that merge. Here you must come to the only conclusion that nothing is true and everything's true of everything else.

'Now, occasional events cruise by, trying hard to look like they mean it. The show is accepted just as it is, without an ounce of understanding or judgement. I'd sing, I'd dance, if I dared risk the disturbance because, in this instant, I'm almost alive.'

An envelope arrived from Norma. It was the first mail that I'd received from a girl. I was surprised because I'd only seen her a few times in the café. There was just a photo of herself, looking so young and beautiful with the close-cropped hair of a boy. She'd had it chopped off and had sent the photo to prove that she'd seen 'Au Bout de Souffle', as I'd urged her to do when I left.

There was a Hungarian waiter who stood like a bull and got all of the girls. He told us unlikely stories about his heroic escape through the Iron Curtain in a hail of machine-gun bullets. He was proud and dramatic and so vulnerable that he could have been slain with a well-aimed word.

He asked me to play table tennis because he wanted to impress the new waitress by wiping me out. Perhaps he wanted to win too much. Perhaps I could see the white ball quite well in the semi-dark room. Or perhaps I also wanted to impress the new waitress. The difference between us was that I'd nothing to lose, because the girl was already destined for him.

Whatever the reason, I started by winning and continued to win. I won almost every point, so blatantly that it had to be mind over matter. I was the mind and he was the matter. But he so desperately needed to win that I had to relent.

My mother had taught us that it's unkind and un-sporting to win by too much. You should never humiliate your opponent. Sometimes, the honourable thing was even to lose. Well, I'd not had much practice at winning and really couldn't care less. Besides, there was no option; I quite simply couldn't bear the macho-man's anguish. Within one point of victory, I'd proved myself to myself. So, taking care not to make it obvious, I let him win point after point until he'd achieved a miraculous comeback. I told myself that, if you win, there's a winner and loser. If you lose on purpose, nobody's hurt, and everyone is a winner.

That was a great day because, later, I sold my first painting. It was a fantasy of Spain which was where I was planning to hitch with the money from work. The cost of living in Spain was extremely low, and this island called Ibiza had no airport, no cars and no tourists. It was peopled by locals and artists, so maybe I could stay there and paint.

That painting was not at all like the series I'd brought with me to finish. They attempted to depict the fragility and transitory nature of this latest blast of existence. They were each in blue and white; shapes folding out of space and fading away. The twists and spirals of infinite possibility that occasionally coalesce into a form that we slap with a name. Like a body, which we inhabit for a moment, before we move on with a further slight shift of the patterns. The waxing and waning of life, in the form of the face of a girl; its features coming together and passing, before you have time to reach out to its brief fluidity.

One afternoon, I climbed up from the end of the beach and followed the coastline through farmland. As I walked the cropped grass of the headlands, the thought that I was probably not meant to be there aroused a feeling of heightened significance. Each gate made it less likely that the public ventured this far into the ongoing layers.

I came to a track and two great ivy-grown gateposts of stone. Skirting the hill, I looked down on a group of old buildings. They stood together on the edge of the cliff. Below them and beyond was nothing but endless water and space. It was like the picture that I'd been carrying in my head since school. The career-choice of a dream that I wanted to build. The previous year, while walking alone in the Lake District, I'd seen such a place by the lakeside. What impressed me was not just their spectacular positions, but their complete isolation from a world that had receded beyond location and time.

I was inspired by the thought that, if I kept seeing this place, one day it would come true. Or were my dreams no more than sky castles in the clouds of a lonely youth? I continued along the cliffs, through the gates of the various dimensions that would filter me back into Devon. There was no doubt at all once I got there. I climbed back down into the exquisite claustrophobia of Budleigh Salterton, and its lace-curtained peek at the past.

I finished my job and hitched away in late summer. Arriving in St Ives, I walked through the town to 'The Wall'. There was nobody there but the tourists, packed like oily sardines laid side-by-side on sand in the sun. The council knew the symbolic significance of 'The Wall at St Ives'. It had become an icon of a new generation over whom they were losing control. Restless young people hitched from all over Britain to meet there. It was a metre wide, built of stone, and ran along the back of the beach. We'd roost there and play there, perched above the ice creams and the burning flesh. Then we'd walk the headlands to Clodgy, and sleep by driftwood fires on the sand.

Since my last visit, the council had cemented a ridge to the wall to prevent us from sitting on it. I climbed up and sat on the apex to read. Then Perry Foster, a guy from the Black Country joined me, to sing Leadbelly songs with the aid of his twelve-string guitar.

Longhaired, navy-blue kids slowly appeared from cracks in the system. We passed round a bottle of milk and sang to the naked tourists of England. Soon, a flock of dishevelled young waifs had covered the wall, and the council could only complain that we misbehaved by keeping our clothes on.

I stayed for three days in St Ives, but it was no longer the same. They'd hired heavies with guard-dogs to stop us spending the nights on our beach. They'd prevented the pubs from letting us in, so threatened were they by our peace and our hair. So we gave up on Ives as it turned its back on the times that were changing. For gone was the moment when we danced to the roar of the surf and our urgent new songs of tomorrow, when the future was ours and the thought made us rich, though our pockets held little but sand.

Back at home, I found a message from my parents who'd gone sailing with my brother Simon in Wales. They'd invited me to join them at a cottage in Newquay. I was afraid that I'd be terrible company, what with my book and the magic that arises only to those on their own. Fortunately, my selfishness was rendered irrelevant by Mother, who was happy to spend her time painting while the others were sailing. I was free to drift through each shining day, only now and then nudged by the pulse of events. I ambled the empty beaches and the flickering light of the cliff-lands. Everything was momentous, poignant and instilled with implications that had long since discarded their burdens of meaning. I came to rest in the endless stillness, in love with a love that is aimless and free, because it has nothing to love or to lose.

And everything being already perfect, how could I not have encountered Jack Patrick's? Outside the village was the old Black Lion Hotel, which they said had seen better days. Did they not know that there were no days better than these? Its overgrown garden had statues, cracked and half covered in ivy. Paint was peeling from weed-grown walls and its door was invariably bolted. I was told that Jack Patrick, the landlord, had been cut off by the electricity board, by the brewery and everyone else. They said that if I knocked he might let me in, but I wouldn't if I was them. Since I was particularly keen not to be them, I knocked on the door and he did. A couple of old guys were drinking pints at a table. Although it was daytime the shutters were closed, and the room was lit by the light of various candles. He'd managed to acquire one wooden barrel of Bass. It perched proud on the bar, in front of the shelves whose rows of bottles were empty.

On the table, where I sat, lay an open book of poems by Theodore Roethke. Flashing like a beacon, waiting for my eyes, the first line read, 'Was I too glib about eternal things, an intimate of air and all its songs?' I wondered if it meant that I should tame my youth's exuberance and come down from my tower. Or, because it spoke of the magic in the past tense, was it a warning that these sacred times were coming slowly towards an end?

On the floor there was a scattering of books. The first one that I picked up, I recognised by its shape. It was *Finnegans Wake*, but it was I who had died. I must have lost my life somewhere out there in the splendour, and migrated to this inn, in the back streets of a personal heaven.

I split the next days between deserted beaches and this empty, overflowing page from the past. I learnt that Dylan Thomas used to stay there to write. The landlord told me stories of the time of the poet; of agents arriving from London in search of a script; of them standing behind his chair, making him write, to protect him from himself and the bar.

I'd already questioned the likelihood of life as it appeared to take place. Now, this place was one more proof that the whole thing was no more than a humorous projection. How else could I have stumbled into these dusty remains, suspended for a last moment in time, before the improvers moved in to hoover the magic? Though entranced by the flawless unfolding, I was clear that it wouldn't last like this for much longer. I wondered if I'd arrived at some sort of a turning. I couldn't read what was written on signposts of tomorrow, but I lingered, loath to forsake the arena. Loath to let go of this lonely haphazard of years, where I constantly expected to be stopped in my tracks by a sudden intervention of wonder.

So of course, as soon as I returned home, I was only half surprised to hear that Norma had been trying to call me. She'd heard that I was planning to hitch around Europe and could we meet before that? She came to my attic where we talked and played music. Kissing her quickly on the lips as she left, I wondered if I was beginning to get my first girlfriend. In the morning, I sent her a dozen red roses, and hitched to the Dover ferry.

From the Sunday Times, I'd cut out some words by Sophocles. I glued them onto the first empty page in my passport, as my own visa to enter the fray. They simply read, 'Lost peaks of the world, beyond all cares. Wellsprings of night and gleams of opened heaven. The old garden of the sun.'

I hitched to Paris, left my sack at the Gare de l'Est and sat down with a glass of wine and a pencil. But I was so in awe of the place that I couldn't defile it with words. I decided to catch a train to meet Harvey and then start to hitch south. He'd finished at college and taken a job at a Munich hotel. He'd urged me to hurry, to be in time for the start of Oktoberfest.

In the bahnhof, the early Germans smelt of aftershave and polish. Their smart clothes and close-cropped heads made me conscious of my tramp-like appearance. Outside the station, the streets were seething with people. No cars in the road, just crowds behind barriers lining the pavements. It was 23 September and some special event was about to take place. I could hear a brass band from somewhere behind me.

The police checked my passport and directed me to Harvey's place on Maximillianstrasse. They told me to follow the tramlines, expecting me to walk behind the crowds on the pavement. But in order to see the tramlines, I needed to get one on either side of my feet. It seemed quite logical to me. So I found myself walking straight down the middle of the empty street, while on either side, the crowds were standing ten deep.

There was no way back. I was trapped between twin banks of staring Bavarians, as I marched up their tram tracks alone. They were craning their necks to catch a glimpse of some event that I was inadvertently leading. Groups of them started to cheer, whistling and catcalling at me, as I reached the stands at the Opera. I wondered if it was because of the sack that I carried over my shoulder. Why, when I kept trying to hide, did I always end up on the stage? Was this latest chicken-run just one more page of the curriculum that I was supposed to absorb, in order to nudge me? Had I laid it all on to surprise me?

I was relieved when Frau Speiser showed me into Harvey's room. He explained that the first day of the Oktoberfest came in September and he'd been watching from his window, astonished to see me leading the inaugural procession. He opened a bottle of wine and we perched outside on the sills, high above the parade. I told him my plan to hitch through to Venice, Florence and Rome, then back across France and down to secret Ibiza. He asked me when I was going to grow up and I told him, 'later'. And we did go to the Oktoberfest, but I was itching for the anonymous road. I knew it wouldn't be easy, but I had a world to see and a need to get thoroughly lost.

The one slight problem was that I couldn't see what might be coming towards me, so I thumbed every noise that approached.

Sometimes it was a lorry and sometimes a tractor. Maybe an ambulance, the police, or a car crammed with people, waving that they were already full. I just kept on hitching until the noise had gone past. At first it was sometimes embarrassing, but then I got used to the looks that I couldn't see. And to the catcalls, most of which came from my head. I just hoped that nothing would hit me, as I put my faith in the impertinence that made me continue. And then, a few days out, I completely lost the need to care about my concepts, or the concepts of others.

On the first day I made good progress. I found a supermarket and bought a bottle of wine and some bread. These new supermarkets were great, but still quite rare. They meant that I could get close enough to see what I wanted to buy. No need to speak the language. No need to point at an item behind the counter. An item that I couldn't quite see, and which had a fifty-fifty chance of being a loaf of bread or a bath sponge. From those sorts of shops, I sometimes emerged with strange things to put in my sandwich.

A car picked me up in the twilight and we drove with one star and a rising moon along the wet strip that led like an arrow towards the unknown. It was dark when they dropped me on a Danube bridge. I climbed down the steps and walked a short way to some trees. I crawled into my sack with my books and my bread, my wine and the sounds of the river. I was now exactly where I wanted to be. Out of the city, away from the noise of the judgements of others. No one in the wide world knew where I was. I drank the wine to wash down my excitement and slept.

I arrived in Vienna where I stayed at a hostel with other kids from the road. We were shocked by the strength of the Viennese grip on the proper order of things. They were so certain that they were correct and had no idea what to do when we asked them to play. I and a friend met two girls from Paris, bought bread and fruit and attempted to sit on the Viennese grass. Wherever we sat, someone in uniform arose from the postcard and moved us away. We'd set off from different parts of our planet in search of something that would never be found in Vienna. So before we went our separate ways, we bought bottles of wine and we danced all night, with fat old women in a bar by the river, to songs like Lili Marlene.

From Vienna I got lifts, here and there, in and out of the Alps. I had no idea of where I was going, and not knowing was better than knowing. Then, on reaching the plain, I slept in a cornfield. The mountains were a jagged blue memory, like smoke from a bonfire of junk from the past. Finally, the next day, I came into Venice, unreal in a drift of watery light. We sat on steps by the Grand Canal, anyone with long hair, a guitar or a dream. We made music and drank to the spontaneous congress of disaffected youth that was gathering, here and there, all over the world.

From Venice, a single lift took me to Rome. Two men were tasting wines for their restaurant in the south. We kept taking side roads into the hills, to fairy-tale farmhouses nestled in hideouts from time. As they tasted, they insisted that I drank. We travelled through dense dimensions of green, to doors in walls that were there before time began, and would remain until long after it was all over. Doors that opened into renaissance kitchens where fat farmers' wives slap-sticked laughter and pasta all over my cries of 'enough'.

I spent a few days in Rome, almost awe-struck but never inspired. The decadence of the Vatican and Colosseum were just ticks in a sightseer's guide. Creepy reminders from Caesars and Popes of what too much power can allow.

Meanwhile, the Romans were having problems with my appearance. They were so natty, with their short greased hair and their high-shining shoes that mirrored their razor-sharp suits. In France, I was completely accepted, not even noticed, but Italy was still in the grip of its past. In some quarters I encountered open hostility towards my growing hair. At the Colosseum, a group of school children actually started to stone me. I was relieved that history had confiscated their chariots and lions.

I hitched north to Florence where I smoked my first hash on

the steps of a church with a stranger. And Florence relaxed and showed me her treasure. But I wanted to get to Ibiza, to stay in one place for a while with people who were open and easy. I hitched over to Pisa and then took ten days to walk much of the way round the coast.

After Genoa it got almost impossible to hitch the Italian Riviera. I walked it and slept in any bit of green space. With the season over, there was a melancholy feeling to the shuttered grandeur of the towns. I was finding it hard to get fed and my earlier confidence died with the absence of lifts. I felt lost in an alien world.

Although I was relieved to reach Menton and get back into France, it still took a long time to walk through the cold Cote d'Azur. I arrived in Marseille, one windswept evening, as it began to grow dark. I took a bus towards the hostel, asking the driver to tell me when we arrived. It grew darker and colder, until it was black and I could see nothing outside. One by one, the silent passengers left, until there was no one but me, clattering into the night. Finally the driver muttered that I had arrived. I got down and watched the bus-lights rattle away.

I was in total darkness and there was no one around. I could hear the wind whistling in invisible wires. My eyes made out a dim light in the distance. Stumbling towards it, I found that it shone on the hostel sign which read, 'Closed for the winter'. There was nothing and no one else in the world, but me and an icy wind. And then it started to rain. I could just distinguish, by the watery light on the sign, a stack of concrete sewer pipes. I gratefully climbed into one near the top and slept, hungrily, on and off until dawn.

Word from the road had informed me that the best hot showers in France were in the railway station at Marseille. On arrival, I found that the station was closed for a holiday. I was dirty and itching from too many nights in ditches and hedges and decided to wait for two days until it was open again. I slept on the Grand Escalier with two dozen Algerians who'd just escaped from the war. The police searched me every few hours, suspicious of what I might have in my sack. When the station opened, I found that they were right about the endless hot water. As I undressed, three cockroaches fell out of my clothes and into the shower.

I got a few fast lifts to the border and then one of Franco's cheap trains to Valencia. I found myself last in a long queue for the ship to Ibiza. As I presented my ticket, they said that I needed a stamp from the office. The office was back down the quay, but the ship was leaving and there was no time, so I'd have to wait three days for the next sailing.

I ran to the office and hammered until they opened the window and stamped my ticket, and then I raced back to the ship. It had cast off and the gangway was gone. Where it had been, in a gap in the side of the ship, three sailors stood ready to close the steel doors. The ship was moving along the jetty, inching out, to reveal a boiling sliver of sea far below.

I shouted to the sailors and threw them my sack. They caught it and started to wave their arms wildly, yelling at me not to do it. The gap was widening fast and I was running beside it. I peeled away from the ship, in an arc to give myself speed, then I raced in and hurled myself at the hole in its side. The outstretched arms of the sailors caught me, hauling me in, and I was on my way to Ibiza. The men marched me to the bridge, where a furious captain screamed at me for a while in Spanish. But I knew how close I had come, and I couldn't explain why, when you are young, it's better to die on the way to a dream, than to give up and live in its wake.

On approach from the sea, it was clear that Ibiza was no Spanish resort. No high-rise hotels, only old houses, stacked between narrow dirt streets. Ashore, the shop windows were covered in messages from people trying to sell anything to raise cash to stay on the island for longer. Like second-hand books by all of the authors that I'd searched for in Paris and London. Like discarded clothes and jewellery, and someone wanting to share an apartment with anyone who'd read *The Doors of Perception*.

Around me, in the cafes and bars, there were no normal tourists. There were people of all ages and nationalities, who were singing a similar song. It was a song about freedom, love, and to hell with the status quo. Perhaps this was the community that I dreamt of founding, and it was already done. I was bemused and slightly unnerved. I'd never been in the majority before and I wasn't sure that I liked it. There was nothing to rebel against here, except rebellion itself. My only option was to enjoy the scenery, to watch but not to join in.

Unthreatened by tarmac, the old town of Ibiza was perfect. I drank in a bar by the harbour that flooded with every tide. The only policeman stood in the square and blew his whistle at donkeys. He protected his world from the twentieth century and sold contraband cigarettes.

But there comes a time when the nights close in, and you've lived enough dreams and drunk enough wine. I was tired of being a sight, and a sightseer who couldn't see sights, although I wasn't sure that I'd ever be anything else. After eighteen years' looking on, why should anything change? But for now, I just wanted to get off the road and into a bed.

At Toulouse I stopped hitching. I had my fare from Paris to London. With it, I bought a meal and a ticket to Paris, from where I'd get the British Embassy to repatriate me. This was an old trick of young travellers. They took your passport, and gave you enough cash to get home. When you paid them back, they returned it.

Finally, I had a few hours in Paris. Time for a last 'coq au vin', and a carafe of wine at the station, while my battered perceptions submitted to a perfect ending that France had laid on.

There was a train-load of soldiers bound for the Algerian war. They and their lovers were kissing and crying goodbye. I drank, not with nostalgia for the end of an era, but with relief at the success of an impossible task. My summer, like maybe my childhood, was over, though I'd made it last to the end of November. I waved them goodbye with the tears of the lovers, as the train pulled me slowly away.

6

In Love and Elsewhere

The day after I returned was my birthday. I decided to surprise Norma in the fashion store where she worked.

'Oh my God, you're back. She won't believe it. Don't move, I'll go and tell her.' I was not expecting *that* sort of reception. From the back, I heard Norma's voice.

'It's not true, you're teasing, I don't believe it.' Then she was running across the store, and with a 'yes', she was throwing her arms round my neck.

'You're back,' she kept saying, 'you're back. We were just deciding that you'd gone to North Africa, and here you are. Happy birthday.' I wondered how she knew, and was slightly overwhelmed as all of the girls joined in. I wanted to keep looking over my shoulder, to see who they were talking about. 'Perhaps it's the power of a dozen red roses, or perhaps she really likes me.' It was such a long way from those nights in the ditches of Europe, and all of those years on my own.

For the rest of that winter I drifted the streets of the foggy old city with my arm around a beautiful girl. She'd arranged a position, 'au pair', in Paris for the following April. I told her that I'd find a job there, in a hotel. She said that work permits were impossible to get and it couldn't be done.

I wrote to the French Tourist Board, received a list of six hundred Paris hotels and began to write to each in longhand, starting from 'A'. By Christmas, I'd sent three hundred letters, without a single reply. Then one arrived from a hotel on the Rue de Rivoli, where I could start in March. We'd go to Paris for Easter, then Norma would go home, to return in late April to work.

The winter slipped by and, before we knew it, our train was pulling into the Gare du Nord. In a street near the Opera we found the Hotel Richelieu. It was small and perfect and like everywhere in Paris, it was old and beginning to peel away from its postcard.

With her inch-short hair, Norma looked fourteen and I looked a year or two older. We were a bit nervous because, in England, you needed a wedding ring if you wanted a bedroom together, but there was no problem in Paris. They gave us a room on the first floor with large windows and an old iron bedstead that was ours for a week. We went out to buy food and candles and bottles of wine. And when we'd eaten, we went to a burlesque show in the next street. I may not have seen the dancers, but I got the idea, as the beat and the swirling of silk was singing out, 'Now'. Surely Norma could hold out no longer. The scent of her hair on my shoulder in the darkened theatre kept pumping the surge that was flashing between us.

There was a brief interlude while we ran through the electric night air of the city. Then, back in our room, we continued the show, while long dammed-up yearning seared along seams in the space that no longer existed between us.

Hours later, she sat up in bed with my typewriter and actually wrote to her mother. Her letter skipped the part which said that we'd realised an unspoken ambition. That each of us, in love with the other, would lose our virginity together in Paris.

We ordered breakfast in bed and, when the knock came, I asked the chambermaid to put the tray on the table. She was staring so hard, as she crossed the room, that she almost tripped on the rug. She put the food down and came across to the bed. In the tenderest voice, she asked Norma if she was all right.

Young, in love, and entirely un-alone, we gave ourselves to those days by the Seine. We danced for joy at the rain of events that had somehow fallen on us. I'd arrived at the other extreme, and rejoiced in the warmth of its daylight.

On the last morning I went down to reception to pay. Then, instead of leaping them three at a time, I climbed the stairs slowly back to our room. In the corridor, I noticed that the pretty, rose-coloured wallpaper was actually grey. Norma was sitting on the floor by the open cupboard, running her fingers over our empty bottles.

'Why are you crying? You'll be back in three weeks.'

'It's because I don't believe that I'll ever be so happy again,' she replied.

'Oh yes you will,' I said, as a pigeon outside on the sill tapped at the pane to remind us to remember her breakfast.

'No,' she whispered, 'this was the moment. You only get one, and it's gone.'

After Norma had left, I found a room at 318, Rue St Honoré. I made it ours with catkins and candles and colourful rags from the flea market at Porte de Clignancourt. And when it was done, I said, 'There *will* be more than one moment. It's just that the first is a gift to show how it is done, and the rest you have to create.'

Later, I stood on the platform at the Gare du Nord, watching the incoming London express. People were tumbling from carriages and, there she was, running towards me and then spinning round and around in my arms with another bunch of red roses.

In the morning, I made some excuse and ran to the Place Vendôme. I collected the antique diamond ring that I'd purchased, with the first part of a small inheritance that I'd wangled prematurely out of my parents. With it and the champagne concealed under my coat, we walked to the river. The first flush of green was draping its veils through the trees of the city. Down by the Seine, a pretty young girl in a long dress stepped out of the past with a basket and sold us a posy of violets. There was no one around as we sat in the sun with our legs dangling over the water. A seagull flew by, dipping its wings, as I slipped the ring onto her finger. When she said 'yes', I uncorked the bottle and we drank to our dreams, and wherever they were planning to lead us.

And all of that summer I worked in the hotel by the Tuileries Gardens. Norma lived with a family at the end of the Avenue Foch, and sometimes I walked there from work. I painted in my room on Rue St Honoré and tried to sell the results on the streets. I had no luck because they were awful, and I was too happy to care. And when that summer was almost over, we got on a train to Lausanne. Back to the mountains and the tides of the mist that wipes out the prints of the world. Back to the secret domain that's hidden from those who forgot how to look without breathing.

'Are those mountains or clouds?' she asked, and I knew that I had come home. I remembered my return from last summer, tired of travelling alone. But I also remembered those solo encounters with stillness and the small things that once made me gasp. Was everything losing its lack of necessity to sparkle with anything more than its nature? Would I ever again round an ordinary corner to be stopped in my tracks by the world? That place's main ingredient had been 'being alone', but now I was tired of the selfish struggle to protect my seclusion. Besides, I was in love with this girl. And in love with these days in the mountains, where we lay in a meadow surrounded by clouds that shut out the noise of tomorrow. And then, one day, we had to go back to tomorrow. It seemed that somewhere, in all of the excitement, I'd become engaged to be married. So now what?

I looked for a flat and found a filthy basement in Moseley. I started to clean it but, as I scrubbed, it only got damper and dirtier. I peeled my way through decades of wallpaper while cockroaches splashed into the slime. 'Not for you,' the cockroaches clamoured, 'this path to a mortgage and waking up dead before you are born.'

I thought of the rest of that cash from my grandmother, that remained after the diamond ring. There might be enough to rent an old shop and open a coffee bar. A place for painters and poets and for people to meet and make music. Not exactly my Van Gogh community dream, but at least it might be a start.

I rented a building in Harborne High Street and gave myself two months to transform it. I painted the inside dark blue and covered the walls with colourful posters of art exhibitions and theatres that I'd collected in Paris. They'd been stuck on the restaurant windows and, when their events were over, I'd saved them.

While a coffee bar and restaurant by day, it turned into a club at night. That was to restrict the clientele, to avoid trouble while staying open late in a city that closed up at ten. There was a Gaggia espresso machine, two fruit machines and the only jukebox in Britain with Edith Piaf, Thelonious Monk and Dylan Thomas reading his poems. With Juliette Greco, Django Reinhardt, The Stones, The Big Bopper and Mozart.

The first few months of the venture went well. Customers for the elaborate French menu were few, but the club showed a profit from the start. Then, by Christmas, we wanted a break. With my younger brother, Simon, the three of us caught the train north, to my parents' new home in Northumberland. It was the day before Christmas Eve, and exciting. I loved these journeys by train that were like living inside an extended drum roll, building up slowly towards an arrival. With seats in the bar, by Burton-upon-Trent, we had the barman's life story. He was in a bad state, ill, with six children and no money for presents. I told him that we'd fix it. So, hauling him out from behind the bar, we sat him down with a whisky. He protested at first, but our confidence, his flu and my pretty fiancée enabled him to give up.

Simon and I took over the bar of the Edinburgh express. We placed a soup plate on the counter and, as we served people drinks, we told them that there was a surcharge to enable the barman to buy Christmas presents for his kids. Almost everyone responded that day. Perhaps it was the slightly outrageous situation. Perhaps it was our whispered good humour, as we pointed at the woebegone barman. Or perhaps it was because half of the train was singing, as we hurtled towards Christmas together.

For me, it was a joyful wiping-out of that memory of Christmas three years before, when they'd tipped me with an insulting song. By Sheffield we had enough for a few presents and by Darlington we had half of a sack full. We washed the glasses, totted the till and, as we pulled into Durham, we handed everything over. Our reward was the thrill at the beneficial breaking of rules, and the tears in the eyes of the barman.

The club began to succeed but there was no chance of it being the prototype of my dream. It was in the wrong part of the wrong city for poets and painters. Instead, it attracted a crowd who drank at 'The Sportsman' and came on to the club in fast cars.

There had been a bit of trouble with teddy-boys. Nothing too serious, though I could see that things would get worse. One morning, I was behind the counter when one of the Daly brothers came in. This guy always carried a knife or a razor. I passed him his coffee in its glass cup and saucer. Picking it up, he said with a snarl, 'It's fucking cold. Give me another, you cunt.' So saying, he threw it at the shelves behind me. I said nothing and made him another, wondering if the same would happen again. But he took it to a table and drank it. From the same table later that day, an old lady complained that she'd found cigarette butts concealed in her bowl of sugar.

I wondered if it was a fringe benefit from my schooling that such situations always made me feel calm. They happened at a distance, and yet seemed so real that they threatened you into awareness. One evening, I was sitting on my own in the window, eating before opening up. Some of the heavy guys were gathering outside. They rattled the handle, banged on the door with its 'closed' sign, and then started on the plate glass. They showed me their arsenal. One swung a bicycle chain, while another was armed with a razor that flashed in the streetlight as he shouted, 'We're gonna kill you, you fucker. You're dead.'

I knew what a tough life these tough guys had led. They'd always been locked out of wherever they wanted to go. Above all, I couldn't bear to find myself on the side of authority, so I resolved to give them a chance. One night two of them were belting the door. I took a deep breath and went out to talk. I got them to promise not to cause trouble and I let them in. They were all right that night.

The following night, upstairs in the crowded club, they were standing next to a man in a suit. One of them stuck an elbow in the man's ribs then grabbed him by the throat. 'You fucker, you spilt your fucking coffee all over my jacket.' Blood sprayed as he smashed his head into the customer's nose. So I banned them for a while and then relented, and something similar happened again.

One night, the smart crowd had booked the place for a fancy-dress party. The lads were hammering at the door and shouting. I opened it, slamming it shut as I slipped outside. They'd summoned the rest of the gang and they were looking angry and dangerous. I knew the ringleader, having spent hours talking to him and the others, and a certain respect had grown up between us.

'What the fuck's going on?' I asked.

'Your lot came out and one bastard kicked Jimmy's head in while he was down.'

'Those fuckers are not my lot,' I said. I couldn't explain to them, why I had no time for those rugby thugs, but they sort of knew that I meant it.

'Peter, we've got fuck-all against you, but if you don't send that fucker out here, we'll go in and fucking kill him.' They were looking menacing now.

'I'll go in and find the sod and get him out here,' I said. 'Give me five minutes before you come in.' The smart cowards had been listening, scared, inside the door.

'What should we do?' they asked, as if I was an authority on English class warfare. I wanted to throw the culprit out to the wolves, but I knew that I should probably not judge the rich for putting the boot in, any more than the poor for their razors. There were thugs in every class and, although it was with the guys on the outside that I'd go for a pint, I'd seen from my schoolfriends that privilege can screw you as much as poverty can.

'Right, here's the plan,' I told them, hoping that they wouldn't see through my complete lack of confidence. 'The person who put the boot in has got to leave, or they'll wreck the club and everyone in it. I'll get them across the street, so that the culprit can run for his car.' I went outside. I edged the angry lads to the opposite pavement, explaining that we needed to talk without being heard from inside.

'The bastard won't come out,' I said. 'We have to make a plan to get him.' At that moment the door of the restaurant opened. Our rugby hero, dressed as a gladiator in mini skirt and a helmet, was running for his life down the street. Two of the boys peeled away from our group. One pulled a pickaxe handle from his trousers and the other was flashing a razor. The gladiator leapt into his sports car and started the engine. The guy with the razor flung himself onto the roof, slashing the elite-looking canvas from one side to the other. With one mighty swipe, the lad with the pickaxe handle smashed the rear lights as the car roared away and they both fell into the gutter.

The boys seemed satisfied, but that night's entertainment was only beginning. While all of this had been going on, furious neighbours were complaining about the noise. They'd lifted a manhole cover and turned off our water supply. I explained to them that this could explode our coffee machine. These people were more threatening than the boys with the razors, because they *knew* they were right. An hour later, a house brick crashed through our plate-glass window. I went outside but no one was there. I never found out who was responsible but, from then onwards, the turning off of our water became a nightly occurrence.

At this time, in London, I met the first specialist not to insist that, with my glasses, I had perfect sight. He diagnosed a rare condition which resulted in the obscuration of central vision. Seeing only with peripheral vision, my eyes presented an overall picture but missed out the detail. This explained the difficulty in reading and seeing the features of faces.

On crossing a road I saw no black hole in the centre. Instead, my brain joined up the lines, inventing the bits that were missing. When I looked, I saw the whole of the road, but minus the car that was coming towards me. This had resulted in various near misses, due to the impatience which made me a compulsive jay-walker.

Having long since decided that we invent our own worlds, this news from the consultant was encouraging. If my ingenious mind could fill in bits of the world that my eyes didn't see, why should it not compose the whole picture? Perhaps we pick up stray clues, projected from previous dreaming, and round them we build the next story. I was elated. I thought, 'Perhaps this is to tell me that the universe is a magic colouring book, drawn by projected experience and wetted into life with the brush of our senses.'

By now, the trouble at the club had almost finished it off. The customers dribbled away and we had trouble finding the rent. We decided to close, renovate the interior, get married, and start all over again.

A friend was running a pub in an Oxfordshire village. On the night before the wedding, some of us drove down for a meal. My best man, John Christopher, said that a cute looking waitress was giving me the eye. Never having seen anyone's eyes from a distance, I asked the others how to respond. They quickly assured me that the only reason she was looking at me, and not them, was because I was the unobtainable star for one night. But I didn't believe them. I wondered how many chances I'd missed during those last lonely years. How many girls had I looked straight through? Perhaps there were women, all over France, still gazing into their coffees and dreaming of me. I decided to atone for my rudeness and be nice to the pretty young waitress. We left the pub at three in the morning.

The wedding was perfect and the bride looked beautiful. The country club reception even had a 'Last Year at Marienbad' feeling. Everything was as it should be, and everyone had a great time, except for the respective parents who despaired at our lack of a future.

We arrived at the ferry with 'Just Wed' written all over the car in blancmange, and coins clanking around in the hub caps. At the Paris hotel, we wanted to hide the car in a side street but there was nowhere to park, so we had to drive into the courtyard. That was a big mistake. We didn't need A-level French to decipher the comments. They actually cheered when we went up to bed.

Now, honeymoon or not, Norma and I were exhausted. We fell into bed and were asleep within seconds. Then Norma suddenly woke me. She was sitting up in bed with a nosebleed. Blood was everywhere. I got some towels and we attempted to stem the flow. Finally it stopped, with her head held backwards over the basin. In the morning, the towels and the sheets were covered in blood. We left the hotel before they could make any further assumptions.

We drove to Spain and played in the sun until we'd achieved a wedding. Then we went back to the mountains where the old longing swept in with surprise summer snow. I watched each flake, as transient as my time by the streams of the silence. I looked in the mirror at a strange man with short hair and a tie, who tried hard to give me a smile.

Back in the city we opened the club. I'd re-designed it as a cave. I'd smoothed two tons of dental plaster onto chicken mesh with bare hands. There were cascades of stalactites and grottoes with concealed coloured lighting. There were tables in candle-lit cave-lets, and a sculpture that I'd made from typewriters sledge-hammered together. Surely this would bring people in from the Birmingham gloom.

We had few customers on the first night, and less on the next. We tried various tricks, but blood and house bricks had taken their toll. Week upon week of slow decline had put a strain on our marriage. It wasn't the fights but the empty chairs that began to stack up between us. We sold the car to pay bills, then decided to sell up and get out.

Harvey had written to say that he and Rosemarie were driving to Israel at the beginning of May. They were going via Greece and wanted someone to share the expense. That gave us a month, but we had little hope of selling the business. Then, at the last minute, we received a derisory offer. It was just enough to get me on the road, out of that cardigan, and back to the life that I loved.

They were leaving from Nuremburg a couple of days after we completed the sale, so we moonlighted out of our brief 'settling down'. And we never returned to the city that had spawned our dreams and then frozen the spawn in the ponds of convention.

Rosemarie met us at Nuremburg station and said that we were to leave the next day. We stopped for the first night on the way to Verona, and slept by a stream, high amongst Lombardy pines. I rose early to watch the sun hit the tops of the mountains, and to steal a secret meeting with May as she skipped through the woods in her skirts of light. She forgave me for my brief turning away, and offered again the grace of her stillness.

Now there was serious seeing of sights to be done. In Florence we gazed at some stuff that I'd already seen. But I was more inspired by a tussock of grass, caught in the lights of the sunrise, or the nobility of trees and the breath-catching tumult of water in motion. These were the wonders of my world, but their magic only reveals itself to solitary viewers in silence. I told myself that, in the confusion of cities it's good to have company, while in the mountains you must be alone.

Then, before we knew it, we were looking down on the lazy blue haze of Naples. It was like an exaggerated portrait of this business of living; alluring when viewed from a distance and heart-breaking when you get close. So we ambled on down to Brindisi.

Greece was still unspoilt, they said, because few people travelled that far. You couldn't get past Albania by road, and only the super-rich cheated by flying. The only route was by sea from the foot of Italy, and most got no further than Rome. Could it really be that this land of the gods was not yet corrupted by progress?

I opened my eyes, on deck, in a temperate mist with a new feeling of well-being. I'd been woken by the sudden cessation of sound from the engines. We were slicing through the first light of dawn, on a limpid sea, in absolute silence. From a dimension that occurs on the outskirts of dreaming, I watched green islands slide by on a rose-coloured mirror of milk. The forward movement, combined with the calm, suggested that something momentous was coming. We were breaking our journey in Corfu, and this must be it. We landed on another planet from Italy and in some different epoch.

We drove out of town and stopped at the first beach down the coast. It was a place called Benitses where we could swim, sleep on the sand and do nothing but be for a while. So we idled the day into evening. In the fading light the world had grown warm and its warmth invited you in. Small boats dipped and rose with the swell. Fireflies sparked in the deepening night, while cypress trees pointed out stars. A donkey sawed through the spell and it was time for retsina.

For all of the night, the two boys fished from their boats by the beach where we lay. A lantern shone at the stern where they stood like young gods with their spears raised, waiting to strike. There was no need of sleeping through the easy perfection of that ancient island in May. I stayed up to keep watch with the fireflies and the lights of the gods on the water.

In the morning we heard two girls singing some haunting Greek song as they came down through the olive groves. Reaching the back of the beach, they called to the boys on the boats. And everything was utterly silent, except for the girls and the sunrise, and the low slap of the sea as it lapped at the sand.

The unblemished sky was a colour that doesn't exist, and the water was a shade or two deeper.

At first light the next day, while the others slept, I heard the girls come singing through the olives again. Their song was as old as the path that had led them for thousands of years to their boys at the shores of the dawn. Then they were running down the beach in their long skirts, their dark hair tossing against slim brown arms. Their laughter was a cascade of life-force, as free as their bare feet on the sand. They turned and ran in towards me, as I sat there entranced by perfection. Kneeling, they took from their aprons oranges, a lettuce, some cheese and a small loaf of bread and laid them before me. Their white teeth were flashing, and I felt their eyes shining with so much light that you wouldn't dare look. Then laughing, they turned and ran with the rest of the food to their fisher-boys on the water.

The simple purity of this offering was a stunning gesture from the last days of a dying world. I mourned the passage of our planet from grace into greed. I thought of how open I'd need to become before I could perform one act that was half as noble as this song of the girls of the island.

I sat watching the timeless unfurling of waves on the sands of a time that was passing. Soon there'd be apartments along the back of the beach and bars where the olive groves were. And these carefree nymph's daughters would be driving to work in make-up and trousers. There'd be motors on boats pulling skiers, and none would recall how you fish with a spear. They'd have forgotten the stars, and the names of the flowers, and how to offer some of the little you have to a stranger. Hurrying past, they'd scowl at these tramps on their nice tidy beach. They might even inform the police, who'd bring dogs to see you off, in the way that they do at St Ives.

I wanted to learn from these girls, and live as simply as they did. I could see that the innocence had to be lost, in a process as sure as the sunrise. I could see how it had subjected the people to the tyranny of centuries of unquestioned church. But I could also see that there *is* a way back to the garden. It was when I possessed nothing that I too ran barefoot through enchanted aisles of the morning. I needed to be reminded of that. It's why I'd come to this land of the past.

We travelled throughout Greece and everywhere we were met with a similar welcome. And then, one evening, we arrived at the Pirene Fountain. As usual, there was no one around and we had the ruins of old Corinth to ourselves. I climbed through a gap and along a dark dripping passage. Inside you could hear the rush of the spring of the muses and the tears of the mothers of all the dead heroes of time.

I was feeling my way back down the centuries, through the wreckage of empires that had lasted for no more than a moment. There was a message hidden for me in this place, waiting for time to rust open its locks. In the darkness I felt strangely relaxed, yet aware that my fingers were trembling with anticipation.

I emerged from past darkness into the fading light of a twentieth-century sun. The others had disappeared and an old man was shuffling towards me, out of history and nowhere. He motioned to me to sit down in the dust, and he started to talk about Corinth.

He said that we were sitting where Diogenes had sat at around the time of the Buddha. He told me that Diogenes rejected all institutions, and the man-made order of things. He despaired of the human obsession with achievement, possession and status. The old man scratched at the dust with his stick and continued.

'The less that you need, the happier you will be. Live simply. Keep away from the crowd and its organisation. This is the pathway to wisdom and eventual freedom. It is desire and its objects that chain our souls to the earth.'

And then he told me the legend. To hear it from a shade of Diogenes himself, right there, in the dust by the Pirene Fountain. To be told it, where it had happened, twenty-four centuries before, alone in the silent city at dusk. Every movement, every word was inscribed in my mind-stream forever. This message from the past was to exude a stream of continuous influence, through all of the rest of my life.

Alexander the Great came here, to this very spot, to find Diogenes who lived in a barrel. The sage was sitting at the fountain in the early spring sunshine. When all of his questions were answered, Alexander said, 'Diogenes, you are the wisest man on the Earth. I'm the most powerful and richest. I want to repay you for your wisdom. Name anything, and it shall be yours.'

'There is one thing that I want, more than anything else in the world,' Diogenes murmured.

'Name it, name it,' replied Alexander.

'I want you to get out of my sun.'

And I knew that I'd travelled to Greece to receive the instruction on simplicity, from Diogenes and the Nymphs of Benitses.

From Athens the others set sail for Haifa and we hitched around the Aegean to Turkey. We were slowed by each likely taverna, by the evening promenade that blocked the way, and the miles of un-made road that protected the land from its future; from all the wrong turnings of progress, like jet-planes and tarmac and hurry.

Hashish was legal in Turkey. The young had come there to smoke it, while using Istanbul as a base-camp for the rigorous trip onwards to India and Nepal.

I laughed when they told me that the British Embassy was the cool place to meet people, and to score reliable hash. Britain was working off issues with karma at its Istanbul embassy in '65. It was also caught in that instant when something momentous has not yet quite happened; a feeling that you couldn't explain; anticipation with no particular goal. It was a stirring in the hearts of a whole generation that was tired of being told what to think.

The embassy must once have been an imposing bastion of

its empire of greed. Now it was engagingly rundown and could have done with a quick lick of paint. As we entered, the large foyer was lit by candles because of a power cut. Maybe. Kids in sleeping bags were lying crashed-out on the floor. People were talking, drinking tea or rolling up cannabis resin. All over the walls were messages stuck with tape. 'Gone on to Kabul,' or 'See you in Kathmandu.'

It was in the British Embassy in Istanbul that I first felt the extent of the change that was coming. You could see it in the way that the kids dressed and the certainty that preferred the road to the office. You could hear it in what they said, and tell it by the books that stuck out of their pockets. You felt that you were part of a club that no one could join, that had no name, and whose address was the whole of the world.

When we'd had enough, we bought tickets for the Orient Express which, by now, was three carriages linked to a goods train. For the first half of our three-day journey to Paris, our hearts were in Greece, and after that it was all about London. By '65, London had become the most relevant city on earth.

Harvey knew that we had no money, so he scoffed when I told him that we'd look for a cool place in Chelsea. He asked if I'd any idea of how impossible that was. I told him that I'd consider nothing less than the impossible, and left it at that.

7

Sixties London

The impossible happened, not through some miracle, but simply by following our luck and our noses. By waiting on the doorstep of a possibility for five hours, we obtained a room by the river in Chelsea, with the owner away for six weeks.

Next it was jobs and we had to be quick if we wanted to eat. The first few boutiques were just opening. Run by the young, they were a focal point for the change that was coming. Their brilliant colours shone like jewels on the old grey fist of convention. Norma walked into a job in the Jaeger boutique on King's Road.

I had equal luck, becoming second chef at the Institution of Civil Engineers. The pay was good and the hours were only eight a.m. until three with no work at weekends. Being situated between the Houses of Parliament and Buckingham Palace, Norma teased me for finding a job in the pompous old heart of the dying empire.

The head chef, Stan, was a young Cockney with a sense of humour and a heart of gold. On day one, he told me to cut a dozen chops and throw them under the salamander. Five minutes later I was still deciding which was the salamander, and if this was it, how the hell did you light it. As usual, I wondered how long I would last.

Norma seemed happy with new friends on King's Road, but I was still restless. One late summer's night, I couldn't sleep, so I went out to walk around town. There was no one awake, just me with the moon playing 'hide and seek' in the chimneys. I walked through the streets by the Thames, looking up at the darkened windows. It's strange how everyone lies down at the same time, like obedient children. I imagined their faces on pillows. The boss, the lover, the child and the bully, each at rest with their eyes closed. They seemed so vulnerable, so precious and unprotected, asleep in rows by the river. When they awoke, they'd don their personas and start to shout at the mirror again. But in those few hours before dawn, they were all alone and the same. Overwhelmed by the sheer scale of the issue, I was filled with love and a longing to find a way to free us all from the nets of our own limitations.

Meanwhile, the taxman was asking questions about my disposal of the club. We both knew that there was no tax to be paid on a loss, but he needed me to jump through some hoops. A few times, I caught the Friday night coach to meet him in Brum. It meant that I could see Pamela. She was a crazy art student, and a stunning, high-explosive free spirit. We felt that we could indulge in the bewitching intensity of our liaison, as long as its innate sexuality was never made active. We said that we were rubbing our souls together, to produce the pure energy of the element fire without any flames.

As platonic lovers we were perfectly matched. She'd kill for attention and I couldn't take my eyes off her face. This was the pedestal girl, jumped into my world, to lead me through lines of the music, while I whispered the words in her ear.

On one trip to the tax man, I left a drinking club at two in the morning with a new address for Pamela. Walking all night, I got there at dawn and a girl let me into her flatmate's room, saying that Pamela wasn't yet back from Friday. I'd fallen asleep and was suddenly woken. An explosion of obscenities announced

Goldilocks' return, to find someone asleep in her sheets. She calmed down, changed into her nightdress, climbed into bed, and we slept.

There was a frenzied knocking at the door. The girl who'd let me in was panicking because Pamela's parents were downstairs. I spent half an hour in a cupboard, wondering how best to define 'platonic'. When they'd gone we went back to bed to talk of a love that transcends desire and the desire that's consummated by desire itself, when you relax into the heart of its own intensity. I was feeling my way along a thought that I was, as yet, too inexperienced to grasp. So I gave up and gazed at the vision beside me, fascinated by a shaft of sunlight that was celebrating its arrival in the golden chaos of her hair.

She wanted to read the notebook that I always carried. I said that it was just more words and words should only be used as a last resort, when you've run out of things to say. I told her that I lived in the last resort. And then, more seriously, I said that she was in it. As an awkward student, I'd written to her, at a party that I'd gate-crashed at her house before I'd dared to make contact. I found the place and she read:

'Parting the curtains, I see that it's snowing. The magnet of serenity pulls me outside, onto the whitening field. I look back at your windows whose music is muffled by flurries of silence. I want you to join me out here in the night. We'd step out of our selves and into the stillness that blankets the sorrow.

'I can feel that you too have encountered the secret significance; that mysterious light that flicks here and there in the garden; that leads you beyond the point of resistance, where things no longer require explanation. Where measureless love puts out the fires of the right and the wrong.

'I carefully tread a few words on the snowfields that surround you. You'll know what they mean in the springtime, but first they must melt back into the earth. Then, when we've grown a bit more and the winter is over, they'll rise in the sky, to fall as rain that will wash you and wake you, like the first birdsong of the morning.'

Pamela closed the book and we lay there, for a while, without speaking.

'Don't you want anything in return?'

'The less that you want, the more you rejoice in the vastness of what's already yours,' I told her, trying to live up to Diogenes. 'Meanwhile, should you and I indulge in satisfaction, we'd be subject to things like jealousy, and the justification of action. We'd be fighting before the leaves have fallen, and apart before the first snow.'

'You're insane,' she said. 'You're my insane poet and I want to kill you.'

Pamela came on the bus into town. We had separate seats because the bus was crowded. When we arrived at the terminal she said, 'I was watching you. I've never met anyone so alive. You sit on the edge of the seat and notice it all.'

Laughing, I explained that it was only because sitting on a bus was the one time that I could get close enough to see what was happening. There was some catching up to be done. I was activated by a childish fascination that is dulled by familiarity in those who've seen it before. And then I added that it's vital, at all times, to sit on the edge of your seat, and to remain totally relaxed while you do so.

In March, a 'To Let' sign appeared outside 65 Earls Court Square. It was unusual for an unfurnished flat, in a quiet leafy square, to come onto the market. I raced round to the agents for the key. They said that it was unlet because it had a problem with access. The three-bedroomed flat, in a Georgian terrace, had a large main room with French windows onto a balcony that overlooked trees. Even better, it was very cheap at ten pounds a week, because of its access problem. We couldn't believe our good fortune.

The so-called 'problem' was that the front door was on the

first floor with a private spiral staircase to its flat above. This staircase was too narrow for furniture to pass but, for us, it was a beautiful bonus. I rejoiced at the lack of imagination that had saved this flat for us. We could saw down some of the banisters. Or, with ropes, we could haul stuff up the outside and in through the windows. Or hell, we could make our own furniture or live on the bloody floor. I ran back to the agents and paid a month's rent in advance.

It was a large flat with a passable kitchen, a wide corridor and telephone alcove large enough to be slept in, as well as two halls and the stairwell. 'Unfurnished' meant that I could re-design it, in any crazy way that I wanted. I could furnish two rooms, let them to someone, and that would cover the rent. This was my best den since 'Bamboo Island'. Hey, I was in London, around the corner from the Troubadour, where Dylan played, a short walk from King's Road, and it was nineteen hundred and sixty-six.

We bought a dozen gallons of brilliant white paint, to celebrate the coming of light. The girls from Jaeger came to slap it onto every surface, to the pulse of The Rolling Stones and the upsurge of London in springtime. Young Sammy got paint on her dress so she took it off and, in white underwear, she fluttered back up to work on the ceiling. I asked her, if I took the steps away, would she stay up there forever?

From floor to ceiling in the entrance, I made a brightly coloured collage and varnished it. It included the remains of my posters from Paris, headlines about cannabis and Vietnam, with poems and slogans, and anything that reflected our rebellion against the gloom of the past.

On advertising the rooms, we were overwhelmed by the eager response. It was heart-breaking to turn anyone away. Most of them had traipsed around endless ghettoes and were in love with our crazy province of promised renewal. In the end I settled on Irish twins, Anne and Mary, who wouldn't clash with our minds or the decor.

Meanwhile, work wasn't taking up too much of my brain. I learnt how to use the screaming bacon-slicing machine, without seeing it, and yet retaining my fingers. Sometimes, if I misheard an order, the Cockney chef would yell across the kitchen, 'Cornish, yer deaf, blind cunt, come 'ere.' But he shouted with a chuckle and I enjoyed his directness.

My younger brother, Simon, came to visit me from Marazion where he'd been living with a girl called Frances and Niall, their child. We went on a pub crawl from Finch's in the Fulham Road, via World's End to the Six Bells, Chelsea. I was so at ease with this guy who'd navigated the years by my side. With his innate honesty and generosity, he was a good influence on me. We clanked our tankards together and toasted each other with our slogan, 'You can never live life to the full, if you hold its jug by the handle.'

And all of the while you could see the colours in the streets growing brighter, and miniskirts defiantly inching up knees. Everything was on the move. A generation was holding its breath and dreaming of going all the way.

Chef called me into his office. There'd been a phone call. Simon had had an accident and was unconscious in a hospital in Penzance. We hired a car and, in May sunshine, we drove out of London.

In Marazion we stopped at his house which was a stone's throw from the beach and St Michael's Mount. Frances told us that Simon had bought a motorbike with cash that Father had sent, a few days before, for his twenty-first birthday. He was riding home for lunch, along the deep coast road, one early summer's day at the start of everything. He overtook a bus and hit a lorry emerging from a junction. They said that his brain would be damaged if he lived.

At the small hotel where Simon drank, there was a line of people at the bar. Standing behind them, I ordered a pint, and the line of heads spun around as one. They told me later that, so like Simon did I sound, that they thought I was his ghost. The doctors explained that he could live for years or die in an hour. Sometimes I talked to him and told him, 'If you're not returning, Simon, it's all right. I learnt at school that there's no beginning or ending. Things only change state. You're just sloughing your previous skin. You have to do it, now and again, in order to grow.'

We went back and forth to Marazion until, six weeks later, I was in London one Saturday morning. It was the first weekend that we'd not gone to Cornwall because Simon was being flown to Plymouth. Norma had gone to work at Jaeger and I was sitting by a window in the whiteness. A crowd of thoughts was jostling me for attention. Mostly about the times when I'd ignored him, or received the treat that should have been his. And then I heard the telephone ring from a far-away shelf at my elbow. A voice was saying that Simon had died. I talked to myself to condition the news, 'We constantly reify phenomena until we convince ourselves that they truly exist, then we're shocked when they fail. If we could give up this need for false stability, we might notice the strange perfection of everything's dance. We might even see that the only stability comes from recognising the sacred insubstantiality of ourselves and everything else. Then, devoid of expectation, we'd see the precious nature of this race of days, and start to laugh at our pitiful demands. We might even grow by letting go of the desire for one or two items of suspect validity.'

After a while, I got up and went down to the street. Despite all of my lectures to myself, a vast part of everything was suddenly missing. I wandered towards King's Road with the idea of seeing Norma. I'd lost the best friend that I'd ever have, and I knew that I'd wasted him.

My father had been advised that Simon would receive better treatment in Plymouth, so they'd flown him there. It was on the journey that he died. I was glad that he'd received the rare honour of dying in the sky. It was appropriate for him.

He and Frances had split up and he'd found a room nearby. Before the funeral, it was my task to clear up his stuff. The worst part was when I came across the piles of blue Embassy vouchers.

These were coupons included in cigarette packets, which you collected to claim an object. He'd sorted them into bundles of a hundred, bound with rubber bands. As I wondered what he was saving for, I was overwhelmed by the sheer scale of apparent futility. And in the pain I wished that I'd died for him, because he was better than I was. And then I realised that he'd completed this life and needed none of this now. I realised that the only vouchers actually saved are the vouchers of our past actions. So, I knew that Simon would receive a radiant prize, whereas me, I'd hang around, steal his coupons, send them in and get myself a saucepan.

And in his room I bowed my head, guilty from the luxury of being. I thought of Simon drilling for tin and coming home exhausted from the mine. I wondered why they never taught us how to handle all this. Why no one had even explained how to die, never mind what we should do once we're dead. And I thought of how I'd betrayed the promise that we'd made, when we were young together, to never sit down while the music played. I'd strayed into the tangled net of events, where I'd mislaid myself in dreams of ordinary freedom.

Back in London that summer, I was selfish with my sadness. It was mine and I refused to share it. I liked to be alone on long walks through the streets. The sorrow brought moments of extreme closeness with Norma, but those soon wore out. Four years before, I'd have given all that I had to hold the hand of a girl like her. Now, I put the hand nearest to her into my pocket, on days when we walked by the river.

I wondered, as a child did I spend too long on my own? Did all of that early dreaming become too real for the mundane to stand a chance? Why was I less lonely when making forays into self-expression with myself for company? Why was I happier, talking excitedly to an uninspiring stranger, than I was when making love to her? Was I still chasing the elusive spirit who'd lead me to a clearing in this forest of thought? I liked to think that

I was on some urgent quest that would take me to the stars, but I suspected that I was simply finding an excuse for bad behaviour. I wrote things down to prove that I was working with reason, but knew that I was thinking of only myself. I was stuck there with this yearning; this ache for all of us who are going wrong while we search for the turning.

From time to time, Pamela sent me cuttings of what was going on in Tibet. The Chinese were committing genocide, yet there was almost nothing in the press. Just the odd paragraph, while six thousand monasteries were being turned back to dust. The news was all about Vietnam, where the Americans were doing something similar.

Norma and I drifted further apart and she found a friend. I was sad for us, and glad for her and me, because I knew that it was all for the best. We didn't argue, but there was a certain sad warmth between us, brought about by acceptance of the inevitable. One evening she came home and said that she'd decided to move. She'd put so much love into making our home that I couldn't bear to see her lose it, so I offered it to her. She said that there was too much of us in the place, and she needed a completely fresh start.

One day, at the far end of that summer, I sat down and replied to Pamela ...

'... Of course I remember the day that you were leaving for Greece. Simon had just died. We stood in the sunshine at South Kensington station. We couldn't speak, but your tears did the talking. Can it still be that same summer now? I haunt fragments of his life, hold photographs to the half-light of the street and shiver at the frailty of our brief connections.

'In my tree-top room, halfway down the rain, I lick tears from the face of promises made when urgency outranked convenience. In our search for permanence we unearth only change as we wander the background flick of events. The sad little trail of litter that we leave behind us is of no importance then. Whether it consists of a few old letters, some photographs, a crate of empty bottles, or an empire that we built. These things are but reminders to the living to make good use of their time.'

I came home from work to find Norma sitting on the floor at the foot of the stairs. She was crying as she held her guitar. She'd been clearing out the cupboard in the hall; the two-storey lobby where I'd papered four walls with kitchen foil, so that you couldn't see where anything started or ended, as you went up the spiral. Upstairs, the music from 'Zorba the Greek' was providing heart-rending reminders of our brief adventure together. She said quietly, when the music stopped, that a taxi was coming at nine.

I saw the joy of the young girl, laughing in the spring-light as I carried her up the steps of Sacre Coeur, or chasing a snowflake across an afternoon in the Alps. I looked at her and knew that nothing is lost; that yesterday is there to burst the banks of assumption and bring new life to the fields of tomorrow's potential.

I found her in tears, washing glasses at the final sink, while the slow Greek music haunted the unwritten chapters of our plans to construct a new world. The open front door reminded me that the November night had arrived to come in between us. As they carried her dressing table down the stairs, she came over.

'It's all right,' she whispered, as they took her last things to the taxi. 'Nothing ends, because in each ending a brilliant new birth is beginning.'

Then it was time for my next lesson, and it came at work. I had to pull the guts from worn-out battery hens to make chicken pies. Scores of emaciated corpses arrived in brown paper sacks. When you slit them open, you had to hold them at arm's length and turn your head from the stench. They were egg-bound, and all their insides were dyed sulphur yellow, and full of slippery, shell-less eggs.

I looked at their heads, with red plastic blinkers stapled to their faces. Any species that could inflict such a crime on its fellow beings had become so depraved that it had no right to survive. Surely it'd be best for everyone if we destroy ourselves quickly.

I collected the wishbones of the hens for my memorial to their suffering. In the end I'd almost a thousand, which I soaked in bleach and then dyed them red. I saved seven, seven-pound pea tins, sculpted them with countless layers of kitchen foil and hung them, as lampshades, in a cascade with red light bulbs, from the high ceiling of the flat. Then I tied the red wishbones on scarlet thread and hung them from the ceiling rose, in drifts down to the floor. They formed a delicate bone curtain of red light. It was a poor memorial but, as my flat became more public, I used it as a reminder to us all to watch who we're eating.

And I liked working in a kitchen. I liked the unpretentious company of life's so-called nonentities. At least I wasn't wasting my potential, sloshing around some professional backwater, paddling my ego upstream to oblivion. I preferred kitchen porters who spent their days in khaki overalls, soaked and greasy, scouring burnt aluminium. They came from the streets and hostels and all social classes. Living rough and drinking hard they had, in common, some shattering experience that had ripped up their lives. I'd take them to the pub across the street in Parliament Square, to drink with their elected leaders.

This pub had a division bell, connected to the House of Commons. It'd ring in the bar, to summon the members across the square to vote, as they were told, at the end of some debate that attempted to dictate my future. It was the sort of place that no self-disrespecting kitchen porter would ever have dared to enter, because KPs had no self-respect, their MPs having bagged it all for themselves. It made sense, I thought, in the interests of social cohesion, to enable the two of them at least to appear to mix.

It was here that I took Harry, the Australian KP. He was a well-educated man of forty. Although only a kitchen porter, he'd won the confidence of the management at the Institution of Civil Engineers. He was charming, polite and plausible. He lived in doorways and never spoke of his story.

Finally Harry confided that he'd found himself a better place to live. He'd unearthed three different ways of entering, at night, our august Institution. His favourite being through a trapdoor in the old coal shed, which led directly to the boiler. He laid his bedroll on a heap of fire-sand beside the boiler in the vast empty basement.

Harry had his own way of collecting the debt that society owed him. With access to the entire building, he found the director's vintage claret, which was kept in boxes of two dozen bottles stacked on their sides. Each night, he'd remove another bottle from the bottom of the stacks and settle on his heap of sand. He talked about the ratio between the rate at which the director was drinking his way down the stacks and he was drinking upwards. He said that, by January, there'd be one row between them and he'd have to leave.

I asked if Harry might let his friends enjoy the Institution's rent-free hospitality. He said that they'd blow his cover, so I suggested that it was his duty to at least give them a meal, since he'd the place to himself from Friday night until Monday. And so it was that, in a pub by the Thames, surrounded by Members of Parliament, we planned a banquet for Harry and the homeless of London.

He'd let the others in through a side door, which he could unbolt from within, saying that he had the keys for one night. He'd lead them to the Great Hall, with its ornate painted ceiling and its chandeliers of crystal. He'd place tables down the centre with white cloths and gilded chairs. I'd leave the main fridge unlocked for him and lay out everything from a side of smoked salmon to liqueur chocolates and a sirloin of beef. Harry would provide vintage claret. I knew that nothing would be missed, because the manager used to take stuff home while Chef looked out of the window.

It was late in 1966 that a party of Britain's poorest citizens enjoyed a stolen night of grandeur, at the expense of the Establishment and within the chambers of its heart. I felt that I'd helped to strike one small blow for democracy.

In the same square as my flat, I found a hidden bar, deep in the back of a rundown hotel, next to the Poetry Society. The BBC, and various theatres, rented rooms there for rehearsals. The owners welcomed a handful of artists, outsiders and trusted eccentrics who could ignore the licensing laws and drink all day and all night.

It was there that I met Pat Jennings who introduced me to Pan's People, who used the hotel to rehearse their dance routines for Top of the Pops. He was going out with Louise, one of the dancers. We'd go back to his flat in the square, sometimes with, sometimes without a couple of the girls, while Dylan punched his urgency into the playful night. Pat was a wild guy who helped me to celebrate my new single life. He drove a souped-up Austin Healey and used the metropolis as his race track. We'd drift through Hyde Park Corner with him fighting the wheel, in the half empty streets of the evening. The hub caps would scream as they kissed the kerb, and their streamers of sparks were our fireworks of freedom.

Of course, I'd heard and read of various great writers' experiments with mescaline. The news was that a synthetic form was now available. It was known as LSD. It was legal, it had just arrived in London, and the young and creative were celebrating its arrival. It came in an eye-dropper. You drew a grid of squares on a sheet of blotting paper. You squeezed one drop onto each square, cut it out and swallowed it. Some dropped it onto a sugar cube, but sugar was considered uncool and a danger to health.

We treated the taking of 'acid' with respect. It was a spiritual experience for which you prepared with diligence, choosing somewhere safe and beautiful, with incense, flowers and candles. Was this the catalyst, the secret key for which we'd been searching? Was it *this* that would release the war-torn twentieth-century from the tyranny of solidified perception?

At the same time, I was concerned. Selfishly, I feared that everyone would soon be able to see things as I did. I'd no longer be special. My arrogant, self-appointed status as some sort of an artist would be stolen from me by a chemical. I ridiculed my self and asked it various questions. Like, did I really want the world to change? Or, did I want the world to stay the same, so that I could go on rebelling from outside of it? The answer didn't matter. It was time to take the trip and see where it would lead me …

'It's 10.30 on Saturday morning, 16 December 1966. I'm in my flat with some friends, a pencil and a large sheet of paper. I've just swallowed one drop of pure LSD …

'… now it's 11.10. My hand is shaking slightly. I'm conscious that we're the guinea pigs, performing vivisection on our own minds. I ate an omelette last night and a plate of sprouts for breakfast. I'm beginning to feel something. The scary thing about this is that there's no turning back. The next few hours are out of my jurisdiction. I've given up control for the first time in my life. That, in itself, is significant. The inevitability of what's about to take place is both terrifying and exciting. A sort of death, a sort of beginning …

'… some hours later now. This pencil is making so much noise that I can't hear what I'm writing. I can't explain what happened because you have to leave your words outside the door of the luminous expanse. But back here, a room no longer consists of four walls. It has innumerable planes that are vividly outlined in light; ephemeral and vitally irrelevant. It all flickers on and off, like everything with which it is dancing. Phenomena are radiant events that collide and quiver with exquisite energy. They overlap and interchange, devoid of separate identity. The walls of this room continuously hold nothing back. Everything is wafer thin and oscillates, slightly, in its mansion of liquid glass. It pulses with momentary existence, then surrenders to the weightlessness of its evolution into space. Words like 'now' and 'here' shoulder pretentiously into the mind-stream from yesterday's pre-supposition. They merge and unite to write 'nowhere' and shuffle off in search of applause. I'm having trouble with rebellious words. They weave through all of this insubstantiality, searching for the dignity of meaning …

'… it's night now. Two bright candles, or binary stars revolving, radiate photons like sparklers into space. The reeds have settled down and stopped waving from their vase. The curtain has dried up, and ceased its display as a cataract of diamonds. The mind is shrinking back into the shell of its own conditioning. There's a sense of loss and a vast peace that's arisen now that the corners of the room fit.

'I've a feeling of relief; partly because I've survived; mainly because my understanding has been challenged and given a brief slap on the back. My conviction that we create our own reality has been ratified in depth. By altering, slightly, the chemical balance of my brain, I loosened the knots that bind me to limited perception. I've enjoyed a universe that is, in every way, more plausible than this dingy old solidified projection that we've been building, stuck together with the sweat from millennia of fear.'

So it was that I proved, to my own satisfaction, that nothing is ever as we see it. Our perception of 'reality' depends entirely on what's happening in us at any given moment. This may be altered by what we eat or think, or by various emotions. I wondered if there was a way to adjust the balance from within, without the use of a dangerous chemical. I wondered if I hadn't once caught a fleeting glimpse of this, in the seclusion of the mountains. I wondered if, in the first months of life, we all see the world like this; see-through and shining with a rainbow light. Maybe our education is no more than the gradual development of a habit for concrete. And we cling to that drab, trustworthy world, even when we know that it's a lie. With it, we can make great business,

but we'll never see the light-showers that shine from the dust of
our dismantled prison.

8

1967

It was 1967 and everything was fizzing. They'd built a rudimentary stage in the centre of the bare floor of the Roundhouse, where Pink Floyd played with flashing lights of red and green. There'd never been anything like this, and no one had a clue as to what was going on. Beneath the stage, we sat on the floor and scored small bottles of liquid LSD. It was sold at cost price because it was considered uncool to profit from a noble cause.

At Whitsun, three couples escaped to the country, driving west towards my old school. We were stoned on leaving Notting Hill Gate, and more stoned as we came into Dorset with the dawn. The ultra-violet of an early summer's daybreak had increased the definition and turned its colour up high. We danced out through the first light and fell in the grass, silenced and released by the splendour. A fluorescing clarity had drawn back the veils of humdrum perception to reveal the innate display of the mind. You could feel the vastness of the earth as it rolled over to submit itself to the sun. We drifted past spinneys of discarded thought that went missing while searching for order. Memories and dreams slunk off, not daring to look in our eyes. Now we were living at last, and feeling it all. We couldn't care less if this was it, or if there was some place still further in than this astonishing suspension of action.

The sun climbed from the haze and we turned towards Taunton. We drove through the gates, past the ancient acacia tree that still guarded the jail of my youth. We looked festive for the Whit weekend, with Indian bedspread shirts and beads and faded jeans. One girl had an ankle-length, floral dress and the other two wore miniskirts. All were outrageous to a frightened world which judged them far too long, like our hair, or too short.

It seemed that now the kids were allowed home for the holiday, so there was a gathering of former pupils and staff. We walked into the dining hall, barefoot, while the 'old boys' were feeding from a buffet. Everything went silent and stopped moving. They wore grey suits, just as they had a hundred years before, when I was a prisoner too. As out of place as I'd always been there, this time it was I who was confusing them. Having failed to question anything at all, they'd simply fallen into line behind centuries of their seniors. And now, instead of fighting amongst themselves for a crust of bread, they were helping one another to oversized portions of somebody else's cake.

In June I went to Marazion for the anniversary of my brother's death. On the train I met a girl and we spent the journey in the bar. By Bristol we were deep in conversation, or at least, I was. It turned out that she worked as a nanny for Lord and Lady Someone, who lived next door to my rich cousins in Phillimore Gardens. In spite of my recognition of a train journey as the optimum length for a serious relationship, we arranged to meet in London in July.

Back in the city, you could feel the excitement growing. Each day, some new event carried the flame a bit further. Amidst controversy, the Beatles were chosen to represent Britain in the world's first television link to half a billion viewers. The young awaited the message that their icons would be singing to the stars. Could this be the puff of smoke that would signal the election of a different order? I went to watch with the girl from the train. We compared sun tan marks and turned on the television. The

Beatles sang 'All You Need Is Love', like urgent angels, high in the diamond sky. A fresh pulse of excitement encircled the globe and we knew that our time had arrived.

Pink Floyd now played weekly and all night at 'UFO', a basement on Tottenham Court Road. They inspired an audience whose awareness was heightened by anything other than alcohol. There were strobe lights, and psychedelic images projected from slides of oil and coloured water. They transformed the environment to imitate the trembling radiance of its inner nature. Everything was based on the assumption that LSD was the catalyst. It would blow the ordinary mind into pure ways of perception. Bereft of its concrete disguise, everything would be observed as fluid. And all of this brilliant fragility would lead us to treat it, and each other, with the utmost respect.

As a symbol of my right to freedom of expression, in honour of simplicity and the sheer release of it, I gave up wearing shoes. Barefoot and carefree I went, on pavements, escalators and the tube. And in all of that summer I never trod on anything that I didn't mean to, which might have been because my feet never touched the ground.

In morning sunshine I walked through London to my work. Longhaired and barefoot in sun-bleached bright colours, I sat on the grass and blew bubbles for ducks and furled umbrella men in bowler hats. 'If this is me, and that is you,' I asked, 'which of us would a fair-minded alien consider as weird?'

At the Institution it was time for the Conversazione, or gathering of the clans of engineers. Because we'd finish late, two of us got permission to sleep on the kitchen floor. From the Great Hall, and all down the elaborate staircase, the place was festooned and drenched with flowers. We'd persuaded two waitresses to stay, so when it was over, it was four of us who climbed the steps to the flat roof. Borrowing rugs from the president's office, we laid out food we'd saved from the feast, embellished with vases of lilies, candles in silver candlesticks and a small chunk of 'Mellow Yellow'.

We lay on the rugs, with the clock face of Big Ben hanging like a malevolent moon at the parapet's edge. Its hands pointed, imperiously, to a time with which the British had ordered the earth. Below us was Parliament Square. To one side was the Treasury, and behind us was the Palace. In the fine warm night we lit candles for the world that had been repressed and pillaged from this place. Whispering at first, before long we were laughing, and yet there was no one to disturb us, but the quarterly chimes of the moon.

I thought of the lives that had been ruled from here, on an Irish farm, in an Indian village. Lives ticked off by the clock, rung out by the bell that had tolled generations to dust. I wondered, 'who has the right to rule anyone else?' I gazed over the edge at the lines of pigeons, obediently asleep on the ledges below, and marvelled at the scale of the organisation.

We wanted change, but external revolution only brings another bunch of tyrants to haunt those ghostly windows. True change has to well up from within. I promised to work on it, as we kept watch with our candle of freedom, until it and Big Ben were put out by the sun.

One evening, while lamenting the lack of female company, there came a ring on my bell. Standing on the steps were five blonde Swedish girls. They'd been hoping to stay at a house in Putney with Donovan and co., but there was no room, so they gave them the address of my crazy flat.

They explained that they were from Gothenburg University, where they'd been warned to watch out, because everyone in London was experimenting with this stuff called LSD. They said that Putney was full of drugs and, for one night, could they make use of my floor?

The next night, I was walking up Earls Court Road with three of them, on our way to the chip shop. A young stranger stopped me to ask if I knew where he could get some blotting paper. He said that Smith's had sold out. The shop girl had asked him why it was suddenly selling so fast. In just one week they'd cleared a year's supply. It was obvious that the first tidal wave of acid had now washed into London. I had to explain to the girls why young people were wandering the night, looking for paper used to dry the ink from an old-fashioned fountain pen.

It was important to clear up a few misunderstandings that were rife at the time. I explained that coffee and cocaine, nicotine, heroin and alcohol were extremely addictive, but LSD and cannabis were not. Otherwise why would we go anywhere near them? It was freedom, not slavery, that inspired us and dared us to dream. I said that the oldest civilisations on earth regarded alcohol as a gross and addictive narcotic that induced violent behaviour. Whereas cannabis just made you cool. I must've been convincing enough because, by the weekend, they'd all turned on to hash. Then we found a room across the square for four of the girls, while Margareta stayed on with me.

So I had the statutory, long-blonde-haired, slim Swedish chick to help me fly the jet streams of that summer of love. When I told her that, she said we were quits, because every Swedish girl wanted a longhaired, cool-looking London boy and that's why they'd come.

Sometimes she wore, as a dress, the Indian bedspread shirt that I'd got from a girl at Biba. Sometimes she wore the lace tablecloth dress that I'd bought her from Granny Takes A Trip. Always she looked stunning and, bedspreads or tablecloths, barefoot and laughing we ran through the shimmering streets of the times of our life. And everywhere that we went there were flowers, and one of us was weaving one into the other one's hair. They'd become the symbol of the love that was to stop the war, the greed of the leaders, and promote a new millennium of peace.

By candlelight, we lay in my room, on a hot night with French windows wide open. She talked, excitedly, about the changing world, while I wondered if anyone could be as beautiful as that, or if everyone was, or if it was only the light. When there was a rumble of thunder and a flash in the rooftops, I told her of a

Dylan song that perfectly mirrored the moment. As I put 'Chimes of Freedom' on, the night sizzled white as thunderclaps rolled into London. We turned up the music and ran to the balcony to catch the display of the storm.

The heavens split open and emptied while we stood with arms held aloft to encourage the deluge. We were one with the power of the lightning, and the lightning was one with the words of the poet, whose time had finally come. All of the pain and the love of the world soaked through our clothes, through our skin. We were alive, wired to the sky, washed inside out and ready to die. As I kissed her, I could see the lightning flash in her eyes, feel the life-force streaming between us. Laughing and crying, we peeled off our clothes like sticky concepts cling-filmed to freedom. On a balcony, high in the midnight square, we dared the world to give up, undress and unite.

On another still and sultry night, I suggested a swim. Some of the girls had boyfriends now, and together we numbered eight. There was a lake in a park that I passed on the way to work. Unlike Hyde Park, there were no railings. It was surrounded by ornamental water birds, a garden of flowers and empty Westminster windows.

It was quiet when we got to St James's Park. Not a soul to be seen but pelicans asleep in the rose beds. A full moon lit the warm, scented air. We looked as pretty as the gardens, which looked like the gardens of heaven in June. We took off our clothes and I ran down the grassy slope, laughing at the feel of the dew. It felt so right to be naked and free in this beautiful night, especially here, with the Foreign Office beside us.

Reaching the water, I threw myself, full-length, into the lake. There was a sickening splat. A thin film of moonlight had disguised a millennium of duck shit. The others had halted at the edge. Very slowly and blackened by slime, I gouged my way to my knees. When my friends had regained their senses, one of the girls found a hose at the gardener's shed. They hosed me down while I refused to look as ridiculous as a shit-covered show-off in paradise park.

So. That was why there were no fences. Not to be deprived of our midnight swim, we tried the Serpentine next. Hundreds of young people had had the same idea as us. The police were manhandling bathers out of the gates. I tried to reason with them, politely, but they politely threatened to arrest me if I didn't shut up.

What was freaking out 'the authorities' was precisely these spontaneous gatherings of the young. There was no precedent for this. The new underground press asserted that the police should allow us to play. They knew how to respond to trouble but had no idea of how to handle illegal outbreaks of peace. Especially events spread by word of mouth or, as in this case, by a common thought and a well-timed moon.

Outside boutiques we watched posters appear, that read, 'You can get IT here'. They told police that 'IT' was the secret energy that was changing their world. Actually, 'IT' was *International Times*, published from Indica bookshop, where you met people who almost understood. It was the place that the establishment feared the most. It questioned their ethics in a language that they couldn't understand and certainly should never be printed. It spoke out about everything that the straight press avoided. From hidden facets of the Vietnam War, to some crazy theory that humans were destroying something called the ozone layer, and how the CIA had arranged the marriage of the King of Sikkim to one of its agents.

By mid-'67, the rulers were thoroughly rattled. They'd lost control of their children. They weren't aware that their best weapon was their lack of understanding. By getting it all completely wrong, they began to trivialise what was beyond them. The press couldn't sell sincerity but, by God, there was a fortune in sex and drugs. We watched this beginning as the summer faded. We'd lived through a spontaneous refusal to be told what to do, based on the realisation that all laws become irrelevant once we take care of each other. Through commercialisation the purity of our simple message was slowly perverted.

But in spite of their ridicule, things were still changing. The old institutions hadn't been swept away, but we were experimenting with alternatives. For example, the Arts Lab had opened in Drury Lane and The Congress of the Dialectics of Liberation had met at the Roundhouse in July. This led to the foundation of the Anti-University of London, two of whose courses were to be held at my flat.

Meanwhile, Margareta and the girls had returned to Sweden. One October night she rang me, begging me to go over and see her. At that time, flying was quite a big deal and most people had never been airborne. I told her that I'd see her in the morning, put down the phone and found that my passport had expired. It was Friday night and everything was closed. 'Come on,' I told myself, 'you know you can do it.'

I tried the Passport Office, rang the head post office, some travel agents and insisted my way through various departments of police. Everyone was adamant that nothing could be done until Monday. Finally, a patient policeman promised to investigate. He discovered that, under exceptional circumstances, a temporary passport might be obtained from the Foreign Office. He asked me, what was the emergency? I lied that my grandfather was dying in Sweden, and I had to get over there fast. Uneasy about using my beloved grandpa, I convinced myself that his Irish sense of fun would have encouraged me to go to my girl.

They told me how to get there, past 10 Downing Street and turn left. I didn't tell them that I knew exactly where the Foreign Office was, from nuclear disarmament rallies, from a night spent smoking hash on a nearby roof, and from jumping naked into the duck pond round the back, with the real reason for my trip to Sweden.

I was escorted through the dimly lit halls of a bygone empire, and into a lift that was actually disguised as a bookcase. When the Resident Clerk asked if I was genuine, and I assured him that I was, he pulled out a parchment embossed with the crest of the Queen. 'Travelling to Sweden on compassionate grounds,' he signed it and sealed it and I was away.

At Gothenburg, all five girls had come to the airport. They were jumping up and down and waving, while I tried to look sad for passport control. We all went for a coffee, and then I spent a few great days with my beautiful girl until, one lunchtime, the telephone rang. Norma had traced me, through a friend, to tell me that Grandpa Mac had died in Hampshire.

Now I had to get the whole system working for me in reverse. I needed one of the emergency seats that airlines kept on crowded flights. The airline wasn't convinced by my grandfather story, although this time it was true. They demanded telegraphed confirmation from the British Foreign Office that my grandfather had died in England. All of this only served to confirm my doubts about our version of 'real'.

The girls saw me off and, as I flew towards London, the unreality of the situation subsided and I mourned the loss of Grandfather Mac. I'd assumed that he'd be sitting with his 'Times' and his tortoise in the garden of my childhood forever. And when I was old, I'd pull up my chair next to his, and we'd talk wisely about the cricket and weather.

In November, Margareta came to see me in London. We had a wild week, at the end of which I was exhausted. Too much drink, little food and almost no sleep. It was time to give up my job and start painting again, while I still had the sight to see it. I decided to return to my parents and stay there until after Christmas.

I let my room at the flat and shivered my way to the Edinburgh train. My innate optimism had given way to a mood that I hadn't encountered before. At Earls Court station the lift was broken. It meant taking the long spiral staircase down to the Piccadilly Line. It was a mesh of black steel that screwed down into hell. I got stuck on the wrong side of the spiral which was six deep with demonic strangers hurrying intently below. Being on the inside, I had to balance my feet on tiny triangles of polished metal that

I couldn't see. I clung to the cold black pole and lowered myself into the abyss. The silence of the flying spectres was enhanced by the clank of their metal heels on the steel. The feeling of menace was intensified by bare bulbs whose weary light sucked itself into the blackness. I, who never had bad trips, was having a bad trip now. It escorted me through the underworld to Kings Cross.

Above ground, things were no better. I gazed from the main-line train at a world that was grey and tired and without any point. In the last year I'd lost my brother, my wife and my dear old grandfather too. I'd no job and no prospect of ever achieving my ridiculous goal. My eyesight was changing and I could hardly read a page anymore. The summer was over and the dark forces of materialism were snuffing the dream. All of the energy that I'd thrown into the past few years had suddenly departed. I wiped condensation from the window and watched the desolate landscape. It'd been such a struggle. All of those years of pretending. For the only time in my life, the thought arose that I could put an end to this bit of the story.

That was the nearest that I got. With the thought, a small feeling of release came and nuzzled my shoulder. Tied to the rope of the thought of death, I'd thrown myself a life-belt. Self-induced death was no way to change course, but only a way to increase the confusion. However bad things might seem, I was alive and that was a miracle. It took the possibility of death to remind me of that. Then the sun came out. It was warm on my face in the window and it sent me to sleep.

On walking into the house, I surprised my mother. She had friends coming to tea, but she said she'd get rid of them quickly. Meanwhile, she brought me blankets and pillows, tea and cake in the sheltered garden. Lying there in unseasonable sun, I felt the colour return to my life. And she never questioned me, she simply looked after me with the unconditional love which was the only way that she knew. My instant recovery made me doubly aware of the gratitude that I owed to this gentle person whose kindness had floodlit my youth.

I stayed home for Christmas. As always, Father flapped before guests arrived and then turned into the perfect host. As always, he offered my mother a sherry which she refused. As always he insisted and she submitted to make him feel good. As always she waited until he'd gone, gave me a wink, and poured it into the sink.

I painted through the winter and then, when the daffodils showed their first slivers of yellow, it was time to go south to the city.

I found an agency where I got work as a char. It involved ringing in, each day, to be told the address of a house that had to be cleaned. The pay was bad, but the agents were idealistic and young. They employed penniless artists and tried to match them with a householder in their own genre.

Another slight problem was that I'd let all of the rooms at my flat. I couldn't return like a landlord and kick someone out, so I stayed with friends, until I hit on the broom cupboard. It was at the top of my stairs, had a good door, shelves for my things, and was exactly the size of a mattress. Furthermore, I had the use of my bathroom and kitchen.

Lying in my cramped but cosy new quarters, I laughed. Working as a char and living in a broom cupboard. Brilliant. Occasionally, the humour of the absurd perfection breaks through. Usually, we're too busy complaining to notice. Even so, titbits get fed to our ordinary mind-streams, as clues that we're not really lost.

I was getting to enjoy my new life as a char. I met a great variety of people in parts of London that I'd otherwise never have seen. One job was for an author called Stephen Potter in Hampstead. I tried to clean his house for him, but the trouble with me was my eyes. They made everything look all right as it was. Dust sparkled with diamond lights and I didn't like to disturb it. I spent hours sitting on stairs, wafting a duster at space between shining phenomena. This author was kind. He'd pour me a glass full of whisky, and talk about writing and the rioting students. I wasn't sure that he could see a lot more than me, and he probably admired the dust more than I did.

Then there was the other side of the story. A neurotic woman with a skinny house off Kensington High Street. She had a fetish about stairs, of which she had many. They were narrow and carpeted and always perfectly clean. As I hoovered them, she'd stand behind me and snap. 'You've missed a bit. You've missed a bit, there.' We would proceed up her stairs like this, until she broke off to get some more pills. On my first day I got to the top and into the nursery. Above the noise of the vacuum cleaner, I heard her nagging again. 'You've missed a bit.' I turned around but she wasn't there. I vacuumed slowly into the nursery and nearly bumped into the parrot. From its perch it mimicked its owner. 'You've missed a bit, missed a bit there.'

I had no intention of quitting, like so many of her helpers before me. She needed someone to badger and chivvy, to give herself the illusion of having a role. I felt sad for this lonely woman and a society that turned beautiful young girls, full of hope, into tortured old dragons like her. A system that took them right to the top, and then threw them backwards downstairs.

In my arrogance, I wanted to throw her pills out of the window and talk. But being rich and from the Royal Borough, she must already have had a psychiatrist to mangle her psyche. So I turned the vacuum cleaner up full, and leant it against the drawing room door to keep her away for a while. Then I lay on the rug by the drinks cabinet, and remunerated myself for my kind thoughts and pitiful wages, with the help of her husband's single-malt whisky.

In early summer, the couple in my main room left and I moved out of my cupboard. My eyes had almost given up reading. It was tiring and taking too long to finish a page, scanning backwards and forwards to distinguish unfamiliar words.

Next to being alone on a mountain, my greatest joys had been painting and reading, and so I'd been delaying and deceiving myself. Now I had to accept that the time had come to read my last book. One afternoon, I walked slowly to a King's Road bookshop. London's plane trees rustled their skirts in a midsummer breeze. There was a feeling like that of first falling in love, with someone who's in love with somebody else. It was neither happy nor sad. It went way beyond mundane emotions like that. It was an end, and like all ends, it would surely become a beginning. There was no more time to hang onto the words of the world. It was like the day that my mother got me to throw my dummy onto the dust cart.

I wondered which book other young people would choose as a farewell to reading. I knew exactly which one I was going to buy. There'd been plenty of time to decide. It was the definitive story of the outsider. I'd been dying to read it, but was determined to save it until last.

I paused to look in the window, at the blurred titles, and it no longer mattered that I couldn't see them. I felt a sense of relief pass through me, that all of that was now over. As I pressed my thumb on the cold brass latch, I felt it down to my toes. I went in and asked for *Crime and Punishment*.

'But of course, darling,' the woman responded, with her Chelsea literary inflection. Her tone implied that Dostoevsky was a personal friend, although he was dead and she'd never read him. If I'd cared, I might have been glad that I could now never be a part of her circle. 'Jolly old Crime and Pun. Should have a copy somewhere,' she said. She handed me the book so casually that I wanted to kiss her or scream to awaken her.

Meanwhile, the underground press campaign to allow the people to play in their parks was nearing fruition. The news spread by word of mouth that maybe, in Hyde Park on 29 June, Pink Floyd might give the first free open-air concert.

When the day came we sat on the grass and drifted together on spiral updraughts of the crazy new sound of our revolution. It soared through the summer city and wove a mesh of impenetrable energy, to hold back the rape of our dream by the moguls. For a moment we regained the initiative. We could do this. We could bring an end to the greed and the fighting. Looking back as we left, where thousands had gathered, there wasn't one shred of litter. The kids had picked up their own, and whatever had been there already, as a sign of our love for our planet.

Then suddenly, in August, the Russian tanks rolled into Prague. Their rumbling increased to a roar that echoed round the world and we awoke from the false dawn of our dreaming.

9

A Dream Turns East

Having learnt how fragile this precious life is, I was inspired to look harder for answers. It seemed that our thinking pointed to a door that was bolted by thought. There must be a way through that door and out into the sunlight.

From my mother, I'd received a foundation of unconditional love. From my father, I'd learnt to respect each occurrence. From the mountains, I'd learnt the relevance of stillness, while Diogenes and the girls of the island had sung me their song of simplicity. Then my eyes told me lies by filling in gaps in the fabric, to insist that this world is imagined by mind. A shimmering dream which we turn to clay, and get stuck in, until we're convinced that it's real.

I'd learnt that perception depends on our chemical balance, which is constantly changed by our emotional response to phenomena. Phenomena such as objects and people, memories, situations, the food that we eat and even the weather.

Various incidents had convinced me that the apparent solidity and boundaries between things are a contrivance of mind with its fists up. In reality, everything overlaps and constantly changes its place, because 'reality' is energy that knows no barriers or borders. This energy flows in the limitless oceans of space that lap through each illusory atom of everything's being.

By 1968, this was as far as I'd reached in my quest for a basis.

But surely, everything had to be more than an aimless stream of projections. There must be a core that's unaltered by subjective interpretation: a truth that doesn't waver, or wavers truthfully, in the display of its natural dance. The question was how to perceive it. Drugs had provided no answers but only underlined questions. They were too heavy a bomb to drop into the chemical cocktail. It needed to settle, but drugs only stirred it all up. Surely it must be through subtlety that we become aware of the subtle. Like the glimpses that I caught as a young boy in the country. How could I pick up the trail that we abandon as we wander off as grown-ups?

Then, one day in October, I was leafing through a new underground paper called *O*z. There was an article which described the first Tibetan centre in the West. It had opened in Dumfriesshire and was called Samye Ling. After years of scouring the press for word of Tibet, Tibetans had settled not far from the West Coast railway line, within easy reach of my questions.

A photograph showed a white building by a river in the remote border hills. As though distant lights had grown a bit brighter, it stirred again strange feelings that arose with mention of Buddhism. I booked a bed and got on the night bus to Scotland.

Samye Ling had recently been founded by a young Tibetan lama called Trungpa. He'd been studying at Oxford and spoke Oxford English. He was venerated by the Tibetans as one of their most revered masters. His aide was another Tibetan lama called Akong, who spoke almost no English. He looked after the practical things while Trungpa took care of the teaching. There was also a third Tibetan, an artist called Sherab.

I was collected from Lockerbie and we drove up into the hills. It became wilder and bleaker, with no one in sight but occasional sheep. We pulled up in front of an old hunting lodge, set amongst pines, beside the Esk river. As two small Tibetan dogs ran out to meet us, the driver explained that Trungpa was in retreat, at the Tiger's Nest in Bhutan.

They showed me the shrine room, darkened with curtains. There were cushions on threadbare rugs and one table with incense, a candle and three small statues of Buddhas. That was all that there was. It was surprisingly simple and yet there was something deeply sacred and timeless about it.

I was at Samye Ling for a week, but immediately knew that it was where I would settle. It always seemed, to me, unlikely that anything happens by chance. How could chance be a factor, if the world is the outward display of the infinite actions that made us? I felt that I was being drawn by ancient strings of the mind, in the direction of answers.

I spent the week learning what I could about Buddhism. About the vastness of its profundity and the necessity of starting simply with a three-fold basis of intent. To do no harm whatsoever, in thought, word or action, to any being or their planet. To help others in any way that you can. And, again and again, to tame the crazy, flying horse of the mind, until it can fly you to freedom.

At the philosophical level, there was talk of an advanced cycle of teachings from Trungpa. Intimations of a state of awareness that transcends the ordinary, everyday mind and reveals the truth as it is. After a process of preparation and meditation, you travel beyond the confines of limiting thought, to the pure realm of the primordial state. Wow. This was what I heard when I arrived at Samye Ling in 1968. I took it as word from the ancient times that I'd been stumbling along in vaguely the right direction. Suddenly now, I'd caught the first glimpse of a vast store of treasure. Waves of excitement pulsed through my veins and I couldn't wait for Trungpa's return.

A few weeks later, on Christmas Eve, the Apollo 8 astronauts sailed around the moon in their spaceship named after the symbol of light. It was the first time that we'd looked at our tiny blue planet from afar. They sent their Christmas message to a mesmerised world, saying, 'Let there be light,' and for a moment, again, there *was* light. But the young were already talking of leaving the cities in the quest for a more honest life.

One evening, a friend suggested that we attend some fringe event called The People's Theatre. I was about to receive another reminder, flashed into the turmoil of everyday mind. A small, personal guarantee that there was a point to the searching.

We arrived at a little, four-sided arena with three tiers of seats and a hundred people. A master of ceremonies handed us numbered tickets, then placed a chair at each end of the stage. As a girl sat on one chair, I had a sinking feeling that we were going to be subjected to audience participation. It was the old game. The showman said that this girl had never shown any reaction. There'd be a prize for making her blink. He'd pick a number from his hat and the corresponding person would go onto the stage and try to make her respond. The only rule was, no touching.

As he spoke, I looked at my ticket. It was number thirty-one. I knew without the slightest doubt that it was my number he'd call. It was like Russian roulette with six bullets. Reluctantly, I got to my feet. There was no escape. I was so preoccupied with my plight, that I didn't even think it was strange. I stepped down from the top tier, walked the length of the stage and sat in the hot seat. Somebody told me to wait for my turn; the man had to call out a number. He reached into his hat, fumbled around, pulled out a ticket and announced, 'Thirty-one.' I passed him my 'thirty-one' ticket. He said that he'd no idea how I'd done that, but he wished that I hadn't, because the crowd would think that we had the show rigged.

In the few seconds while this was going on, my ordinary mind had been working. It had come up with a plan to save my embarrassment. There was no way that I had the guts to perform some comedy routine. So I rose from my seat, walked up to the girl, put my face within six inches of hers, and stared in silence. Then I blew as hard as I could and she jumped. I hadn't touched her, so I'd won. Won by the mischief of ordinary mind, whose task is to conjure up such tricks for survival. On the other hand, the knowledge that my number was next was the product of what lies beyond our conventional mind-set. I wondered which level of mind had devised the whole episode to provide me with a little encouragement. That was the sort of question that was leading me on.

I was trying to find out about Buddhism. There were few books, so I wasn't missing much by not reading. The books that existed had been written by academics who hadn't practised their teachings, and therefore lacked insight. The rest, it was said, were untrustworthy translations.

In early 1969, I returned to Scotland. The Economic Forestry Group had bought large swathes of Dumfriesshire to plant tree factories as a tax dodge. They were selling the farmhouses and shepherds' cottages as holiday homes. Being so remote they were cheap.

On arrival at Samye Ling, they told me that a girl from Earls Court Square had booked for the following week. Also staying was a man called Tim Field. He'd been a member of The Springfields, a group whose lead singer, Dusty, was still popular. Tim was known as Dr Box, owing to the box of electric wires that he claimed could cure various ailments. He admired two small mandalas that I'd painted. They were no more than sixties trip-aids and trinkets, but Tim, an Old Etonian with the right connections, said that he'd get me an exhibition in London.

Meanwhile, two sisters had been brought to Samye Ling by their mother. To the girls' anguish, she made it clear that her daughters were at Benenden School with Princess Anne, and needed to be treated like royalty. I got to know the two girls. Diana, the younger, was fifteen years old, a gauche and innocent, 'jolly-hockey-sticks' of a 'gel'. She was trying so hard to be grown-up that she kept making awful mistakes. It was obvious that, under her film of misapplied polish, was bubbling a genuine angel. It was why, within a short while, she'd be marrying Trungpa.

The moment that I saw the elder sister, Tessa, I felt an attraction. Where Diana was blonde and bubbly, Tessa was dark with an air of mysterious calm. Before the sisters left for London, we made arrangements to meet there.

Of the Forestry houses, some were very remote and the rest were remoter. I decided to look at two in the valley of the Rae burn which joined the Esk at the back of the Centre. 'Ted the Head' offered me a lift to the footbridge that led to the valley. We turned out of Samye Ling gates and saw a young girl walking alone. 'No doubt I'm to drop you beside her?' Ted shrieked the jeep to a halt. She was wild-looking and unnervingly pretty in an ankle-length, embroidered dress from Nepal. She had slightly unkempt, fairish hair to her waist. She seemed to hover in space with the uncertain air of a waif who would have been lost, if she'd had anywhere to be lost from. She was seventeen years old and had left her baby at home with her artist mother in Earls Court Square.

We stood on the footbridge and watched the Esk racing along through the fields. The sky was full of the tumbling cries of the curlews who sang us a shivering descant of welcome to the valleys of their desolate world. I asked her name and it started to snow and she said that her name was Amalie Swinford. She said that it was strange that we should live in the same London square and yet wait to meet at a Tibetan monastery in Scotland.

A couple of miles into the valley, we came to Raeburnside, the first cottage. We could see a fire flickering through dusty windows. There were foresters inside, so we walked on, across a small bridge to Mid Raeburn. The windows were smashed and it was painted in green and a sinister silver. The whole settlement was in a world of its own, with views for miles and no other houses in sight. Raeburnside, two cottages with a stretch of land by the river, was five hundred pounds, or the price of a cheap mini-van. Mid Raeburn had a field and a garden and was for sale for a little bit more. Both properties were more or less ruins.

The area looked only a bit like the location of the community dream of my youth. In front was a giant twenty-two acre field, which was not quite the vast plain to the south, and the mountains were only the hills of the Borders. Even so, it was beautiful, and maybe this was the place. We'd crossed miles of pot-holed track, two broken cattle-grids and a questionable bridge. There was an access problem, hence the give-away price, and maybe this was an omen.

When the foresters had left, we walked back to Raeburnside. I picked Amalie up and carried her over the threshold. Was everything already decided? And who was this pretty young girl who fell with the snow from a mischievous sky, and just happened to turn up on the road to the future?

I gave her my gloves and we walked to Raeburnfoot through a blizzard. Then, halfway over the footbridge, dressed in snowflakes and the flush of the coldness, we kissed. And there was no one but us in all the white miles of the morning.

On the day that we arrived back in London, Amalie invited me across the square to have tea with her parents. They had a flat of two floors on the corner, where they let rooms to anyone addicted to chaos. Dora Holzhandler was already quite famous and her canvasses were stacked six deep against walls. She had long, black plaited hair and wore an embroidered, ankle-length dress with a Tibetan striped apron. An unlikely grandmother in her late thirties, she'd popped out of one of her paintings, to rearrange the scenery and everyone in it, before she popped back.

Amalie made various attempts to introduce me to her family. Everyone was talking at once about something completely different. No one was the slightest bit interested in what anyone else had to say. After a while I made out Dora's voice. 'Amalie tells me you've got a flat in the square; very nice.' She said it in a tone that implied that her plans were already advanced. She was gazing irritably at her third daughter, a baby called Hermione, who was seeking attention from a rug on the floor. 'Oh look, it's really freaking out. For goodness sake, *somebody*, stick a bottle in its mouth.' Hepzibah, the middle one of three daughters, found a bottle and gave it to Hermione. Amalie picked up her baby, Theodore, and there was a momentary lull, in which I was asked if I wanted some tea. Twenty minutes later, Dora's husband returned from his work.

'Here's George,' said Dora, 'he's terribly straight. He works, nine to five, in Regent Street as a jeweller. Don't know why he doesn't give up. Make us some tea George.' George went to the kitchen with the smile of a man who has learnt how to live in a house with four women. He was slowly becoming enlightened, having happily given up attempting to speak or to think.

Next morning, Amalie stood at my door looking pretty and a bit less than seventeen years. Her waifish appearance was enhanced by the long coat that she might have nicked from the Victoria and Albert Museum. Her hair was brushed, but not quite completely, and she clutched a small bunch of freesias.

'Dora's thrown me out,' she told me. 'She says the house is too small now that I have a baby, and she thinks I should move in with you.' I invited her in for five minutes. I told her that it was too soon. I thought of Tessa and a life of peace. I thought of her family invading my space; I saw the lost orphan look on her face and I smelt the scent of the freesias. I wondered if she really thought that I'd throw away my life for a bunch of my favourite flowers. By lunchtime, the cot was assembled in my room, and my life, as I'd known it, had ended.

An exhibition in Knightsbridge had been arranged and I worked flat out on my painting. Amalie helped, and although Dora had taken advantage of my propensity for letting things happen, strangely, I was getting to like my crazy and exhausting new family.

To wind down, we'd go to Gandalf's Garden or the Dragon Tea Shop which you entered through the jaws of a swirling psychedelic shop front. Inside, it was lit dimly by candles. On the floor were mattresses covered in rugs and cool-looking kids. There was a record player on a table with a stack of appropriate albums. You could play what you liked while one of those girls in long dresses might bring you some tea or, if they were involved, you'd make it yourself.

And always my eyes kept me on my toes with a mix of near misses and miracles. Like when I was walking along Park Lane going home. Not seeing what was coming, I walked slap into the front line of an oncoming march. It must have looked like I'd come, head-on and confident, to join in the protest against the military junta in Greece. Leading the march was the beautiful Greek star, Melina Mercouri. Laughing, she took my arm, and I walked with her to the meeting.

One morning I was painting when the doorbell rang. I picked up the entryphone and enquired who it was. A woman's voice asked if she could come up. She added that if she said who it was, I would probably not let her in. I couldn't imagine anyone who I'd rather meet than someone I wouldn't let in.

It was Tessa and Diana's mother, Mrs Pybus. She was impeccably dressed and in an even worse state than such people are usually in. I showed her into a room, the likes of which she'd never have entered. She turned not a hair, as I unearthed her a seat and she started to talk. The girls had told her that I was a writer, and a responsible person who'd been very helpful to them. They'd given her my address, and she didn't know to whom else she could turn in these times of confusion. She thought that I might have some idea of what was going wrong with the young.

She'd lost control of her daughters who'd run off to this Samye Ling place, against her express command. They'd returned, yesterday, and she couldn't bring herself to speak to either of them. They'd been sitting in their house in a state of unbearable silence.

I always got on well with people's mothers, as long as I wasn't going out with their daughters. At first, I agreed with her, how shocking everything was, while I hid the small lump of Black Moroccan under *The Book of Grass*, and kicked Amalie's knickers under the bed. I tried to explain why Samye Ling was all right for her daughters. That Buddhism teaches compassion and kindness, and the importance of not being selfish. How it was all about opening the mind, so there was no threat of a closed-minded cult, and how, unlike Christianity, it encouraged people to stick to their own religions. It taught meditation as the antidote to mind-scrambling drugs, and stressed the importance of respecting your parents. I told her how I'd just been, with Trungpa, to see Khrishnamurti in Wimbledon. That I'd found him an inspiration, committed to the ultimate well-being of others.

Saying that her daughters were just going through a difficult patch, I lied that they'd both told me they loved her, because I was sure that they did. I avoided adding that it was just her attitude that they couldn't stand, and that I could see why. I offered to mediate between her and the girls and we arranged to meet later.

I walked to the house which was sandwiched between a couple of embassies at Lancaster Gate. Tessa let me in and escorted me to the drawing room. On the wall, above the fireplace, was a large portrait of Mrs Pybus, seated in a wing chair in twin-set and pearls. Beneath this sat Mrs Pybus, in a wing chair, wearing twin-set and pearls, posing as herself, posing as the English Queen. The girls sat at the far end of the room, while I took up a station between them and their mother.

'Do help yourself to a drink.' Her Ladyship waved at a trolley of bottles.

'D'you know, I think that I might,' I replied, trying not to run; appalled at how easily I slipped into the vernacular.

'So far, so good,' I said to myself, 'this is all very grown-up. I'm glad that I decided not to turn up with bare feet.' At the trolley I got my back between Mrs P and my glass. I poured a tumbler full from a bottle that I hoped might be gin, with a 'let's pretend' splash of her tonic.

There ensued a bizarre conversation. Although we were in the same room, Mrs Pybus spoke to me and asked me to repeat what she said to the girls. Playing her game, they replied to me and I relayed their reply to their mother. This process continued with translations and footnotes from me. Finally, with most of the issues resolved, Mrs Pybus invited us all out to dinner.

It was a smart restaurant, as dark as midnight with a sliver of moon. It had little gilt chair-lets, and so much clutter on inadequate tables that you'd only have to breathe and something would break. Such places were a nightmare for someone who couldn't see as far as the end of his fork. I was relieved that I'd not gone in and sat on somebody's lap. If trapped in this sort of place, I'd order a steak, which was easy to deal with. This time, our hostess ordered the food. Apparently, we were to eat sole. My heart sank.

For my first mouthful, I carefully skewered a safe piece of vegetable, only to find that I was chewing the lemon. I decided that the way to proceed was to cut off chunks of the fish and treat the thing like a steak. I'd attempt to separate the flesh in my mouth, then discreetly remove the bones with my fingers. And all of the while, I had to carry on a polite conversation with the matriarch, who seemed unconvinced that she was quite ready to talk to her daughters. By the end of the meal my entire fish had been transformed into a sticky white pyramid on the side of my plate, and I'd consumed nothing but a trickle of sole juice.

I must have got away with it because, the next morning, there was a further ring on my doorbell. This time it was a delivery from a South Kensington florist. I was handed a box with, not one or two, but about fifty sprays of gardenia.

Meanwhile, Old Etonian Tim was pulling his strings. He got a few of my paintings into Asprey's of Bond Street and more in the gallery at Heal's. He also arranged a well-known Indian sitar player for my private view at the gallery in Knightsbridge.

The opening was all right. A few pictures were sold and it got some polite-ish reviews. When everyone sat on the floor for the music, I slipped out of a side door into Sloane Street. There had been a soft summer rain and the pavements were planes of light. I walked up towards Harrods trying to think of something that mattered. A Rolls Royce glided by on the glistening surface. I thought of pushing a pushchair through the potholes, on the track up the Raeburn valley. Was I really going to live in those dark Scottish hills with this little girl and her baby?

Once again, I seemed to have assumed the lead role in a play that had no part for someone like me. Nothing was even bothering to pretend to be real. All of those people back there at the gallery, celebrating my night of success. How great to have a one-man exhibition in Knightsbridge. What none of them knew, and I couldn't tell them, was that I'd done my last painting. The strain on my eyes was giving me headaches and nightmares. It was time to let go of implying that I could see, as solid, all of this stuff that we spread out around us. It was time to let go of this thing that I loved. It could join, in the gutter, my other great passion of reading. I'd long ago resolved never to be negative about the eyes that had once saved my life, but there was no need to make resolutions. I'd come to see them as the brilliant guides on my personal trek towards freedom. They provided precisely enough ordinary sight to get me around, while protecting me from getting lost in the detail. They were watchdogs, who kept snapping me back to attention. Now they were saying, 'Okay, it's okay. It's time to stop painting and try something different.'

I loved this rain that gave me the streets to myself. It emphasised the sad relief that all of this was now over. I felt detached from my tiny moment of triumph, which was the last act in the old competition. It wrapped up my useless attempt at a life in the world. I could leave the cities with hardly a trace of regret. Just the usual feeling of dancing in space, once the crowd was all right and I could slip away without being noticed.

Because I'd struggled, a bit, to survive and succeed, I'd been preoccupied with personal objectives. This had made me self-centred. I looked for a puddle to splash in, but Knightsbridge streets were too proud for a puddle. I stood in a doorway and addressed the mannequins and the myriad Buddhas of the raindrops of evening. Would they please teach me the humility that would open my heart, and let me evolve to a point from which I might actually help?

The rest of that summer passed in a daze, because I'd really left London and saw no point in paying attention. Holland Park was full of colourful people, and there were times when it still seemed like heaven. Like when we kissed by the lavender beds, and a peacock flew onto the wisteria wall, and we were children again.

I'd been sitting inside like everyone else. I was watching the girls' television. It was a hot summer's night and everything was happening too slowly, so I went for a walk. They still had to open the hatch, so it'd be a while before they stepped onto the moon. There was no one in the square and no one in the streets of the world. The planet was glued to its screen. All of the windows of London were open and the same American voice was drawling from each bedsit and basement in town. It droned on the air from everywhere, and there was no other sound in all of the stationary city. And there, above the square, was hanging the waxing lantern of our satellite symbol of love.

I rejoiced at the possibilities created by what we were doing and I mourned for the beautiful moon. How appropriate it was that these were the last days of our decade of dreams. I climbed the fence into the garden, lay on the grass, and talked to the stars. I too was going on a journey to an alien world; out of the city, out of the sixties, hassling the unknown for its answer.

My thoughts trailed away as I let myself drift with the soundtrack uniting the planet. And the lunar light rippled down on the wide-awake town and there was no one to notice. Then the voice said that a man had trod on the moon. It was late. Would we all stay up to welcome a radiant morning, or would we go back to sleep for a further millennium or two?

10

Butterflies and Razor Blades

In early August I arrived in Eskdalemuir. The van bumped away down the track to leave me with a pile of my stuff at the bridge. There was Mid Raeburn and me and the empty hills for as far as the eye could imagine. It was beautiful, desolate and not quite like home. I hauled everything in, and started to scrape out the house.

The first thing that I noticed was the bathroom windowsill. Spread across it were dozens of rusty razor blades, interspersed with dead butterflies trapped by the glass. Butterflies and razor blades, focused into relief by the lonely glare of the hills. Were they left as a signal to a passer-by, of the dangers of chasing a dream? I worked for some days on the house, then walked a few miles to the phone and arranged for Amalie to come.

From the end of the two-mile track, it was thirteen miles to a shop and we had no car. Once a week, a grocery van came to the foot of the valley, laden with stuff that we'd rather not eat. In spite of our remoteness, slowly we got the house ready for winter.

Word soon got around that there was a cool house in the Raeburn valley. People began to drift over the hills from Samye Ling. Amalie would open the door. 'Oh, wow, more beautiful people,' she'd say, and they'd roll joints while she fed them. They brought news of the festival that had just happened at

Woodstock and the Bob Dylan concert on the Isle of Wight. We were saddened to hear that the open-air concerts were no longer free.

I spent much of that year picking my way through inert bodies, while lugging buckets of concrete. Occasionally, I'd receive a little encouragement. Like, 'Hell man, that bucket looks heavy.' And yet I got the house built, in spite of the guilt that arose from wasting time working when a real man would be occupied with the full-time business of being.

It was a minority who acted like that and exploited the dream, but we seemed to attract them. Claiming that everything belongs to us all, if they wanted something, they took it. An example occurred in our first summer. My mother brought us a large wicker basket, piled with hundreds of strawberries that she'd grown in her garden. We left them in the kitchen and went out for the day. We returned to an empty house and an empty basket with a pile of green strawberry stalks and two solitary fruits left for us by our friends. Amalie said, 'If they'd waited, they knew we'd have shared them.'

Trungpa was living near Samye Ling, at Garwald House which had been bought by American students from Oxford. He was a 'crazy wisdom' master, which meant that his style was unpredictable. His lineage used shock tactics, where needed, to cut through habitual patterns of survival mind, to awaken students to their innate nature. He taught that, in Tibetan, one word for wisdom is 'yeshe'. 'Ye' translates as primordial and 'she' translates as knowing. So he spoke of wisdom as that which we already know. Every one of us has this wisdom within, but it's blocked by our habit of thinking.

Hearing my uncertain conjectures confirmed from an ancient source was one of the most inspiring events of my life. The flickering starlight that I'd once held in my hand had returned as a radiant orb. Here was the verification for those hints at a truth that is out of reach of our reason. Trungpa now gave it authenticity, with names like 'intrinsic awareness'.

Thought can lead us to learning, or knowledge; the accumulation of facts about the container, and everything in it. Thought can also deliver the curriculum that teaches us how to let go of our thinking, so that we can become available to a state beyond thought. Not a dull, unconscious state of non-thought, but the scintillating array of unimaginable awareness, beyond the limits of conceptual mind.

Trungpa was standing at the open door, pointing to the way for which I'd been searching. Yes, there *is* a place where reality can be known as it is, and yes, he knows how you can get there. I rejoiced that the trail had grown warm again, but knew that I was only at the beginning of the beginning.

Trungpa was tentatively revealing, to the West, the supreme teaching of Dzogchen which, in Tibet, was kept secret to protect unready students from confusion, and itself from corruption. It was treated with such respect that it was whispered, by a master, to the few students who were ready to receive it. Could it be that the Western mind was already sufficiently evolved? To teach it would be an experiment and a gamble. Trungpa knew that it could easily go wrong, and cause all kinds of upheaval, but maybe it was worth trying out, on these fresh minds of the West. After all, having come from a society which had yet to make use of the wheel, he was interested in minds that had just put a man on the moon.

Sometimes we'd go to see him at Garwald, and sometimes he visited us. Students would bring him and some whisky for tea. I got to know him in those cold afternoons in the shade of the hills of the Borders. You couldn't help but like him. His magnetic personality invited affection. While his openness made him seem vulnerable, his presence was unnerving, and his spaciousness left you completely at ease.

As I watched his students treat him like an errant god, I thought that this refugee prince could use a friend in the alien world of the West. Why not? He was roughly my age. My arrogance was based on the fact that I'd no clue as to how to become a disciple, and no inclination to do so. My schooling had provided no evidence that subservience to authority ever produced a beneficial result. So I was relieved when he asked me not to use the honorific title of 'Rinpoche', but to call him by his first name.

An interesting group of people were living at Samye Ling, or in the valleys nearby. They had nicknames which aptly defined them. There was Samadhi Bill who drifted about in search of his body which was continuously smiling. There was Junkie Jenny, the good-looking chick with long, long hair, and a heart of easy-going gold. She belonged to the stars and was on loan to anyone cool. There was Jonathan Egg, and Americans like Long Ron, who were avoiding the Vietnam War. And then there was Psychotic Kenneth.

Psychotic Kenneth was a tall, thin Texan with piercing blue eyes. His head and chin swam in a halo of curly black hair. He was permanently stuck between life-threatening decisions, like whether it was safe to get up, or better to first eat an apple. He was as gentle as a lamb and great fun, provided that you'd taken patience as part of your path. My first encounter with him was a three-hour tea break spent urging him that there was no need for him to take acid. He followed my advice, bought a black Quaker hat, became an evangelist and changed his name to Solomon Broadsword.

Kenneth was a little paranoid. One day he gave me a lift. We were doing twenty on the inside lane of a four-lane highway. He slowed down and stopped. There was a 'state-of-the-art' cattle grid stretching across the four lanes ahead. Cars were streaming across it, in both directions, at speed. Kenneth got out, bent down, grabbed the first steel rail and tried to shake it. He proceeded, on his knees, across the grid, testing each rail until he reached the far side. Then he came back to the car. 'You can't be too careful,' he said.

One afternoon there came a knock at the door. It was Tessa and a few others. Walking up the path behind them was Trungpa. Amalie made tea while we talked and played music. Then the others went to our shrine room to practise the saddhana that Trungpa had recently composed at the 'Tiger's Nest', in Bhutan. Thinking that you could practise at any time, I took the opportunity to be alone with this extraordinary being.

We talked and then Joan Baez stopped singing. I could hear the ebb and flow of chanting from the far end of the house. It seemed to be filtering in from a dimension that someone had left on by mistake. I wanted to ask him how I could find out who I was, but I wasn't sure if that was the question. I was a novice at this, and I didn't want to get heavy. Besides, I'd heard that it was all right not to chatter. Better to simply allow yourself to become available to the wisdom mind of the master. Otherwise, however carefully you worded your question, it would seem irrelevant in the presence of someone like Trungpa.

I looked at him, sitting beside me on the floor. He smiled. Instead of feeling self-conscious, I felt completely at ease. A sudden trickle of raindrops splashed into a bucket from a leak in the roof. He laughed. I laughed and relaxed to a state where thoughts and other phenomena fizzled away, like ribbons of mist in the sun of the morning. I would have found myself in a state of immeasurable grace, had there been any 'I' to have been there.

The far-away chanting ceased and the others came back to the room. Years later, a wise old lama, called Tulku Pegyal, told me that this was known as 'the showing of a sliver of the moon'. It was an unfortunate fact that I was far too unaware to truly receive it.

A young Tibetan lama called Ato Rinpoche was coming to dinner with Trungpa. Knowing that I'd trained as a chef, his students asked me to cook. I'd heard that Tibetan nomads tenderised meat under the saddles of their horses. I had no idea whether they cooked it, or ate it raw, or whether these lamas had ever tried the fare of the nomads. Nonetheless, impressed by the story, I decided to give them a treat of best Scottish beef. I'd remembered a dish that was, at that time, considered exclusive and rare. It was finely chopped fillet steak, eaten raw, with a raw egg yolk, chopped onions, tomatoes, capers and parsley.

When they'd finished the first course, a student came for the steak. When he saw it, he freaked and refused to serve it until it was cooked. With my confidence faltering, I assured him that Steak Tartare was a classical dish of Lhasa cuisine. By the end of the meal my cold feet had got frostbite. And I never knew whether they were just being kind when they thanked me for introducing them to this dish which they said was delicious. I suspected that they'd have said the same had I served up a strangled cat. I told myself to curb this arrogance that deluded me into assuming that I knew.

It was in those days, observing Trungpa's interaction with his students, that I began to understand a little about the unfashionable topic of 'devotion'.

He was trying to encourage them to open. This quality was essential if they were to absorb such a profound philosophy. In his tradition, in order to transform habitual resistance, teachers would constantly push students to the edge of their self-imposed limits. They'd tear down the lace curtains of worldly conventions from behind which we peek out to judge all that is passing. And this process would test the student's commitment. They'd need this commitment in order to negotiate the wreckage of pre-conceived notions that would litter their paths, as they shuffled about in the market, trying on pretty ideas. They'd need it to open their minds to allow the stream of instruction to flow. After all, they'd asked for the ultimate prize of enlightenment, of omniscience, the ability to really help others, and eternal freedom from pain. If we set out on a quest for such treasure, should we not be prepared to die once or twice on the way?

It seems that confusion concerning enlightenment remains

the main problem, both in the West and everywhere now, as materialism tightens its grip on the mind. We talk glibly about it, or are embarrassed to mention the word. Perhaps most of us need to concentrate on the meaning of enlightenment for a decade or two, until we've fully understood that it's beyond our understanding. If in that time we catch a first glimpse of what it might mean, we'll do anything to reorient ourselves towards it. We'll probably start shoving one another out of the way; be so single-minded that things might get a bit rough, until we realise that the only way there is via compassion and love.

Past teachers of most religions threatened their students with gory stories of hell. That trick may have worked in the dark age, but today we've rejected all of that heavy repression and guilt. The way ahead is a direct aim for the radiant light of our nature. What we're really like when we let *everything* go. That is enlightenment. When we begin to gain the vaguest impression of what it might look like, we realise that, compared to enlightenment, this ordinary life of pre-packaged concepts is already a ramble in hell.

However we look at it, there's work to be done. We can move slowly and surely or we can risk a short cut. The difference between these approaches is not the goal but the length of the journey. The short cut is the lightning path of direct experience that Trungpa was teaching. It's a vertical climb up the mountain with avalanches of doubt to sweep you away, and then a leap from the top. It's not for most of us because we're restricted by our judgemental bias. Until we're ready to risk even our lives, we should probably keep off the rock-face and stick to the reasonable route. As long as we're going in roughly the right direction, we can enjoy the scenery and, hey, who cares if it takes a long time?

But quick path or slow, in either event, we could do with a guide. On the slow route we can change guides each time that we enter a different terrain. On the fast track, although we may share many porters, we need to commit to one leader. This is because we may cross dangerous ground and will require someone we trust; someone who's been there already. This trust will get us across. Like the chuckling blind man being led across a ravine, with devotion that grows at the end of each non-fatal journey.

These days, there are doubts concerning devotion. True devotion is unlimited and opens your heart to the world. Although it may coalesce into pure love for one person, it includes all that appears to exist. On the other hand, limited devotion is the problem. It's a deluded and possessive attachment to one particular being. At worst, its clinging can lead to the exclusion of imaginary rivals, and makes us the pawns of dictators. It actually closes our eyes until we believe that only *our* teacher is authentic, only *our* way is the right way. It's this sort of jealous, fair-weather loyalty that is actually all about 'me'. It leads to the formation of cults, and gives devotion such a bad press.

With genuine devotion we see the teacher as a mirror that reflects both our true nature, which is perfect, and the confused and temporary self that covers it up. If we look in the mirror and fail to recognise those faults as our own, we may blame the guide and turn away from our path. This is called missing the point. We've reacted and retreated behind the lace curtain. We should ask ourselves if we really want to see our original face, or just want a kind old mother to tuck us up in our cosy bed of delusion.

It's said that for some of us, when we're ready, the right guide will appear and we'll make an immediate connection. Others need to seek and check out a teacher with care. The nineteenth-century adept, Patrul Rinpoche, warned of the prevalence of false teachers who are attracted to power like moths to a flame. He said that, if necessary, we should keep watch on a guide for twelve years. This is because, for the fast track, we need to be utterly certain, and then make a total commitment. If we're not happy with that, we should buy some books, attend inspirational lectures by various teachers and, like a hawk, keep an eye on our ego.

Of course, on the deeper level, there's no such thing as false teachers because we learn and evolve from whatever takes place, but most of us aren't yet ready for that. In any event, one day we may find that our mind is slightly more open, our actions less coarse and our warmth towards others increased. At that time we may safely conclude that we chose the right teacher or teachers.

Now Trungpa's students had all read *The Life of Naropa*. They admired the skilful way in which the wild guru, Tilopa, had trained the academic Naropa, so many centuries before. How he'd put him through a series of life-threatening ordeals, slowly opening him to the point at which he was ready to experience the nature of mind.

Trungpa started to train them in a gentler way. They had asked him for this. Could they take, in real life, even a pale shadow of what they'd enthused about in the cloistered comfort of Oxford? I was told that he picked up their lives and shook them a little, to let some adornments drop off. If they really wanted to see the stars, he'd have to flush them out of the forest.

I witnessed only a small part of the process. For example: many old houses still had a glass-fronted box, high on the wall of the kitchen; a relic from the days of servants. In gold circles on the glass, a series of room numbers were painted. When someone upstairs called for a maid, a bell would ring and a number would light. I remembered playing with one of these fiendish devices in the house of my parents. What fun such a toy might be to a Tibetan who'd recently come from a time before time and electrics.

Patience is one of the first things that you work on. It's the antidote to anger which puts you in hell, as anyone knows who has tried it. Well, what a fascinating patience-machine Trungpa had found, built into the fabric of his house in the West.

Upstairs in his room he'd ring the bell. A student would run up from the kitchen. With an angelic smile he'd ask for some tea, wait until they'd just got back to the kitchen and then ring again. He'd repeat this over and over, while they ran up and downstairs getting more and more angry. And they forgot all about their hero Tilopa, who'd left Naropa half dead in a ditch full of leeches.

The more that Trungpa tested them, the more most of them proved they weren't ready. He used various techniques but they only reacted with growing resentment. They'd read the book and they knew the story but they weren't yet up to a part in the movie. And to be fair, they were the guinea pigs. What was on trial was the aptitude of the West. Were the brightest young minds, from its best universities, daring enough to leap onto this express that was thundering through their stations? Later, most of the few available masters who held this tradition felt that they weren't. Not yet. Not generally. There were plenty of other radiant cycles of teaching that you didn't have to be quite so ready to die for.

On the night before my birthday, Amalie stayed up while the rest of us slept. She painted a picture of us, for me, showing herself holding a baby. In the morning, she gave it to me and said, 'Happy birthday. Our baby is due in July.' I was thrilled and puzzled that someone else had arrived to fly with us, this crazy flash in the sky.

Then, before Christmas, Tessa came to stay. She said that her mother had given up on her, but was keeping a close eye on her sister. Diana wanted to come to Samye Ling, but Mama was threatening to make her a ward of court. Tessa suggested that, if I invited Diana to stay for New Year, then their mother might just relent. I said that I'd ring if they really thought it'd help. Actually, I couldn't refuse. This girl was intent on escape from an empty, upper-crust sham of a life, to study the electrifying philosophy of Buddha.

I doubted that any mother would let her sixteen-year-old daughter stay in the wilds of Scotland with someone like me. Then I remembered that I was already living with the teenage child of another mother from London. In fact she'd thrown her at me. Perhaps I was becoming too bourgeois and safe. I resolved to grow my hair longer.

Adopting my best English manners, I rang Mrs P, and was surprised when she seemed to say 'yes'. I urged her to send Diana, first class, on the overnight train. I meant it, but I knew that that would impress her. It was arranged that Diana should come for New Year. Meanwhile Dora had invited us to spend Christmas with her and the family in London.

On Christmas Eve we caught the train south. The next day we sat around talking amongst Dora's paintings and chaos. At one point a table got cleared and I thought that Christmas dinner might be in the offing. This small flurry of activity quickly subsided and things settled back into their natural state of static upheaval. I'd long known that only the unexpected took place in that house. I tried hard not to expect food, in the hope that it might surprise me.

Eventually, someone called out that dinner was ready and plates were brought from the kitchen. In the centre of each plate sat one bright orange tablet of LSD.

Like many artists, Dora regarded the responsible use of acid as a sacrament for expanding the consciousness. I was beginning to realise that the true opening of mind takes place through meditation. Chemical stimuli might cause a breach in the walls of the prison, but they disturb the very equilibrium for which we are searching. Awakeness takes place in the stillness of the high pastures of mind. Or, when startled for an instant of absolute freshness, by a confrontation with a scene in which something has shifted.

I was happy to get back to the shivering vastness of Scotland. With a few days of December left, we constantly expected a knock on the door from Diana. Then, on New Year's Eve, Trungpa came to visit with her and with Tessa. They came out of the night in a halo of light hearts and laughter, which made New Year's Eve come sparkling to life.

I'd seen Diana with Trungpa before, but only as one of the usual group that surrounded him. This time it was obvious that they were together. 'Brilliant for Diana,' I thought, 'but, oh dear,

Mrs Pybus, I can only tell you that I had not the faintest idea.'

They stayed a while, for a drink and some stories and then they were gone. They were on their way to visit others in the valley and, perhaps, to celebrate their engagement.

But people were possessive of Trungpa and most had their own agendas for him. Diana told me later that, after leaving us, that night turned into a frenzy; a vortex that flashed with the lightning of jealousy and unleashed resentment. People were angry when they realised that they had to let go, and angrier when they found that they lacked the commitment to do so. These emotions turned them against their teacher and Diana, as they thrashed around looking for someone to blame. Who the hell did she think that she was, this chit of a girl, come down from the rarefied reaches to snatch their pet guru away?

Meanwhile, Amalie and I had been left with a feeling of warmth, through which blew the fresh air of renewed motivation. I watched shadows flicker on the saffron ceiling, and the ceiling flicker between me and the stars. This Trungpa had made the stars dance. One day I might gain a little understanding of what it had all been about, but right now, only one thing was for certain. Never again would I be so alive, or be so excited to be so. It was thus that an era came to an end, on this the last night of the sixties.

In Edinburgh, on 4 January, Trungpa and Diana got married. It was all over the Sunday papers. 'Sixteen-year-old Benenden schoolgirl elopes with a monk'. They'd called him 'a monk' for the sake of their audience that was only alive when saying 'tut-tut'. Diana told me later how her mother received the news. 'Oh no, not Tessa, I don't believe it.' And then, when they told her that it was Diana, she fainted.

The difficulty that Akong was having with Trungpa's approach was growing. Their two perspectives were too far apart. Both had been current in Tibet when the two young lamas had escaped. The step-by-step path that was slow and safe, and the swift and brilliant short cut to the essence. Akong wrapped up everything, to protect it, in the cling-film of tradition, which Trungpa tore off and threw out.

One day at Mid Raeburn, Trungpa showed his qualities as a bodhisattva. He noticed two of my mandalas that I'd rescued from Asprey's and said that he liked them. I was embarrassed that a Tibetan lama should even see them, but he insisted, so I offered them to him. He hung them in his room, alongside a large and exquisite scroll-painting of the Pure Land of Amitabha, which had been given to him by the Queen of Bhutan. I was touched that he'd been so chivalrous in order to encourage me.

Trungpa's son had joined him, from India, and was now staying with him at Samye Ling. We were in his room, playing Monopoly, when Trungpa asked me to take over his hand for a while. He went and sat on his mattress on the floor, next to his son. I felt such a feeling of love for him. How had he coped with all of this? He'd lost everything; his family, monastery, teachers, status and country. He'd lost the world as he knew it; a world where he'd been showered with respect and with plenty. Now he had nothing but a see-saw suspended in space. And the cold Scottish darkness, that made me shiver, as I tried to buy him a house on Park Lane.

Trungpa went to America in March when the curlews were calling, and although we met many times in my dreams, I never saw him again.

II

Time to Wake Up

The forestry group were covering the hills with millions of commercial trees, but they were still small. It would be a few years before they'd grow together, excluding the light and all forms of life. For a moment now, with the livestock gone, the grasslands celebrated in an up-rush of profusion. For so many seasons, wild flowers of the Borders had been bitten to their roots, to bloom without stems in the sheep-shorn grass. Now they raced upwards, into the toothless sky. Meadowsweet filled the valleys with scent; fizzing with light, on the verge of dissolving, transient, ephemeral, and as unlikely as the mind that enabled their splendour.

We had a couple of acres of this. On one of them I dug a vegetable patch, and rejoiced in the dirty work that was so much more real than painting. As I dug, I thought of how much we were going to miss Trungpa. He'd sent me a letter from a 'York Hotel' in Montreal, asking me to forward his mail. It seems so final when someone asks that. For those of us stumbling around in Buddhist philosophy, with no trustworthy books and no guides who spoke English, how were we to progress?

Amalie and I were struggling on the cash that we had coming in from my London flat and my paintings. I found encouragement in a further letter from Trungpa which told me what he was doing in the States. It touched me by ending with the words, 'Thank you for being my friend in Scotland.' Then, one day in June, Amalie came into the garden to tell me that a taxi was negotiating its way through the potholes and up the valley towards us. It stopped at our bridge and Diana got out. She'd come to collect Trungpa's son from Samye Ling, and take him back to the States.

We sat in the garden and listened to stories of New World promise and plenty. I remembered the dark of the previous winter and the grasping of those around Trungpa. It seemed that we were still too petty to deserve the light that this messenger had come out of time to deliver.

Diana recounted a meeting that had taken place before they'd left Britain. Her South African mother couldn't believe that she'd married a 'black man', who she called a 'Tiebettan'. Now, to compound the fracture, that 'Tiebettan' was whisking her off to the States. This prompted the arrangement of a meeting in an Edinburgh hotel. There was Trungpa and Diana, with Mrs Pybus and the family solicitor. Over coffee, at the end of a silent dinner, Mrs P finally addressed her new son-in-law.

'And you, do you people have surnames?' she asked. 'What will my daughter be called in the future?'

'Why of course,' said Trungpa, in his Oxford accent and radiant smile. 'The family name is Mukpo. From now on she'll be Lady Mukpo.' This time, Mrs P failed even to faint. She was simply not equipped to comprehend the perfection of this rendezvous with her karma. Later I heard that, in a great transformation, she became devoted to Trungpa.

Diana said that the Americans couldn't believe how few possessions they had. Just one suitcase, the Pure Land of Amitabha and my two painted wood mandalas. The mandalas were now hanging on the wall of Trungpa's room in the States, which meant more to me than had they been bought by the National Gallery.

Diana left and then, at first light one morning in mid-July, with Amalie's contractions increasing, I cycled down the valley to ring for friends to collect us. We sped to Lockerbie where the driver took a wrong turning and we found ourselves hurtling up the motorway, away from the hospital, with Amalie about to give birth. We finally arrived, just in time, and Tara was born with a name that is sacred in both Ireland and in Tibet. Three days before the birth, a white dove actually settled on our roof and stayed until the baby arrived. When everyone noticed, we told them that it was a racing pigeon blown off its course and taking the piss, while secretly, common sense assured us that it was a sign.

A few days later it was time for my divorce. I'd instructed Ambrose Appelbe, a solicitor who helped artists and rebels from his Dickensian chambers in Lincoln's Inn. My case was handled by a woman barrister who said that Norma needn't attend. She insisted that I leave time after my case for a little 'get together' with herself, her secretary, and 'another nice young client'.

So, in the bar at the Royal Courts of Justice, we went for our drink. The barrister and her fizzy blonde secretary asked questions about young people's obsession with sex and drugs. 'You wish,' I thought to myself. The barrister said that she'd used amphetamines to help her to slim, but was giving them up. Then she pushed towards me a cigarette packet containing hundreds of yellow Preludin pills. There were officers of the courts in full fancy dress, detectives, police and people in wigs all around us. I told her that I'd no need for such things to get me high, that 'speed' wasn't good for your head, but I knew some musicians who used them, and slipped the pack into my pocket. What got *me* high was the thought of scoring drugs from a barrister in a wig, under the nose of the British bulldog, at the Royal Courts of Justice in the Strand.

Back in Eskdalemuir it was high summer with warm afternoons and the doors open wide. I threw the drugs in the river and sat in the shrine room with its yellow silk sunlight and silence, where Tara lay in her basket and gazed at the red-tasselled lantern above.

But soon the nights began to draw in, as the winter came early that year. The gallery had sold no more paintings, so there was almost no money, but at least that meant that the guests had moved on. We were alone in our house at the epicentre of nowhere, with no fuel for the winter. Our spirits slid down the hill with the sun.

By November it was bitterly cold. Our sack of brown rice was almost empty, and we had nothing else left. I hated brown rice. I took our last two shillings and walked to the mobile shop, through a light drizzle of snow. What was I doing? I'd no job and no prospect of a job. We'd no food, no fuel and the vegetable garden was rigid with frost. I walked by the burn that was slowly freezing and talked to a crow that picked at the corpse of a sheep. 'It's all right for you,' I told her, 'you were born to all this.' I wondered if this was why Norma had said that dreamers were dangerous. I walked on to the shop, my dreams as distant as the memory of sun. Like the dream of sitting by my own log fire, with the girl that I loved, in a cottage by a sparkling river. In the first winter we'd been unable to get near our fire for a small cluster of silent strangers. This winter we huddled close to some smouldering twigs that only got lit in the evenings. Then there was my old dream of starting a community of wide-awake people. What people? The ones who'd spent the last year watching me work, and were gone as soon as the money ran out?

Arriving at the shop, I bought four bars of Fry's Peppermint Cream, and took them back through the snow to Amalie Swinford.

We'd moved our bed into the gloomy little room at the back, thinking that that side of the house had fewer draughts. We took the chocolate, climbed into bed to keep warm and lay without speaking. Everything seemed hopeless. We'd reached the bottom, and then, in giving up hope, a strange sort of peace seemed to settle.

Within minutes, there came a knock at the door. I took a letter from Geordie the postman and sat on the bed. It was from the landlords in London. I guessed that they'd found out that I was sub-letting and were giving me notice to quit. I opened the envelope slowly. Unlikely words swam into some sort of order. They'd offer me fifteen hundred pounds for vacant possession of the flat that I'd already left? I gave it to Amalie to read. 'My God,' she said, 'we're rich; we'll go to Brazil or Peru.'

What I didn't tell her was that, if they'd offered fifteen hundred, I could probably get three thousand, which was the price of a house. I kept quiet because, if Amalie got anywhere near the money, it'd all be squandered or given away before spring.

It was no time to be lying in bed. That cash would keep us alive for a couple of years and turn Raeburnside into a meditation retreat for students of Trungpa. I went to the kitchen to scrape out the empty jar of damp instant coffee once more. There was another knock at the door. It was Pamela Woodman from Garwald House. She had to go away for a while and would we consider moving into her place for the winter? They'd provide food, if we'd look after the children while her husband was working. Now at Garwald they had things like a washing machine and a huge Aga cooker that you could lean against to keep warm.

A complete solution to our problems had arisen from two unconnected and almost simultaneous events. Two messengers carried them into the frozen expanse of the moment that we'd given up. 'Remember,' I said, 'in case it ever gets that bad again.'

We spent that winter at Garwald, and let Mid Raeburn to Beatrix Lambton who wanted to be near the Centre, or 'Samye Ling Shrine and Dine' as she called it.

I went to London and brought back the rest of my mandalas. At Lockerbie, the train was too long for the station. Normally, it would stop for passengers at the front, then pull forward to disembark those, like me, at the rear. This time it pulled forward but, instead of stopping, it kept gathering speed. I found the guard and insisted that we make an unscheduled halt, to let me off at the next station.

In a panic, at a tiny deserted stop called Beatock, the guard threw the mandalas, one by one, from the still-moving train. As it disappeared, I sat on the platform at the head of a trail of my rainbow-like spheres. Nothing moved but a steady drizzle that varnished the strange little scene. I thought of Trungpa receiving R. D. Laing at Lockerbie station. To the astonishment of the locals, dressed in his suit and a mischievous grin, he'd prostrated himself to his guest three times, full length on the wet Scottish platform.

There was no one in this desolate scene to whom I might prostrate. The last person had died of sensory deprivation in the middle of the previous century. There was nothing but Sunday from horizon to horizon, and me playing pig-in-the-middle of nowhere. After a long search, I dislodged an off-duty official and the system collapsed under pressure to spew out a free taxi which drove me the long journey home.

Moving back, in the spring, to remote Mid Raeburn, we decided that it was time to teach Amalie Swinford to drive. With a mind that could see in three directions at once, she was great at shedding new light on old propositions, but from behind the wheel she might be prone to dangerous assumptions. Amalie lived in a world that only rarely coincided with yours. If you wanted to meet her, you had to catch her when she'd strayed into the overlap. Otherwise, you could just *watch* her, dancing out there on the corpse of your last mad suggestion.

In Carlisle, I sat in the back while she took her first lesson. What was really terrifying was her confidence. As we pulled out into the traffic, I realised that she thought that a motor car worked on the same principle as a rowing boat. If you pull to the right on the wheel, you go left. As we got too close to the lorry she kept turning the wheel towards it, waiting for the steering to kick in.

We were taking a breather in a side street. The instructor told her to drive, slowly, to the end of the road and turn left. A double-decker bus, in a stream of traffic, was blocking the junction. It was stationary, a good fifty yards up ahead. Amalie drove slowly and purposefully towards it. Without flinching, or losing speed, she drove head-on into the side of the bus. I decided that it might be safer if I did the driving. Perhaps I could teach Amalie on the dirt roads of Eskdale. So I found an ancient Ford Anglia for sixty-five pounds, which we could both drive legally on the forestry tracks, and illegally on the mile of main road up to Samye. It wasn't an ideal combination of driver and co-driver, but it was all that we had. If there was an obstacle, Amalie could see it but couldn't avoid it. I could avoid it as long as she said where it was.

Now Amalie and I had started to quarrel. It was partly because of my frustration at her inability to organise anything. Partly her resentment at my expectations, which prevented her from being herself. Sometimes I'd come in from building and have to make us both lunch. She said that she couldn't get it together. We'd argue and she'd tell me to stop laying trips on her. Our future together didn't look good. It was only years later that she was diagnosed with a thyroid condition, which robbed her of much of her strength, and taught me not to make judgements.

The lulls between storms were wrapped in a hopeless tenderness, and there was no animosity between us. I felt that we were witnesses to an unravelling of circumstances over which we'd abandoned control. We soothed each other as we pulled slowly apart. Then, one lunchtime, I came in from work on the vegetable garden. Seeds that we'd sown were beginning to bloom. The air was full of the fragrance of honeysuckle, released by the warmth of the sun. I wanted Amalie to come out and share it. I called her name, but as I did so, I already knew that she'd gone. The 'I Ching' was on the table. Beside it she'd written down the six lines of the hexagram that she'd thrown.

'Abundance' was its title. 'Clarity within. Movement without'. So she'd moved and left me the hexagram. She'd underlined a passage for me. It read, 'Be not sad. Shine like the sun at midday.'

The house was empty and I'd no desire to be there. The vegetables, flowers and trees that I'd planted all seemed pointless now; a self-indulgent waste of time that I could have spent with my daughter and her beautiful mother. I supposed that Amalie belonged in the city, not in this crazy hermitage of another guy's dream. Our time together must have fulfilled its purpose with Tara, and now she'd probably gone to Moodlaw over the hill. I picked a bouquet of the apricot foxgloves that I'd grown, and carried them through the fierce afternoon, pretending that I no longer loved her.

'Oh wow, look,' she said, 'he's brought me some poisonous flowers.' I got a bucket and stood them on a high sill in the courtyard of stables and barns.

'Don't know why you brought them here,' she grumbled, 'they're dangerous for children. They're the main reason I left you.'

After that, we talked in soul-searing snatches of tenderness and tension, in the only way that parents can talk, when the world is falling apart and there are nappies to change. It took a lot for her to make up her mind, but once that was done, it was done. She'd been offered a place to stay for a while in a cottage at Heriot, next door to Jenny Richardson who was later to turn up in Ireland. Amalie suggested that I should visit her in Heriot, and her words made it all sound so final.

Then, one August morning, I walked out into the dew before sunrise. There was the first bed of flowers that Amalie had grown but not seen. They were blooming with a shout that poured scorn on my sorrow, so I picked some for her, and started along the track by the river, to the road that would take me to Heriot.

It was too early and there were no cars going north. I walked out of Eskdale, climbing towards Tushie Law and, as the altitude rose, so did my spirits. I'd forgotten the splendour of the high places. I remembered the mountain days as a boy, when I loved with no need for a lover; when I barely dared breathe, in case I blew out the magic; when I realised that I owned the world and there was nothing to be done but enjoy it.

At the Selkirk border the first two cars went by, but I didn't bother to hitch them. I wanted to speak to no one, nor get to anywhere else. The skylarks knew that all you had to do was keep singing your heart out. Up there in the stillness you did it without making a sound, so that then you could hear the hum of perfection. Perfection that sang its own song of total fulfilment that knows of no end and no purpose.

Then a bread van stopped without me asking, and I got three easy lifts to Heriot. To Amalie, I held out a bunch of dishevelled flowers and said, 'Oh well, at least this time they won't kill you.'

12

House in the Border Hills

With Amalie gone, I set about filling the vacuum of my new-found freedom. I was able to get up early and use the shrine room that I'd built to attempt meditation. On the shrine was the handful of books which existed on Tibetan Buddhism. I gazed at the pages that I couldn't read. Did I hold the secret in my hands, but lack the merit to receive it? I told myself that Trungpa had given me all that I needed for now, and besides, he'd said that these texts were not to be trusted. I looked at the pictures of the mysterious statues of Buddhas Aksobhya and Amogasiddhi. I loved the photographs of retreat caves and a hermitage high in the snow-covered mountains. I sat and let go and felt that it was right to be on my own.

It was in those pre-dawn mornings that I developed my technique for calming the mind. Sitting, observing my breath coming and going through not quite closed lips. Hearing the air in my teeth was the sound of the sea. Like waves washing a long sandy shoreline in the shimmering light of the dawn. The in-breath, drawing the backwash into the ocean of being. Briefly holding. Uniting. Then the wave of the out-breath breaking along the wet sand, on the primordial strand of existence. With a sweep of white freshness, it wipes out the footprints of wandering mind.

When there comes a storm in the ocean of mind, the surf

of the breathing increases and its breakers grow louder. Then the wind that blows words to whip up the surface begins to die down and the ocean calms slowly. The sound of the breakers whispers 'ssssssh' with each out-breath, as the breeze of mental activity dies, and rogue thoughts that lap at the edge dissolve into freedom.

Meanwhile the car sat in its garage and quietly jangled its keys. I started to drive, at ten miles an hour, the empty roads to Samye Ling, mostly without any mishap. One day, I steered a bit close to the bridge and shaved off the passenger's door handle. Over-compensating on the way home, the same bridge removed the one on the driver's side.

Then there was a party at Garwald. The Raeburnhead crowd requested a lift, which was fine, until I had to drive home in the dark.

'Don't worry, I know this road like the back of my hand,' I told them, wondering why the verge had gone missing.

'Then how come you're driving across a field, heading straight for the river?'

'It's a shortcut,' I said, 'this is the quickest way home.' But a girl in the back freaked out, so I offered the wheel to someone who could see, renewed my resolve to give up driving for good, and this time I pretty much kept it.

At that time, Samye Ling was about the coolest place in Great Britain. It was visited by an ever-changing array of creative youths and brain-damaged dropouts. Apart from the draft-dodgers, there were rock stars and daughters of the aristocracy coming off drugs. There were dancers and painters, lunatics and poets and unemployed dreamers like me. They were almost all in their twenties and their eyes were alight with the mischief. Most had tried acid, except those who were on a permanent trip and had been advised not to do so. Some of the latter thought that they'd arrived in a flying saucer, or had yet to be disembarked.

I was standing by the front door when a guy came staggering out of the building.

'Wow. Too much. Cosmic bombardment. They've put a time-warp machine in my room,' he explained.

'Oh dear, very nasty, what does it look like?' I asked him.

'It's an evil, glowing, white colour. It's made of weird metal and it sits there and clicks,' he said, and then added, 'they've tried to disguise it as a radiator.'

And the musicians came to Mid Raeburn to play. One, Larry Coryell, was regarded as the world's finest jazz guitarist. He and his wife Julie were looking for somewhere to stay for a while, so I offered them the house and moved into the roof of the ruin. Larry was arranging a tour with The Grateful Dead and spent his time walking to Samye to phone. In between times he played his amazing guitar.

But most of the time there was no one around. Just a vast expanse of silence, in which stray events flapped like fish out of water. I'd experienced brief spells of loneliness in a school, a city, and a marriage, but I'd rarely felt it when I was alone. Now I felt it swirling through the moors, like black fog on a darkened day. I could stand at my window, with a view for miles, and there was nothing out there but weather. And the autumn weather was wind. Wind that sent banshees to scream in the chimney. Wind that shredded the summer and blew it away to the islands. With no distraction, there was nothing to be done but to feel it.

We'd not made it easy for ourselves, but there was no turning back. We'd given up television, media propaganda and the radioed gossip of others' events. It all seems so important when you're plugged in, but once you've been for a year without it you ask, how could anyone justify such a reckless squandering of days?

I built a pond and a rockery along the back of the house. In the pond, I kept my bottles of Carlsberg Special to chill them. It was weird stuff, but it was strong. The stronger the drink, the fewer bottles you had to carry for fourteen miles on the school bus, then two miles on foot up the valley. For this reason, the people at Raeburnhead started to brew nettle beer which was really disgusting.

I'd been asked to design a sleeve for the debut album of a group called 'Sattva'. I hitched to London and took it along to their inaugural concert at the Wigmore Hall, with a girl from my old flat. After the gig, I was walking with this rather smart girl, when a stranger crossed the street and, without a word, slammed his fist into my face and walked on. I was knocked onto the pavement. My sweet companion ran off in a panic, and I couldn't chew for a week.

A similar thing had happened on a previous visit to London. I was sitting with friends outside some upper-crust pub on Cheyne Walk, Chelsea. Maybe I was looking a bit too longhaired, bright-coloured and pretty. When I went to the bar, a guy turned around and punched me in the face, again knocking me to the floor. I'd no idea who'd hit me, or why, except that it was some stranger; part of a group that kept talking politely. All I could do was to stand up and order the pints. The landlord had continued to polish glasses, to the background hum of his elite clientele. I drank for a while at the bar, for the sake of my pride and its increasingly stiff upper lip. Then I went back outside to my friends. When I told them, they jumped up ready to fight. I had to persuade them not to react; insisting that violence only spawns violence and someone has to take it on the chin if the old cycle is ever to cease.

I thought of how London had changed from the dazzling arena that I'd roamed with no shoes on. I'd been walking down Earls Court Road, in the summer of '67. As a cool-looking couple of strangers passed by, the girl grabbed my hand and squeezed it. We walked on without looking back because this was love without grasping. It was one simple gesture whose warmth still wipes out a punch in the face.

After the concert, I walked through Holland Park, looking for Amalie in the fog. The summer, and the history of our moment together, were gone in a flicker of days. I shuffled around kicking leaves, trying to reach her, or find a way past her, or catch a syllable of a song that had faded forever.

Back in the hills I made plans for the winter. Although drinking was already restricted by cost and by distance, I decided to give up completely for now. I had to maintain a clarity that would be fugged by even an occasional use of the bottle.

The idea of meditation had now become fashionable. Some people were earnestly searching for the way onwards, while most simply followed the trend to look good. I'd discussed this with Trungpa. The momentary fashion had no fuel to sustain it. Soon the Tibetans would learn English, texts would be translated, centres founded and then, in a few years, it would spread through the West in a real way. It seemed that my role was to prepare for that time by establishing a centre for meditation retreats. It was the natural progression of my dream of a community of artists. I resolved to start serious work on Raeburnside as a retreat centre, as soon as the winter had passed.

Of course all of this serious stuff didn't mean that I had to give up on living. I loved dancing as an expression of freedom and because you didn't need to be able to see. Sometimes there would be girls from Samye Ling to share my desire for release. More often, alone in that house by the turbulent river, I'd dance for half of the morning. With two large speakers in the window, I'd put on something like the Stones' 'You Can't Always Get What You Want'. I'd turn the volume up full, run into the meadow and *dance*. Then I could laugh or cry or the sky could fall in and it wouldn't matter at all. And when I was tired, I'd sit on the grass by the dry-stone wall. The sudden cessation of movement silenced the words of the brain. It rinsed the emotions with the peace of the vastness in which worldly concern frays at the edges and fades.

And rock stars and film stars like David Bowie and Charlotte Rampling continued to come to the Centre. They'd usually end up at my cottage, drawn by the reputation of its crazy décor and unusual location so far from the world. One such was Leonard Cohen. He was one of the few whose interest in Buddhism was more than a knick-knack found on the shelf of a curiosity-shop called The Sixties.

He walked over from Samye Ling in the mornings, a serious young man in a black leather jacket. His humility emphasised the sincerity with which he joined in our quest to find a way through the lies and the myths. Someone asked him to sing 'Suzanne' and he shyly sang his beautiful poem, while I gazed at my 'place near the river'. Black and white tiles, inspired by the Pure Land painting of Trungpa's. Blue and red panels, silver hexagrams and bright red curtains to keep out the cold. There were wind chimes and mobiles amongst bunches of onions that hung from beams of the ceiling. Images of an era whose children sat on the floor and inhaled its incense, lost in the sounds of its song.

Now the government announced grants for owners to renovate derelict houses like Raeburnside. It seemed that always, at the last minute, just enough money turned up.

It was time for the 'I Ching' to prove, once again, that there exists a level of 'knowing' beyond the reach of our ordinary mind. I was about to undertake a double divination, the results of which were, by any measure, out of the ordinary.

There being no water supply at the house, I needed to find a source in order to access the grant. I'd marked it on the plans as the old spring well which was said to be somewhere out there on the hillside. The forestry group had ploughed the slopes to make ridges for trees. With this grown over, there was no trace of a well, which could have been buried within half a mile in any direction. Day after day, criss-crossing that land and finding no trace, I began to lose heart.

There was a small stream that ran off the hill at the end of the Raeburnside acre. Should I get my water from there? It was not what I'd drawn on the plan. It was subject to pollution and might run dry in the summer, so I kept scouring the hill. After weeks of frustration I decided to let the 'I Ching' have a go. I would ask it the specific question, 'Is it to be the invisible well, or the stream?'

I'd developed a great respect for this oracle, since it had been taught at my flat, as part of the curriculum of the Anti-University of London. I'd use it only rarely, maybe once in a year, when a vital decision was proving impossible to make. Then I'd sit quietly for a while, and throw the hexagrams with my mind in a state of ease.

You can use yarrow stalks, or three coins. You throw them six times, and the way that they fall dictates the make-up of two hexagrams, which you then look up in The Book of Changes. The first of these hexagrams answers your question and the second indicates its development into the future.

I sat at the table. There are sixty-four hexagrams. Having given up reading, I was familiar with only a few. I expected to get something like 'The Preponderance of the Great' or 'The Taming Power of the Small'. I'd then have to decipher the commentary, in the hope that it would tell me clearly which choice I should make.

I threw the coins and wrote down the lines, until I had two hexagrams on a piece of paper. I looked up the first on the chart. It said, number 48. I looked up number 48 in the book. To my astonishment, it was 'Ching', 'The Well'. I'd not even known that such a hexagram existed. I was elated. I looked up the second hexagram that I'd thrown. It was number 29. It was 'K'an', which is 'Water'.

So the 'I Ching' had spoken with spectacular clarity. 'The Well', changing to 'Water'. 'That'll teach you to go consulting the oracle,' I thought. My ordinary mind had settled on the easy option of the stream. Now my hands were tied and I had no choice but to continue to search for the well.

As it turned out, I hadn't yet finished with divination. I met a builder in Langholm and asked how I could locate the well. He came to the Raeburn valley with divining rods and his lad, and walked the hill for a while. The rods indicated a spot between two rows of trees. He dug his heel into the ground and told the lad to start digging. Soon there was a hole, three feet deep, and no sign of anything other than earth. We'd almost given up when there was a 'clunk' as the spade hit a house brick. With more digging there appeared a small box, from beneath which bubbled a spring.

So. Divination upon divination. Chipping away at the arrogance that leads us to think that, by subjugating phenomena with our rules and our reason, we can ridicule anything that refuses to fit. Was this not the pure unreasonable, at work in its garden, allowing a flash of diamond light to shine through?

For me, it was the scientists who were trapped in their cages of logic. I had the proof. I could drink it. They'd require further tests. You can't test with the brain that which works beyond the scope of the brain, and kicks in when the brain comes to rest. I'd been handed the lamp of certainty, protected by the shade of humility that is part of its radiance. The humility that arises with the realisation that we'll never know, until we learn to make contact with the awareness that's innate in us all.

Before Christmas, I got a lift to Edinburgh. At her flat in Spittal Street, Amalie flung her arms around me with a warmth so absent at our last meeting. Tara was lying asleep on a mattress amongst a chaos of toys. Amalie looked thin, beautiful, and not of this earth. I felt such a pure, non-attached love for this person with whom I'd shared a moment of struggle.

On my previous visit, Amalie had told me that she didn't want to get involved with anyone again. This guy Alan, who owned the flat, was kind but no more than a friend. Now she began nervously to tell me that she loved him and they'd probably marry. I watched her serious face in the streetlight and saw that I was already no more than an episode out of her past.

She said that Alan had been summoned by his parents to Yorkshire, where they were freaking out about her and her crazy family. She said that his father was quite famous and lived in a mansion. He disapproved of her and her babies because she was no one and poor. She was going to procure a marriage licence and take it to Yorkshire, and once he'd signed it, his parents could no longer keep them apart. I told her that it didn't work like that, and she should slow down or she'd lose him. She said that she must send a letter at once then, no, no, not a letter, a telegram, and please would I help her to write it?

So we sat there, Amalie Swinford and me, in her flat by the Edinburgh castle. We sat there united in our task of trying to help her, as it slowly sank in that this was 'goodbye'. And we worked on a message to the rest of her life, from the last part of our journey together. Past the part where we lay in the long grass of that summer and she read to me, while Tara slept on her rug by the sun. Past the part where we sat on separate sides of a table, eating chapattis and nettles. The part that was cold and searching for answers, while the black hounds of hopelessness bayed in the hills of our heads. 'Keep going,' she said, as I stood with one hand on the gate of our garden. Had I really needed to bitch at her, for sowing those carrots in a wandering line?

With tenderness, we talked far into our last night as a family together. We laughed at the craziness of this latest dream that we found ourselves dreaming. She said that I could sleep next door, and I told her that she must be kidding. I told her that I loved her with a love that makes sex unimportant. With that she was happy and we went to bed, and she put a small golden child in between us.

In the morning Dora arrived with the family. She immediately started on me about 'letting go' and 'not hanging on when something is over'. She'd moved Amalie in with me because I had a flat and a cottage. Now she saw a better proposal, and was moving Amalie upwards again. She couldn't accept my acceptance that this new affair was a good thing, in spite of a slight residual hurting. And I couldn't explain how it feels sometimes, when too much importance is placed on events. When grasping onto a desired result seems to blind the players to the ridiculous perfection of every step of the dance.

Dora was telling me about the chandeliers and gold taps at the Walker Street flat that Alan had bought them. Then, Amalie and I walked to a posh Chinese restaurant where she bought lunch to take back for the family and a few hangers-on. She ordered almost everything on the menu and said that they did that most days. I remembered last year at Raeburnside. Hungry and cold, at the end of our food and our fuel. I realised that the 'I Ching' had triumphed again. 'Abundance' was the hexagram that Amalie had left on the table, and I wondered if it was going to apply to me too.

'Where are you going to sleep tonight?' Dora was sitting upright in her chair.

'With Amalie,' the devil inside me replied, resenting the woman's intrusion.

'Oh no you're not, You shouldn't even be in the same building as Amalie,' Dora insisted, as Hepzibah and the whole family joined in. I watched them in silence and saw how worried they were. They were intent upon landing the catch of a lifetime and I was a hole in their net. Last night had been our 'goodbye'. I was calm as I watched Dora pick up my things and carry them to the spare room.

The afternoon lapped in and out on the waves of their talking. They tried to involve me, but I was no longer involved. I carried little Tara up the street to the shop. To the old lady, she held out a fist full of dimples and sixpence. Her smile brought tears to my eyes, as she turned her head, shyly, to bury it into my shoulder. I watched her with a lump in my throat that was burning. I watched her and promised to write her this story, and wished that it wasn't 'goodbye'.

Isaac came round to drive me away. The parting was eased by the chaos. Amalie looked like a beautiful whisper, as thin and as pale as an orphaned desire. Isaac, who couldn't take his eyes off her, told me, 'That girl is not of this world. She looks like she's got out of a star-ship that's just flown in from a planet called Wow.'

On Christmas Eve, I sat by the bridge and looked back at our house in its acre of silence. A couple of bipeds appeared, scratched at the earth and dissolved. I listened to the burn that had carved that valley out of forever, and knew that 'forever' is a flash in the actual pan. I had so many questions and they all needed time. I'd stay on my own in retreat, and allow the winter to be my instructor. I'd live simply, in this empty valley, and not try to see what was coming. I'd take advantage of the situation by not wanting much, while there was so little on offer. 'It's desire that causes the trouble,' I said to the river. 'It leads to dissatisfaction if we fail to fulfil it, or satisfaction, which is worse, because that drowns your awareness in sugar. Desire is the weather that stirs up this climate of pain. It's the wind on which we sail our ship into the ocean of sorrow.'

Then came the day when spring bubbled into the caves of the north, and the curlews were calling again. Always in love with bright colours, I put on my finery too. Beatrix had left a pale mauve silk shirt, and a red corduroy beret. I wore them with a crimson velvet smoking jacket from the antique market in Chelsea. I despaired of the sad browns and greys of the people. The Church had brainwashed us into wearing the colours of mud and the shadows, to make their bright-coloured bishops look grander. I wanted to sing out my joy at being alive, not pretend that I'd never happened.

In April, Geordie knocked on the door with a message from Amalie to say that she and the circus were coming. Geordie had hardly left when the whole family, bar Alan, turned up, wanting to stay and look for a house. Remembering her performance in Edinburgh, I teased Dora by saying. 'There's not much room, you know. Amalie will have to sleep with me.'

'I don't give a damn what she does,' said Dora, 'now that she's married.'

But they only stayed until teatime, which was sad, because Richard Alpert was coming. He'd just arrived from an Indian trip. He'd changed his name to Ram Dass and was staying at

Samye Ling. 'Psychedelic Experience', which he wrote with Timothy Leary, had been the Bible for the first generation to experiment with acid. I invited him to Mid Raeburn to find out how far he had got. About thirty of us listened to him insist that meditation is the key, and there's no future in drugs.

I looked around the room. Spring sunshine streamed through the windows to light the bright-coloured shapes of one moment in time. The man newly returned from the East sat cross-legged in a white robe on my bed. The room was packed with young people sitting on the floor, on the windowsill and the table. Was this not what I'd been trying to establish, come unexpectedly to life at the end of a period of trial? Kids listening intently, hoping for glimpses of whatever led on from the drugs and the music. My role was to create an oasis of inspiration, as far as you could get from churches and sects and tyrannical institutions.

It had become apparent that two distinct groups were emerging. One was searching for spiritual and the other for material self-sufficiency. Both groups were looking for a new way and were springing up all over the West. Each teased the other for wasting its time, but there was no rift, because the two paths overlapped.

At this time I met a journalist who'd just returned from the States. For a series of articles in the national press, she'd taken a tour of some communes. She confessed that she was disappointed to find that her 'hippies' had seemed hard-working, serious-minded, young people. She'd gone expecting to enjoy a wild party with plenty of sex, but couldn't get past the monogamy. I told her that she shouldn't believe what she wrote in the papers. If she wanted sex, she should go to the suburbs.

And then suddenly it was summer in the border hills, and the stream-sides were strewn with flowers again. Once the skylarks arrived I wanted to break all of my promises at once. I asked, who was this proud one who thought he could live in the mountains and search for the truth on his own? First sign of the sun and he's out in the buttercups, longing for someone to share his buttercup freedom.

I strolled over the hill to Moodlaw to see who was around. Moodlaw was now the main self-sufficiency scene. I walked past the farmhouse and along the stream to the courtyard of old stone buildings, where I'd given those foxgloves to Amalie.

I found a hive of activity. In one barn, Samadhi Bill was carving wooden toys, while in another was a man making pots. By an open window sat Rose, in a low-cut, antique white blouse with full sleeves. She was seated at a loom like a four-poster bed on which she was weaving. The wool for her work was being dyed yellow with heather tips, on the cobbles in the centre of the yard. Here, three rough wooden poles had been lashed at the top for a tripod. From this, a chain was suspending a cast-iron cauldron over a crackling fire. The pot was being stirred with a long stick by a tall young woman in a felt hat, an embroidered shirt and a red, woven, ankle-length skirt.

I went over and asked her what she was doing. She spoke very fast, in beautiful English, with the words all barging each other out of the way, and yet ending up making sense. The phrases were punctuated with a delightful stammer that almost gave you time to catch up. She was pretty and vulnerable and disturbingly alive, and her presence filled the whole courtyard. I asked her name and she told me that she was called Harriet.

13

Harriet

From time to time Harriet would get into her Renault 4 and drive over to see me. I was wary of losing my freedom, but she was captivating and the weather was hot and it had been a long winter. One morning, I rode my bicycle up the valley to Raeburnhead where she'd moved in with Rose. On the way, I found half a roll of old sheep wire. I gave it to Harriet for their new vegetable garden. 'Oh how romantic, he's brought me some fencing,' she said.

Harriet loved wildflowers and knew the Latin names for most of them. She carried her copy of 'Keble Martin' wherever she went. Whatever less important event was occurring, it would be abruptly terminated upon a glimpse of wild colour. Driving to Lockerbie on our first outing, she screeched the car to a halt. 'Oh my God, it's *persicaria amphibian*' she cried, as she threw herself into the drain with a shriek of delight.

By early July, Harriet had moved in with me and my freedom. The 'moving-in' itself was not a particularly spectacular event. One night she just failed to go home. Few changes had to be made, as all of her worldly possessions remained on the back seat of her car. The only difference was that I now had this engagingly quixotic creature to ensure that never again would I know what was next.

The rest of that summer was dappled with new dreams and

sunshine. We grew love and vegetables in the valley that had slowly grown kind. Harriet was interested in Buddhism, and particularly in Padmasambhava who'd established it in Tibet. She was extremely respectful of this vast tradition and its myriad practices for developing compassion and wisdom. When I told her of my plans to establish a retreat in the Raeburn valley, she said that retreats needed mountains, not hillocks, and she had plenty of cash and would like to help, so we should look somewhere else. How amazing that this dakini should appear with the means, at that moment. Was this the other half of the prophesy of 'Abundance' that Amalie had left on the table?

But things had moved a bit fast. I'd only just met her, so I said that we should wait for a while. At least until she returned from Kinlochbervie where, in August, her father went fishing. So I continued to work on the cottages, until Harriet came back at the start of September. I heard her car coming and went out to greet her. On the path by the lager pond, she walked straight past me and into the house. 'I want to see who you've been playing with, while I've been away,' she said. I learnt not to expect expected responses from this twenty-one-year-old child from Kensington High Street.

Each evening, Harriet would sit spinning sheep's fleece into yarn on her wheel. The mesmeric clack of the treadle was a mechanical mantra for calming the mind. Then we'd pore over maps in search of the place that I held in my head, whose details were clear, but whose origin I could no longer remember. I described it to Harriet. On the edge of a mountain, overlooking a vast misty plain with hills in the distance. Silent and green with mosses and ferns. A strange sense of peace and a scatter of dwellings.

We went on a trip to scour the west coast and failed to find anything like it. In Strontian, Harriet suggested that we give up and go gathering toadstools instead. So we spent the days in the lanes and the forest, and the evenings in the bar of the Strontian Hotel. She'd stride in, with her ankle-length tweed skirt

159

a-swirling and her hair tied back, in honour of *amanita muscaria*, with her red and white-spotted bandana. On her arm she carried an antique cane basket, crammed with festering specimens, half of which dripped with decay. She'd lay them out, with great care, on various unoccupied tables. Then, with the aid of three textbooks and occasional squeals of delight, she'd identify them one at a time. For Harriet, self-consciousness was an alien concept. Such boring states were reserved for people like me, as I watched the landlord mopping his brow.

Christmas Day dawned with a full moon still admiring its frost in the first light of the sun. I awoke alone, like the previous year, with the Christmas tree at the foot of the bed. Harriet had gone to her parents, so it would be Christmas when she returned. It was always Christmas when Harriet was around; Christmas or Armageddon.

This year I was invited to Monkinshaw. I worked on the old cottage and then set off on the five-mile walk to the house in the Garwald valley. As I left, the pheasant who lived on the hill flew down to ask for some grain. The sun was shining and it was Christmas Day. I'd a dream and a girlfriend and a beautiful walk to my lunch. How quickly things change and change again, as we clamber like mice on a turning wheel.

In January, Harriet and I were driving back from Dumfries. It was snowing at Lockerbie and by Eskdale it was dark and there was a blizzard. We turned up the track, past the Cartner's farm and over the hill. As we came down to the Rae burn, the front of the car had ploughed the snow over the lights. I got out to clear them and the ground disappeared beneath me. I couldn't move. We'd stopped on the snow-covered cattle grid, built into the bridge that spanned the river. My left leg had shot through the steel bars and was trapped above the knee, and hanging in icy space. Harriet pulled and pulled, and the knee joint swelled.

Though you could see no more than a matter of yards, we decided that Harriet should go for help. We couldn't move the car because I was trapped against the front bumper. The Walker's farm was somewhere on the hill at the end of the valley, but there was no hint of a light, so she might walk round and around until daybreak. She set off into the snow and was out of sight in a moment. To save the battery, we'd turned off the car lights. I was able to savour the archetypal event, as I told myself that we'd live. Trapped between twin bars of frozen steel; wet leg freezing in the gulley of wind that blew down the river. I thought of a hare caught in a gin-trap like this, with no hope of a rescue. My steel bars didn't even have teeth, to tear my flesh to the bone. Brought to awareness by personal danger, sickened by the crimes that we humans commit, I was prevented from bemoaning my fate.

I'd learnt, in the short time that I'd known her, that Harriet was extremely proficient in a crisis. She'd panic at a twinge in muscle or limb, or any unexpected event in her body, so external challenges were a relief. Faced with a simple life and death situation, she'd come triumphantly into her own. In less than half an hour, I saw a torch light flashing. She was back with Johnnie Walker, the local sheep farmer. Now they took one arm each and they pulled but the leg was stuck tight. Farmer Walker was talking about tractors and oxy-acetylene cutters. Harriet dispatched him back to the farm for a pair of scissors and a lump of butter.

'Butter-up the ears and yank like hell,' she said. 'That was a daily procedure at home when small heads got stuck in the banisters.'

'Well, that explains everything,' I told her.

When the farmer returned, Harriet cut off my trouser leg, buttered my knee, and the limb slipped out with one heave. Back at the farm, by the fire, we drank enough whisky for the long walk home. Then, with a naked leg and much laughter, we hobbled me back up the valley through the deepening snow.

The forestry group organised shooting parties for over-fed Germans. One day, a Range Rover stopped at our bridge and disgorged the game-keeper and four armed men. They marched up the hill, shot our tame pheasant for fun and drove off.

Some friends had got into trouble with this keeper. They'd been caught fishing sea trout from the stream that ran through their land. They were told that the fish belonged to the Duke of Buccleuch who imagined he owned all of the fish, in all of the rivers, of much of the Borders. 'Is all of that old feudal stuff still going on?' I enquired as I asked our friends to teach me to tickle a trout.

Now I was caught between the conflicting philosophies of my peers. The self-sufficiency school said that if you eat meat you should do your own killing, while those on a spiritual path insisted that all life is sacred. These concepts were mixed, in a dangerous cocktail, with contempt for the arrogance of the old feudal system.

I pulled a fine sea trout from the stream. I needed only two but, before I knew it, the savage in me had five fat fish on the grass. I looked at their desperate beauty. Wild creatures are so much more perfect than those that occupy houses. I gazed at the shining eyes that had crossed an ocean, and struggled for miles up the river. I thought of how it must be for fish deprived of their wetness. To be scorched to death by the searing air. The blood-lust of aeons had activated my reptilian instinct, to slaughter the creature who appears throughout history as the timeless symbol of spiritual life.

And I thought back to how I'd shouted at those men who'd gunned down a pheasant for kicks. My hypocrisy made me feel sick, and much worse than them, because I'd done it while I knew it was wrong. I, who spent hours releasing flies who were trapped on the windowpane, with a glass and a sheet of paper. I, who rejoiced as I took them outside, to watch them soar into freedom.

We spent the rest of that day, driving around, looking for friends to take the other three fish. Unusually, no one was in. No one was going to absolve me of the guilt that would force me to learn. That night we cooked all five fish, and made ourselves eat them until we made ourselves sick. Then I remembered how I'd been taught before not to go barging through perfection with boots on, ignoring the sensitivity that is our nature. It was a memory from the last time that I ever used acid.

I had sat, for hours, in a palace whose corners were portals that led from the realms of the gods. Four processions of celestial beings, in an endless stream, led tigers and lapis lazuli deer. Breath-taking girls in a swirling of secret dimensions heaped priceless gifts at my feet.

I went outside to attempt an escape from my ego, in the dark by the river. The night was pitch black but there were bright little points of white light lighting the world. The dry-stone wall and the track were covered in mosses that cascaded and drifted through epochs of green. It all seemed so ancient; older than earth, older than this temporary universe, maybe even older than this knot of experience that ties us to imagined existence. I felt that I was being shown a secret that is everywhere and always on show, waiting for each one to know it.

I knelt to look at the mossy track onto which I'd so carelessly wandered. It was exquisite in clarity beyond definition. It was as though I'd been swimming for lifetimes in a murky sea and had just discovered the surface.

There were small lichen meadows and spinneys of moss. There was an intricate network of pathways with tiny creatures moving about them. There were lakes of dewdrops and one-pebble mountains and motionless valleys of plenty. From each thing that appeared shone an inherent radiance of self-light that needed no dawn.

Most important of all was the sensation of the absolute perfection of everything just as it is. All brought to life by one breath and destroyed in the space of a footfall. How gross are we humans with our big feet and our broken commitments.

There were many adventures that summer; some that we learnt from and some that we laughed at. Between distractions and failed meditation attempts, I built the retreat house. We drove to London and sat on some steps with a row of Harriet's friends who were all in ankle-length, bright-coloured dresses. They looked like a row of Gauguin girls on the south sea island of Chelsea. Harriet opened a Sunday paper, and there was his painting that had haunted my youth, 'Where do we come from, who are we, and whither do we go?' It had first inspired me at school, to ask what really was going on. Little had I known that, one day, I'd sit in the sun with a line of Gauguin girls and one of them would step out of the picture to show me the picture. To remind me not to stop looking. To remind me that, with Gauguin and all of the rest, we have to keep on the trail of the secret.

And, all of the while, we were writing to estate agents and checking the press. We lay on the floor, adrift in an ocean of maps and pictures and dreaming.

Then, one night in late July, Harriet burst into the cottage. She'd been to a course at the 'Weaver's Workshop' in Edinburgh. On the way back, she'd stopped at the Gordon Arms. Now she was bubbling over with more than her usual excitement. The owner, the good Mrs Nettleships, had advised her, 'You should go to the south-west of Ireland. They have donkeys and carts and everyone knows how to spin. It's more spiritual there and would suit you much better than this.'

'She's been trying to get rid of me for years,' I said, but there was no stopping Harriet once she was flowing. 'On the way back we saw three auspicious signs like the sickle moon lying on its back like an offering bowl and, and, and there was a sort of a circle of fire above it and a pure white hare ran along in front of the car and, and it all means that we've been looking in the wrong place and hey let's go to a place that's got space 'cause everyone's leaving. Like Ireland.'

Book Two

IRELAND

14

Manifestation

I'd passed thirty years inspired by occasional flashes of gold in the stream of events. I'd realised that this was the gleam of our nature that sometimes breaks free from its prison of concepts. I'd dreamt of creating a place to assist the release of that nature, and I'd chased the dream in and out of the mischief. Now, excited, I watched the coastline of Ireland rise from the sea with the sun. Could this be where it would happen?

We drove off the ferry in a rundown city called Cork and headed west to Killarney. The scenery was spectacular, but the town looked like something that had followed us over the water, so we kept driving until the buildings fitted into the landscape. At the south coast village of Ballydehob, we rented a cottage in a garden with hedges of fuchsia. It was the real thing, with a chemical lavatory disguised as a bucket, and water from a long-handled pump in the yard.

Straightaway we set about searching. With a large-scale map of West Cork, we followed the maze of winding roads, marking them off one by one. Years of emigration had emptied the land and peppered the small Irish fields with its ruins.

Knocking on doors, I asked if anywhere was for sale. Years later, I wondered how I'd had the nerve, with my English accent, at that time of the troubles. I was protected by my ignorance, pride in my Irish middle name, and the sheer good will of the people of Cork. We continued through Schull, Goleen and back to Skibbereen, as the days became weeks and the magic of Ireland was casting its spell.

Paddy Sheehan showed us some 'rough coastal land' on the Mizen, but it was bleak and blackened by wind, so we drove to Crookhaven for a drink at the Welcome Inn. Ireland was still full of legendary characters like its ninety-year-old landlord called Daddy Nottage. At the start of the twentieth century, he'd come with Marconi to experiment with ship-to-shore wireless, and had never gone home. From remote Crookhaven they radioed the great liners as they rounded the Mizen, to be first with the news from the States.

Ahead of us, two Dublin businessmen walked into the inn for a drink. Daddy Nottage picked four dirty glasses from a table and stuffed them into his old sports coat pockets. He shuffled out to the yard where he washed them under the pump. Stuffing them back in his pockets, he came into the bar, took them out and poured the whiskey. We passed many hours listening to the stories of old Daddy Nottage.

Now we'd covered much of its coastline and had fallen in love with West Cork. With its twisting lanes and handkerchief fields that hid between rocks by the sea. With the scattered perfection of farmhouses made from bits of the land. And the last of the donkey carts which still brought turf from the bog and took churns of milk to the Creamery stands at the crossroads. And the haycocks, with hats on, that garnished the fields of the summer, built by the people whose currency was uncounted time. We were lost in its peace, and the depths of its green that slowed down your step, seeped into your soul, and brought worldly concern to a standstill.

There were so many deserted houses, their doors just tied up with string. It seemed sacrilegious to enter. It was as though the last of the sons had stepped out for a drink, while the years wrote in dust on the cobwebbed dressers of home. There were copies of *The Saturday Evening Post*, sent back from the States, dog-eared and thumbed from the dreaming. And everyone gone, but Jesus and Mary who gazed on the pain from where they were nailed to the wall.

We were having no luck so it was time to try Dingle. On our way north we met Ian Stuart, the sculptor, who'd given up looking for a place by the ocean and started looking inland. He told us, 'Confucius said that the wise man lives on the mountain, the clever man lives by the sea.' The coast attracts people and commerce, while a retreat should be up near the sky in the silence.

We stopped for the night at the wayside inn at Kilmackillogue, a hamlet on the coast road to Kenmare. There was the pub by the jetty, a few old houses, and the Knockatee Mountain adrift on a mirage of Kerry. You could sit outside with a pint while the world ambled by, on its way to the twentieth century. By the bridge, an old man gathered seaweed forever, and every few hours, someone from the past cycled by with a wave.

Joan O'Sullivan emerged from the bar to clean mackerel on the sea wall. She was gruff and direct and as permanent as the mountain that guarded her door. She kept you on your toes while making you as welcome and warm as her laughter. Over the years we often returned to see her and Teddy, her husband. When we closed our eyes and dreamt of old Ireland, their simple pub was the place that we saw.

Next morning, I needed a bank to draw cash for our stay. Mrs O'Sullivan directed us to Castletownbere, a thirty minute drive back to the south-west. It seemed not to cross her mind that a stranger might not return to pay, and that attitude was a large part of what kept us in Ireland.

Now I had, in my file, some mention of a farm near Castletownbere. It had come from an agent in Bandon, but we'd never followed it up. It was towards the end of the Beara Peninsula and sounded like the gale-torn moor that we'd seen at Goleen. However, since we now had to go near there for the bank, I fished out the paper, which read 'Garranes. 150 acres of coastal land with old residence. Mostly rough grazing. Magnificent views of the Atlantic. £12,000.' At the time, that was the price of three new Irish houses.

At the bank, they gave us directions. Garranes was halfway to Allihies, about five miles down the coast on the left. We drove west for ten miles, with no sign of the turning, and arrived in Allihies village. It was known as The Mines, because of the old copper workings. There was a sandy beach, a handful of houses, five bars, a small church, one shop, and ruins in many of the fields. At the post office we were directed back a few miles on the right. We got to Castletownbere, having missed the turning again. Once more we turned west, searching the wild mountain road and, once more, we arrived back in Allihies. One argument said, 'We're wasting our time, let's head for Dingle.' The other one reminded us that in the 'I Ching', 'Difficulty at the Beginning' is the best omen. And besides, if it was so secret, it was already a perfect retreat. Again we checked at the post office where Eily, the postmistress's daughter, gave us directions once more.

Stopping the car, we walked the road at the point where the turning should be. We met some road workers who took us to a grassy gap in the furze. We walked an imaginary way that led east, across a bog and into the mountain. There were no trees, no buildings and certainly no sign of an ocean.

It was one of those mornings, like a stray morning, slipped from the tethers of physics, beyond time and matter and measure. There was the stillness that comes when you brush past the barriers of thought-life, to enter the expectant unknown. The sun came and went through veils of mist, and everything dripped with the liquid green of this hidden land in the waves of the West.

A close-cropped grass path wound up the mountain between rocks that were covered in moss. It was as though no one had walked this way since it clicked into place, a millennium or a moment ago. All was suspended in effortless grace, as we lowered our voices to whispers and then stopped talking at all.

A causeway of stone led up the face of a cliff. We turned south-west down a slope through shoulder-high gorse, then south, past a bog pond and meadow. As we came round the corner, the mist-curtain lifted to reveal an arena of shimmering space. We gasped at the vast expanse, half sky and half sea with almost no difference between them. To the east was a cluster of ruins, built on terraces cut from the edge of the world. In front, sloping down to the cliffs, were small fields with hedges of hazel and fuchsia. Far below was the water, flashing its dance with the sunlight, while behind us, protecting it all from earthly involvement, was the might of the mountain.

I'd entered the manifestation of the dream that had inspired all of my searching. Everything was as I'd seen it, and not in the least surprising, when you think of it all as a dance. On the other hand, should your mind require science, then you might say that I'd searched for an archetype, and had found it. Either way, everything was just as I'd dreamt it, except that my plain was an ocean, and the hills that I'd seen to the south were the last two headlands of Ireland. I laughed as I realised that the Confucian dilemma was solved. There was no need for a choice because we could have both. We'd found our mountain, surrounded south, east and west by the ocean.

Harriet knew, and she also laughed as we ran, hand in hand, down the hill to explore. And then she turned to me and she said. 'Of course, I couldn't possibly live here. Not with my vertigo. I'd be terrified that I'd fall off.' This was a piece of pure Harriet. She had an evolved sense of timing. And of course it was true. She got vertigo walking upstairs. She'd never go onto a balcony, and this place was nothing but balconies, lashed to the rim of the sky.

I felt no panic at this hydrogen bombshell. The extraordinary location had been unfolded from somewhere way out of reach of the ordinary mind. A little light-headedness could never gazump it. It would have been an insult to this place for us *not* to be dizzy. I'd get Harriet back a few times and she'd soon get used to the vertical drop.

And so we returned to Garranes each day, and each day we found something new. Even the foreseen stream and its waterfall appeared, plunging from the cliffs to the west. Then, one day at the end of the process, Harriet announced that her vertigo was cured to never return. We wondered if this was the first sign of the healing potential of the naked elements of Garranes. We drove straight to the vendor's solicitor in Bandon, who turned out to be a relative of Ambrose Appelbe of Lincoln's Inn, but I was no longer surprised by surprises.

They said that the farm hadn't sold because of its half mile of impassable track with three hairpin bends good only for horses. Now each of my refuges had been blessed with an access problem. It seemed to be the way that special places were kept protected for guardians with no common sense or commercial intent. We paid a deposit and returned to Scotland to raise the cash. I'd sell one of the cottages and Harriet would come up with the rest.

It was 1973 and the world situation was becoming daily more turbulent. Harriet, of the self-sufficiency school, said that the corrupt world order was about to implode. Now I was beginning to think that perhaps she was right. It was an appropriate time to be moving to Ireland. We sat in Scotland watching the show and ringing solicitors to hurry them up.

The American president was in danger of being impeached and might do anything to save his own skin. Then, on 6 October, Egypt and Syria invaded Israel and there was war in the Middle East. On the tenth, Vice-President Agnew resigned and on the twelfth, Nixon was ordered to hand over the Watergate tapes. Things were getting out of control.

It was time for Harriet to tell her mother that she was moving to Ireland with me. We sat in a coffee shop on Kensington High Street, opposite where she'd grown up.

'For God's sake, just go home and warm them up. I'll come and knock on the door,' I was saying. 'Introduce me, and tell them it's no longer called living in sin.' At that moment Harriet gave a yelp.

'Fuck, it's my mother, she's seen us.'

'Right, I'm going to the bog,' I said, as I slipped back into my pocket the naggin of whiskey that I was about to pour into our coffees. I disappeared for a minute then, having resisted the temptation to fortify my nerve with a Jameson, I returned to the table.

'And what are you going to do in Ireland?' Harriet's mother was asking her daughter, with the self-assurance of one who was Royal Borough born and bred.

'I'm going to be a shepherdess,' Harriet said with defiance.

The gaze was turned onto me. Harriet's mother had refused to sit down, so I was standing beside her. Although not quite as tall as I was, she peered down at me from a great height. This effect was achieved with the aid of a carefully inclined nose, and a terrifying pair of lorgnettes on a string. She studied me, moving the lenses back and forth, in an attempt to paralyse her prey.

'And *what*,' she enquired, 'are you going to be? A shepherdess's assistant?'

I loved the pure theatre of these situations. I'd learnt long ago to never react. Like when being beaten at school or confronting the Birmingham razors. I felt so distant from my self *and* its assailant that they had no hope of identifying me, never mind pinning me down. Meanwhile, I responded with the good humour that defuses most crises and soon got us back for tea at 19 Phillimore Terrace.

It was 17 October. OPEC countries cut oil production in protest at American support for Israel in the war that was raging. The price of oil went into orbit. Harriet told her mother that the world was running out of energy. Our greed would collapse the system, and that was her real reason for going to the under-populated isolation of Ireland.

A week later, the Dalai Lama gave a talk in London. We went to see him, thinking that he was the only world leader who was sane. That morning, a desperate Nixon had put U.S. forces on global alert. You could feel the tension in the air. The papers talked of American bombers circling overhead, with armed nuclear warheads.

Back in Scotland, the solicitors were insisting that we go back to West Cork to check for a water source on the land. I was sad to be giving up on Eskdalemuir, sad to be abandoning my attempt at a contemplative life, in order to establish the first Buddhist retreat in Ireland. Perhaps I'd end up keeping sheep. As we set off from Samye Ling, a deer ran in front of the car and was killed. The deer is the symbol of meditation.

Now it was back to Ireland, for a week, in search of water. 'Are they serious?' asked Harriet. We drove to the ship in a car packed with things that we might not find at the end of the world. On board the Innisfallen we watched television, until it spluttered and died as we sailed away from the signal. It was one more programme on the world energy crisis. Acres of American gas-guzzlers, new cars with no market, lined up to be scrapped. Televised scientists forecast that we'd run out of oil by the end of the twentieth century.

In the morning, as Ireland appeared from the sea mist, it felt already like home. At Bantry we bought a second-hand mattress, tied it to the roof with baler twine and drove west for an hour, hanging on to it through the windows. Having to leave the car at the road, we carried the mattress half a mile up to the house. We kicked out the neighbour's cows from the kitchen, made a fire and put on the kettle.

Downstairs, there was one room, divided in two by a flimsy partition. One side was the kitchen and the other the priest's room, or parlour. Next to this was a derelict annexe. Upstairs, there was just enough room to stand carefully upright in the apex. A tiny window in the west gable filtered a glimmer into the darkness. It was purposely small, so as not to depress you with what light might reveal.

In the kitchen, the boreholes of sea-worm said that the beams had been fished from the ocean. On the walls, a floral linoleum had been glued, hip-high to keep out the damp. This was hanging off to expose a sticky brown tar. Two broken doors, opposite one another, opened outside to the north and the south. It was small, smelly, awful and ours, and we loved it, as we braced ourselves to move in.

Over time, we became slowly aware of what English schools didn't teach. It was the tyranny of the landlords that had forced this level of poverty on Ireland. We would treat this family home with the utmost respect and restore it with sensitive care. Years later, the Murphys of Garranes apologised for the state of the houses throughout the country. I'd thought that their family had been on this land since the Stone Age. They said, not at all. The landlords kept moving their family, and everyone else, from farm to farm to prevent the establishment of property rights. There was no incentive for them to improve their temporary homes.

We cleared a space upstairs for the mattress, ate cold baked beans and lay down. Boards and ceiling paper peeled from the ceiling. We had to get up and turn the bed around because Harriet said that one bit of paper looked like Henry Kissinger, and it was freaking her out. At some point in the night, the cows decided to join us. They pushed in the door to help celebrate our first night in paradise. Harriet said that they'd keep us warm, so it was all right with her, as long as they stayed downstairs.

I lay and gazed at the chaos. No water, no electricity, no telephone; there wasn't even a road, but all that could be changed in time. What couldn't be changed was the fact that we'd landed slap in the centre of the dream. Now it was up to us. I was thirty-one and ready for whatever was coming.

The point of the trip being to find water, we made enquiries in Castletown bars where local farmers assured us that there were springs all over our mountain. We could have been looking for gold and they would have said, 'Sure the place is built on the stuff.' But we'd heard what we wanted to hear. We returned to Scotland to inform the solicitors that we'd taken expert advice, and there was plenty of water.

On 28 February 1974, we finally moved to our new life in Ireland. A friend drove his lorry filled with all of our junk. Welsh customs were officious as always. They made us empty the entire, tightly packed contents. We spread them out, across the white lines, involving as many lanes as we could. Old furniture and paintings, carpets, two spinning wheels and a dozen jeroboams of home-made wine, bubbling away through their airlocks. There were hundreds of books, a pile of sheep fleeces and sacks of herbs for dyeing the wool. The centrepiece was Harriet's two beehives, each with its swarm of bees.

In the drive-through shed of Welsh Customs, we were forced to mount an exhibition of our way of life. So we decided to do it in style with a re-creation of an old-fashioned parlour. On the carpet, we placed a table and chairs. I found an ashtray and a potted plant, and we sat there smoking and drinking a glass of our foul, half-fermented concoction. All that was left in the lorry was Harriet's piano. A uniform man came over and snarled, 'I told you, *everything* out.' Stepping over the Siamese cat who was drinking a saucer of milk, with his baton he started to jab at the beehives saying, 'What's this, what's this?' When I told him that they were full of aggressive Scottish bees, he jumped back and told us to go.

The Cork Customs were good-humoured and teased us about the beehives. They asked how the other side had managed to search them for drugs and for guns.

On arrival in Castletownbere, we looked for a tractor and trailer, of which there were few. Finally we found one in Allihies, and transported our stuff to the house.

The next morning, Harriet and I drove to town and parked between the bank and Chris Shea's bar. As we got out of the car we were approached by the bank manager. 'Good morning, good morning, good people,' he said. He introduced himself and explained that he'd noticed the number plates of the Renault. 'Welcome to Castletown Berehaven,' he continued. 'In order to celebrate the advent of tourism in our little town, the Allied Irish

Bank is giving away one hundred pounds to each new arrival.' He was waving us into his bank.

'Please step inside and allow me to furnish you with a cheque.' This really was the bank manager who, apparently, was not impartial to a drop for his breakfast. The cheque failed to materialise but he provided a humorous welcome.

'And this really is Ireland,' said Harriet. 'My God, all of those stories are *true*.'

We returned to the farm to see a man leading his horse away, across the fields to Brackloon. On the doorstep stood a bulging hemp sack. Neighbours had heard that strangers had moved into Garranes. Mossy had brought us, slung over his horse, the gift of a sack of the precious potatoes that he'd grown for the winter.

We spent March settling into our new home, new country and life. We bought a frisky young mare we called Soma, who I rode to the post office to buy food. And we kept discovering new parts of the land: a secret field with hedges of hazel, found through a tunnel of fuchsia. A terrace of grass, surrounded by rocks, looking far down the foaming shoreline. And wrapped all around and invading each thought was the vast expanse of the ocean. On a map of the world, I saw the extent of the vastness that spread from our door. If we got into a boat at the foot of our cliffs and sailed south, we might see nothing but water until we hit Antarctica's white walls of ice.

On a walk to the western cliff, I stood on the edge of a vertical drop to the tide. I took off my watch and threw it into the ocean. Now I'd arrived in Ireland. No more would I try to confine the universe and carry it safely tied to a wrist. To hell with the circular stress machine, whose every tick knits one more knot in the net that fishes us out of perfection. From that day, for the rest of my life, I never more carried a watch.

Sometimes, in our idyllic seclusion, we felt a bit daunted by the scale of the task. We knew no one. We had a derelict house and one hundred and fifty acres to fence, a ten-minute walk to the car and almost one hundred miles to the city. Where should

I start? I found myself with a hammer and chisel, cutting steps in the rock by the farmhouse. It was the first job that I did, and the last that needed to be done. Was it blind panic, or a symbol of the slow, solid steps of the coming battle with convention and the westerly wind?

Harriet cooked on the open fire while I drew water from the well at the back of the mountain. We started to dig to get some seeds of vegetables in, but by Easter we needed a break from the good life. We'd take a few days off and see a little of Ireland. The problem was the twelve hens and the Rhode Island Red cockerel that we'd housed in the tumbledown annexe. The only answer was to take them on holiday with us, so I made a wire partition and gave them the back seat of the Renault.

We drove for three days around the Ring of Kerry through magnificent scenery. Everything was a little more developed, the roads a bit straighter and wider. We preferred the natural disorder of Beara, whose ways unravelled in a sequence of mishaps that twisted through history, devoid of rules or obvious intent.

Before breakfast, on our last morning, in the car park of Glengarriff Castle Hotel, the hens finally staged their revolt. While we were feeding them on the tarmac, they decided to make a break for the trees. The owner came out to help us gather them up. His nonchalant humour implied that it was not in the least unusual for his guests to bring their poultry on holiday. Harriet said that it was because only the usual was unusual in Ireland.

Back at Garranes, in the light green excitement of springtime, we talked about babies. Harriet was worried that my eye condition might be passed on. If we couldn't have children we couldn't stay here. I'd have to let Harriet go and all would be lost. A black cloud blew into the dream. I sat on the cliff and sucked nectar from a floret of fuchsia. In the crystal air, the fields fluoresced along the edge of the ocean. A ridiculous thought splashed into my pool of concern. In my favourite story when I was a boy, Ferdinand sat under the cork tree sniffing the flowers. Here I was, under a County Cork tree sucking the nectar from fuchsia.

I laughed. Even that was prophetic. How could all of this be not meant to be?

I wrote to the Royal Eye Hospital in London to arrange an appointment in June. After posting the letter, I sat outside a bar in the Castletown sun. The driver was trying to park the school bus in the square. He was reversing into the space between the only car and a telegraph pole. The battered old bus had no mirrors, so he kept getting out to see where he was. Now he was backing, gingerly, into the gap. I'd noticed a little old man with a stick, admiring the driver's manoeuvre from outside Hanley's, the drapers. Now he scuttled across the road and stood close to the telegraph pole, out of sight of the driver. His stick was grasped in both hands and raised high over his head. As the driver reversed towards the pole, the old fellow gave the bus an almighty wallop. It lurched to a halt and the driver ran round the back to see what damage he'd done. The old man touched his cap as he disappeared into McCarthy's Bar.

'That,' said Harriet, who'd joined me in time for the show. 'That's what lack of television allows. People still have time to be creative.' Electricity had just arrived in Allihies and the first sets were about to be rented. On the other hand, telephones had been around for a while, although there were few, with all of the numbers of Ireland, bar Dublin, in one single book. The phones had no digits or dials, but you had to wind a handle to call the post office who'd connect you to someone that you couldn't hear. West Cork was a generation behind the mainland of Europe.

It was reported that eighty-five per cent of families in the West of Ireland still had no water piped to the house. The roads were used as much by cattle as cars, and livestock had the right of way as they grazed the 'long acre'. It all seemed as it should be to those of us who were leaving a society that had smothered itself with its blanket of comfort.

When we'd arrived, the fields by the sea were studded with celandines and violets. Now the new grass was turning the terraces green. The Mizen leaned on an idle horizon and gave not a damn for the sparkling light. I walked out, each morning, to check that it was still there, and wondered when I'd wake up. The calm of the ocean rose slowly and fell, oblivious to the centuries of sad departures that it had supported. Surely it is sorrow, come to rest in perfection, that opens the heart. Having arrived, so recently, at all of this splendour, was I to lose it so soon? I felt my life like a seabird that rides on the wind, at ease and alert, blown by currents that define its direction and yet allow it to soar.

I received a letter from my mother to say that she'd been diagnosed with lung cancer. Harriet drove me to Cork, to take the next flight to London. In Newcastle I bought bunches of freesias and roses and caught a train north.

My father and his sister had made Mother a bed in the conservatory, so that she could lie and look over the fields. The doctors said that she was too far gone to operate on, but she showed no sign and never complained. She said that she'd only one worry; one bad thing that she'd done. It had been bothering her, and she wanted to confess it to me, and to know if I thought she'd be punished. She'd been dared, as a schoolgirl, to steal an apple from a stall. She said that all the suffering of Christendom had been caused by the theft of an apple.

Although well aware of her self-sacrificing generosity and immeasurable love, I found it a wonder that anyone could have led such a blameless life as this woman. I told her that the true definition of freedom is to be able to die and worry only that you once stole an apple.

I told her that I'd stolen money from her purse, although she had little, having spent it already on me. She smiled and said that she knew. She said that perhaps she'd recover and come to her beloved Ireland in autumn.

I arranged to return in a few weeks and caught the train back to London. I saw a genetic consultant. He said that my eye condition was extremely rare, and that we were all carriers of something, and if that stopped us there'd be no next generation. He told us that there was no reason why we shouldn't breed. I balanced on the scales of a turbulent week: the sorrow at my mother's illness, and the exhilaration that Harriet and I could go on.

Having hitched from the ship to West Cork, I found Harriet sitting on a grassy bank above the ocean in evening sun. I gave her the news that we could have children and she told me that, while I was away, she'd slept with a pitchfork beside her in bed.

Two weeks later we drove into town. At the post office, a telegram from my brother, Michael, said that he'd been trying to contact us for three days. Mother had died and her funeral would be on Tuesday. Tuesday was the next day.

15

Clueless and Determined

We hurried home to unearth my old pinstripe suit. Moths had eaten holes in the shoulders so the lining showed through. On an all-night train to the north, Harriet inked them in with a pen. Arriving tired and dishevelled, the next morning, we found a house full of relatives about to depart for the church.

I learnt that, three days before, Mother had got out of bed in the sunlit conservatory, walked quietly across the room, put her arms around my father, and died. Now he was surrounded by an army of sisters who ensured decorum by protecting him from emotion and his children who, after all, had only half the right blood. Father's Victorian father was pompous and advocated total intolerance, so Father rebelled against this and was disinherited in favour of his younger brother.

Mother's Irish family were less inclined to let prejudice deprive them of fun. Father's busy sisters dismissed eccentricity with contempt, whereas the Irish lot admired it each day in the mirror. Harriet muttered something about the small minds of Middle England. I told her that, from an Irish perspective, the only thing wrong with the English was their almost total lack of an ocean. 'Why not?' chuckled the Irish, at anything that you might suggest. 'Better not' was the English response.

My mother had arranged for Father to live with Aunt Roma,

his Tavistock sister. She lived in a house stuffed with exquisite antiques and out of bounds to all but the most repressed children. In the days following the funeral this aunt whisked through the house disposing of Mother's possessions. As a child, I'd treasured the drawer of her sewing cabinet with its reels, in neat rows, of bright-coloured threads. She was always making something for Christmas, for her husband and boys. I saw her at the end of the holidays, sewing Cash's name tapes into our vests, fighting to hold back her tears. I'd play with the jewel-like cottons and brilliant hanks of embroidery silk. It gave me a life-long fascination with colour. There were patterns and pincushions, knitting needles, thimbles and buttons and bobbins. This was the secure and creative world that had been there since time had begun. Now I found it all dumped in the dustbin, so I rescued it for Harriet to use.

I watched the active aunt flitting around the world of my mother, turning out the lights on her life. 'Life must go on,' she kept saying. When I pointed out that it had just ended, she threw me a look and a duster.

I wanted to talk to her, but could find no chink in activity's armour. I wanted to say that, if death is the end, nothing makes sense. There'd be no hope, no point and no problem. What a relief, you could just get a gun. I wanted to tell her that her doctrine of one life, then heaven or hell for ever, was a barbarous lie, thought up by a power-crazed church to terrify its victims into submission. What a ridiculously old-fashioned and brutal suggestion from the era of darkness. It seemed to me that we continuously evolve by fluorescing in and out of existence, anywhere in a cosmos of possibility so vast that this mind can't even approach it. With us, we take the thread that we spun with our doing, and behind, we leave nothing but a lesson for the next lot to learn.

In the larder was a row of empty jam jars. Each was neatly labelled 'Mint jelly, 1974'. My mother made this every year for my father to eat with his lamb. This year she'd run out of the time to fill them, although the mint was tall and green in her garden.

Back in Ireland I wondered how I'd picked up this habit for such remote places. I watched the waves wash in the sorrow of evening and wondered how long it would take. It was time to be working. A neighbour came over to help me fence the vegetable garden. We stood facing the sea, unrolling the wire along the edge, and fixing it to the stakes.

'Where are those staples?' I asked him.

'They're a biteen to the easht of your wesht boot,' he replied. So well orientated are these peninsular people. No problem with abstract concepts like left or right, which reverse, depending on which side of yourself you are standing. With the horizon always before them they know exactly where they stand on the planet. East is east and west is west, no matter how many times you turn round. I quickly adopted this superior means of orientation, and thought of how Mum would have loved it.

With the winter coming, it was time to start on the house. There was another ramshackle dwelling nearby. It was the only other building in sight and had been deserted for decades. We asked its absentee owner, Michael Joe Lynch, if we could move in while we put a roof on our ruin. The fact that most of its windows were broken, and its door was missing, didn't seem much of an issue. The palm trees and fuchsia hedges persuaded us that the winters were mild, and we were young, naïve and excited. As the days shortened, we searched for someone to help with the building. Dan Flor, who'd a reputation as one of the old school of craftsmen, agreed to start work in October.

With no electricity and the world running out of energy, we decided on wind power, but windmills were a thing of the past. The last few were being ripped out, as mains power reached the remotest regions of Europe. We found one source, with stainless steel blades for lighting buoys in the Arctic, but they were so expensive that we decided to stick to hurricane lamps and our candles.

At this point, the Renault 4 gave up the ghost. Harriet saw it as an opportunity to live without such a cause of our planet's pollution. I thought it might be difficult watching the world flash by on four wheels, while building a house so far from supplies.

Meanwhile, a hundred miles away, in our nearest second-hand bookshop, Harriet had found *Five Acres and Independence*. With advice from this and other such books, she worked on the garden. It was tough enough because the whole farm rested on rock with just a few inches of soil. Only occasionally could you locate a fissure with more, by poking around with a crow bar. In an attempt to provide shelter, I gathered rocks and built walls filled with soil, carried in buckets from where I could scrape it. Into this, I pushed cuttings of fuchsia, the one hedge that thrived on salt and continuous wind.

Tired of carrying everything half a mile to the house, I bought an old cart with wood-spoked wheels. I exchanged Soma for a quiet young mare called Dusty, who'd safely haul the cart up the dangerous track. Driving the rig into town, I realised how shut off from the world we become, in our fast-moving packets of steel. Now I was travelling at a speed at which I could see what was happening; at which I could smell the moist earth; at which I could hear the birds sing. I felt like a king on my old Irish cart, with the reins in my hands, enabled to drive with the aid of my ears, and the eyes of my beautiful mare.

So now we needed a cow. There was an old man who was selling his land in the mountains of Kerry, so we drove to his remarkable farm. There were standing stones and rocks with Celtic spirals, scattered all over the ancient fields. It was a strange, unreal place that left you with no doubt that we are all dreaming; certain that, if you had the guts to stay until twilight, it would prove the existence of fairies.

The man led us into the windowless cowshed. There was a flat stone with a carved spiral, lying in the mud, as a doorstep.

For sixty pounds he sold us the black Kerry cow that he'd milked for almost a decade. We were warned that this one would be a bugger to milk. Having been handled by one man for so long, she'd never take kindly to an amateur stranger. Worse again, she was a Kerry – a breed related to the black Spanish fighting bull, a breed renowned for its temper. Maybe I'd have to give up sniffing the flowers and get in the ring after all.

For the first few days she'd hardly let me milk her at all. Harriet said that she hated me for calling her 'Lupin'. She'd break loose from her tether, bucking and kicking her heels almost up to the roof of the shed. I'd catch her and tie her again to the ring in the wall, and hope that she wouldn't pull the place down on us both. After a few days, the wily old cow settled down. She stood perfectly still and allowed me to half fill the bucket with milk. I'd finally got the measure of her. As I squirted the last stream, she'd give a kick at the bucket, spilling it into the straw. She knew that she needed to be milked, but she was damned if this upstart was going to get it. She followed this routine each day, before finally allowing me her milk. I soon got to love this cantankerous old bag of a being, with her huge, soft, all-seeing eyes.

Meanwhile, the main problem with West Cork was the friendliness of its people. Their open and easy generosity was especially dangerous when mixed in a cocktail with poetry and wit, in the nineteen bars on the short main street of Castletownbere.

Who'd not be beguiled by the music, the crack and the Guinness? I drove Dusty to town, sitting on a bale of straw on the cart. At the shop, I bought another dustbin, in which to store feed for the stock. I filled it with our food for a fortnight. Donnie, the old lady at the counter, had taken a liking to me. When I finished shopping she said, 'There's a free offer this morning,' and with a wink, she cut a large chunk of cheese, and slipped it into my dustbin.

I walked the rig to Jimmy's field at the back of the town and unharnessed the mare to graze. Afloat on a ridiculous feeling of freedom, I walked to the bar. For the first time in my life, I wasn't dependent on others. I could drive, I could drive, and it was perfectly legal. Captivated by the stories of old men from a time that was passing, I lost count of how many times we had one for the road. On more than one occasion, I remembered harnessing the mare to the cart, remembered driving out of the town on the five-mile trip home, and remembered nothing more until I was awoken by sudden non-movement. Dusty had brought me up to the Gap of Gour. She'd turned left and negotiated the hairpins of the steep track, brought me to the farmhouse door and waited for me to wake up.

Before we knew it, October was whistling in the broken roof and it was time to move into Lynch's. With a yard-broom, we brushed the worst of the flaking plaster from the walls. We cleaned out the fireplace and moved all of our possessions into the two upstairs rooms. Because there was no water, there was no sink and no bathroom.

We stood a rough wooden bedstead in the main downstairs room, the other being filled with our hay. The foot of the bed was a metre from the open doorway, across the top third of which I'd nailed some felt so that we could come and go underneath it. Sure, the winters were mild and it was only for a few months. We'd not bargained for storms. Why should we? This was the seaside, and my memory of the seaside was a sun-baked beach in midsummer.

But soon, the winter storms were blowing their rain onto our bed, through the doorway and broken windows. We slept like logs in the freshness, beneath a plastic sheet with a wet bedspread to hold it in place. The wind blew plaster-dust into our eyes, our sheets and our dinner, as our idyll showed us a wrathful side to its nature. Showed us that it wasn't only lapped by the tropical Gulf Stream, but also lashed by the wild North Atlantic. Clueless and determined, we worked until we almost despaired. Then the sun came out and we were beguiled again.

Our first load of gravel was dumped in the middle of the Allihies road. An occasional car and the school bus had to take to the verge and drive through the gorse to get round it. No one complained as we took two days to shovel load after load into a trailer and ferry it up to the house.

We worked through the winter and slept in our windswept room. Each morning, I brushed the puddles from the floor and lit the turf fire. Harriet made breakfast while I searched for and milked the old cow. When the mist was down it wasn't easy to find her. She might be south-west, down by the tide, or north, uphill in the furze. In the sea fog, you might search for half of a morning. So I wrote to the Swiss embassy in Dublin for the names of suppliers. Within a month the problem was solved. Our weirdness was confirmed, to the delight of the neighbours who'd never imagined a cowbell. However, they soon got the point when they saw me go to the door, listen, and hear exactly where the cow was, in the dark of a wet November. They said, 'Fair play to you,' and may have even half-wished that they had the nerve to do likewise.

Soon we were warmed by the news that Harriet was pregnant. We'd go to England for Christmas and see if her parents were truly liberal or if it was only a pose. Would her Chelsea-born mother be concerned at the scandal that she might imagine, when the world found out that her unwed daughter was pregnant?

Harriet gave her parents the good news, and I was invited to join the family in Sussex for a slightly fraught Christmas. In the tradition of avoidance of difficult topics, the subject of babies was little discussed. Instead conversation centred on such civilised topics as the arts, the garden and golf.

Back in the fresh air of Ireland, the building was nearing completion. We had a fair-sized kitchen cum living room, a fine bathroom with no water, three bedrooms and a shrine room. In Scotland, I'd been teased for building the shrine room before the kitchen. This time, I made sure that I got my priorities wrong by completing the kitchen first.

There was a government grant for a septic tank. We had some local experts digging the hole and building it up. When I checked it, I found that they'd made it a metre too short.

'It's not big enough,' I told them, 'it won't pass the inspection.'

'Don't worry,' they said, 'it's the traditional size; quite big enough; you should take no notice of the college-boys' rules. Once it's buried, who can tell? We cover it with a concrete slab, a metre longer than the tank beneath. The inspector comes, measures the slab and is happy. It gets you the grant, saves us some work and saves you some cash.'

In March we celebrated our first anniversary in Beara by moving into the farmhouse, upstairs. Harriet was proud of surviving a whole winter on a clifftop, pregnant and doorless. Mossy showed me the rock of old Patsy Murphy, the father of the family who'd sold us the farm. He was a 'fierce man for the wreck'. It was said that he'd sit on his rock and keep an eye on the ocean. He'd spy a beam or a wooden hatch-cover when it was 'halfway across from the States'. Assessing the tides and the wind, he'd know where and when it would land, go down and fish it out, and that was the way that the houses were built. It was why I wanted to lower the floor, rather than raise the old pitch pine ceiling that had come from the sea.

We smashed the concrete floor, dug it out, levelled it and laid down a screed. Then I spent weeks chipping cement from the backs of octagonal quarry tiles that I'd got in Edinburgh, for the price of a drink, when they renovated the Royal Scottish Museum. I laid the tiles and discovered the Irish drainage system that I'd just destroyed. A summer deluge sent water cascading down the mountain and in through the back door of the house. The whole floor was deep under water. We learnt, from neighbours, that it wasn't meant to be level. It had been carefully sloped from the east and the west to the centre, and then from the north to the south. When there was a rainstorm, the water would flow in the back door, across the room in a neat rivulet and out through the door at the south. You could sit by the fire with the stream behind you, and not even get your feet wet.

The summer of '75, in Ireland, was long and hot. We'd dug a well in the meadow but the water was no good for drinking. Even after leaving it for a month to settle, it still slurped from its pipe like black porridge. The old well by the track had run dry, so I reverted to carrying buckets from the stream at the back of the mountain.

Few farmers could afford fences and cattle were straying in search of a drink. One morning, a note was left in Shea's bar, to say that my Kerry cow had broken into a farmer's barley at Kilmackowen. We'd let Lupin go dry and put her out on our mountain. How had she wandered for so many miles and how did they know she was ours? We guessed that she was heading back to her Celtic spirals in Kerry.

Harriet dropped me at the end of the farmer's boreen. Up at the house I found Lupin tied to a post. The farmer wasn't at all angry but was cheerful and friendly as he asked how I was going to get the cow home. He smiled when I said that I'd walk her nine miles on the road. With a piece of rope, he made her a head collar and then handed the long rope to me. The old cow scowled with a look that said, 'Are you sure that you're ready for this, boy?' Then she turned and ran down the steep boreen, at a gallop. Grimly, I clung to the end of the rope. I concentrated on keeping my feet until we were out of sight of the farmer. Then I let go. She ran a hundred yards and turned right, into a field. I chased her around the field and out into the road again. She turned left then right, up a long boreen, and I found myself back in the yard from which we had started.

I was exhausted and there were still nine miles to go. I remembered that most farms didn't have gates. It took us hours to get back to Castletownbere, and hours more to get home, via half of the fields and farmyards in Beara.

Garranes, because of its spectacular location, and having been empty for years, attracted visitors who we usually welcomed with tea. But sometimes it became a bit much. Never liking to lock the door, once or twice we found people in our house, innocently enjoying a good look around. On some busy Sundays we took to hiding in the barn with the chickens, until the voices had gone. We became fans of Gaelic football because it was played on a Sunday. If Cork was having a good season, everyone would stay at home to watch the match on the new television, and we'd have the day to ourselves. Although we had no television and didn't give a damn about sport, Cork had no keener supporters.

In late July the baby was due and the nearest maternity hospital was three hours up country in Cork. Harriet drove us there and we waited. Contractions began in the early hours of a fine summer's morning. We walked through the silent city at dawn and, reaching the hospital, Harriet wasn't ready to go in. Leaving the suitcase by the front door, we walked the empty streets. On our return, there were sirens wailing and the place had been cordoned off by the bomb squad. An alert had been caused by a suspicious suitcase found against the main door. Harriet was allowed in, while I apologised to the unconcerned guards.

Forty-eight hours later, after a difficult labour, Harriet gave birth to a beautiful redheaded baby called Flora.

Back at home with a crying infant, Harriet felt vulnerable with no one to turn to. Her mother wrote to say that we 'must be thrilled that it's all over now, bar the screaming'. She said that she was delighted that it was a girl but she hadn't told anyone, being loath to become the 'dinner party gossip of the gin-swilling bags of East Sussex'.

Harriet became ill with puerperal fever. I walked to the post office to call the ambulance, which had to wait out at the Allihies road. Harriet walked for half a mile on churned up mud, gone hard with the sun. She had a high temperature and insisted on carrying the five-day-old baby.

After two days in hospital, Harriet returned and the baby kept crying and her mother wrote saying, 'I can't believe that you've called it Fiona.' Each sleepless night we said that the crying would cease the next day. Each restless day, Harriet constantly fed her and said that when west from the door was America and south was Antarctica, at least there was no one to complain.

Now the land was burnt as the sun shone week after week. Walking to the back of the mountain, I filled our two five-gallon containers, and then washed the nappies in the stream. Eventually, the endless sun reduced the stream to a trickle which finally died.

Across the Allihies road, higher up the mountain, there was still water. I estimated that with eleven five hundred foot rolls of the new alkathene pipe, I could get water to our taps. I spent the next week manoeuvring the pipes, rolling them up the mountain, through rocks and brambles, furze and various bogs. I used a bucket of water and a funnel to establish a suction. Then, with much shaking and snaking to remove any air blocks, I worked my way down to the house. After many failures, I finally experienced the exhilaration of seeing a stream, bubbling from a pipe at our door. I took a glass of clear water to Harriet.

Eventually, the baby stopped crying and tension was replaced by cute little giggles and gasps. Then, a week before Christmas, Harriet was breast-feeding the baby in the kitchen. A large black rat ran across the room and disappeared up the chimney. While we had no particular objection to rats, this event seemed to suggest a certain lack of refinement in our lifestyle. We decided to risk a trip to London on Slattery's bus.

Soon after our arrival we were reminded of why we'd been in no hurry. Any lack of physical comfort in Ireland was as nothing when compared to the mental discomfort of Kensington. 'Give me real Irish rats any time,' said Harriet. This was a little bit harsh. They'd simply inherited the superficial confidence of their class, which subtly scoffs until everything wilts without knowing why. I saw this as a survival technique of the system. Most people are motivated by a desire to climb up the tree, unless they perceive themselves to be already on top. In which case they have nowhere to go, so they hang around in the canopy, scowling at anyone who looks like making a move.

Somehow I found that I could hold my own in this polite jungle. Harriet said that it was because I couldn't see what was going on in their eyes. I thought that, in not reacting, I was able to see that their sad, self-imposed suffering was as valid as anyone else's. So I listened to them and they liked that. And I liked them, one at a time, because once you broke through the out-dated veneer, they were as real as the rest of the dream.

16

Domain of the Spirit

Increasing traffic was making Irish roads unsafe for transporting babies by horse and cart. We bought an old Morris Minor for thirty pounds in Sussex. Because the Irish government had friends in the motor trade, they tried to stop people importing cheap cars from Britain. At Cork, the customs told us to return the car on the next ferry. I said that this was unreasonable. I'd pay any tax due on thirty pounds, which was nothing. We sat there for hours, with the baby, while customs officials looked awkward. If I got angry everything would tighten so, with good humour, I said that we'd sleep on the floor. I fetched cushions and duvets and rugs from the car. They brought us cups of tea and then, when it was time to turn out the lights, they told us to go.

It was strange for our bodies to be travelling at speed again. With our minds already careering about at the speed of light, we wished that someone would invent a mechanised rig that would chug along at ten miles per hour. How much better the world would be if nothing went faster than donkeys. We might even slow down enough to catch up with ourselves, and become aware, in the new silence, of the answers that flow from all that surrounds us.

I built a rustic hen house with a turf roof and stone walls. It had no door but there were tree trunks and branches for perches, too high for the fox.

The farm was split into two. Fifty acres of small fields and terraces ran down to the cliffs, where their backdrop was Bantry Bay and the open Atlantic. It was here that we lived. Then, across the Allihies road, to the north, was a further hundred acres of mountain, stretching high up through the gorse and heather. A stream with waterfalls ran down to an east–west valley of peat, where the Murphys had cut turf for their fire.

At that time, most houses still had a corrugated garden of lazy-bed potatoes. Some still cut hay with a scythe, but the old ways were fast fading away. As peat in the valleys ran out, the peat cutters were forced up the mountain and into the mist. Up there it was tricky to dry it and even that source was now almost gone. There remained the ends of old peat banks, rising out of the grass like black tombstones for a time that was buried or burnt.

The peat was running out at the very moment that electricity arrived. Now we were told that oil would last for no more than three decades. Would a new energy appear as soon as the oil had all gone? Such things were the talk of our time. Meanwhile, in the name of self-sufficiency, it was decided, not entirely by me, that I should cut peat for next winter.

I needed a hay-knife, a slean and a pitchfork. The slean, or peat-cutting spade, had a blade bent at right angles along its length, to cut cubes from the bog. It was hard work skinning the bog and cutting the peat. For me, there were further complications, like my inability to see what was going on at my feet. I had difficulty in placing the blade on the right spot in the uncut slab of black butter. Since it was a matter of guesswork, instead of smooth rectangular ingots, I produced an artistic assortment of L-shapes.

The work was hot and slightly demoralising at first. Then slowly I began to get the idea. I had a helper who ushered me out through this doorway in time. A dreamy, slightly spaced-out girl called Floating Cloud had come out of nowhere, to stay. She came to the bog to help me, while Harriet stayed at home with the baby. She was pretty in the sunshine, with her fair hair bound in a ponytail which hung down the back of the dress that brushed her bare feet. She was tripping about in the myrtle, gathering twigs to make fire for the tea. She was young and unknown, a fairy dakini who'd blown in on the breath of a summer. It wouldn't have surprised me had she flown round the sun and settled on the palm of my hand.

All morning I laboured in the hot May sun. I took off my shirt and slid the slimy black bricks up onto the bank where the bog-nymph tried, laughing, to catch them and spread them out neatly to dry. Her body was silhouetted through her long pale dress, as she worked between me and the sky. She pulled the dress up and tucked it in, with the hem a short skirt to hang down. She danced on the grass above me, as I cut deeper into the past, and her long lean legs shouted 'Yes' to me and the morning. And I marvelled at how well I could see when I had to.

Then it felt like time for our lunch. We lay on the moss by the stream in moist shade and ate our bread and butter in silence. The birds had ceased to sing in the heat of the day. The only sound was the giggle of water, as it played with its pebbles, polished from seasons of teasing.

'My old neighbour was cutting turf here, when he was a boy,' I told her. 'He found, deep in the peat, a woman's hair comb that was carved from a bone. They said it was more than a thousand years old. It must have dropped from her hair on a day such as this.'

'So that's why I'm here,' said the nymph of the myrtle. 'I've come back to find something I lost.'

I ran my fingers over the back of her hand and up the slenderest arm. She certainly seemed to be there. I'd wondered if she was a maya-girl who would disappear the moment I reached out to touch her. I was close enough now to imagine the light in her beautiful eyes. I remembered lying with my crazy art student, one Saturday morning, a decade before. I was sure that the only real way to deal with undesired desire was to completely relax and enjoy letting go. It was time for me to try to explain, but she already knew, so there was no need to have spoken.

'I'm not going to kiss you,' I said, 'but you should know that you're perfect, and almost irresistible.' I told her how Harriet and I had an agreement that we were both free to experience this brief life as we saw fit. The only thing that was holding me back was a slight issue with fairness, perhaps also my shyness, but above all, the absolute purity of that energy just as it was.

To go any further would degrade that purity with grasping. Better to stand right on the razor's edge of desire. Not lost in the force that had made us, but so tingling with life that it hurts; so far-awake that you'd remember that moment forever. I wanted to look it full in the face; feel it surge through floodgates flung open by an unlikely meeting, and yet not be swept away by the tide. There is a choice: to tense up and try to feel the earth move, or to relax and stop the universe from revolving. To succumb is to continue the famous old cycle. To resist is to dangerously dam up desire. But to relax in the moment of tension is to enable the radiant awareness that would be dulled with mere satisfaction. To let go with joy, to completely give up, is when we begin to receive. Then, one day, as we journey away from the wanting, we might find that all desire has ceased and we're free.

Wondering whether she understood, I saw that it wasn't a matter of that. It was she who was offering me her wordless instruction. The grass had absorbed so much light that it shone like the green in an evening rainbow. The girl in the ferns by the stream that flashed out of time had come to teach me her silence. We finished spreading the peat and ran back to the sea, as light as the breezes that blew us.

I looked down at the dazzling ocean. The scent of bluebells drifted in from the field of the dream. Spires of foxgloves insisted that it was already June. Their vertical clocks introduced the bustle of time to the timeless. From the base of their spires, the first purple trumpets had fanfared the onrush of summer. Soon the procession of florets would climb up the stem, daily to open and die. Finally, two flags would wave on top and another spring would be buried in crazy July. If I sat on the mountain for a day without moving, I'd see the sun rise out of Berehaven, sail through the stations of day, and then set in the rose ocean, west. I may have thrown my watch from the cliff, but there's no escape from the turning. Not until it all comes to rest in the absence of wanting.

There was a goat that lived on the cliffs and jumped my fences for fun. We decided that it was time for the goat to go. We caught her and walked her down to the road, then tugged her and talked her over the bog, and a long way into the mountain. On the far side, we let her go and sat down to regain our breath. There was gorse, there was heather and brambles and everything of which a goat might be dreaming. We watched her scamper away, occasionally stopping for something to eat. We sat for a while and then walked home with a sense of fulfilment. We opened the gate and there was the goat, back before us and halfway through our last lettuce. If, at any time in your life you begin to fool yourself that you're in control, go out and get you a goat.

Now Harriet wanted goats to milk so that she could make cheese. She assured me that, if we imported pedigree goats from England, we'd find a way to contain them. So we added goats to our list of dependants. We already had two horses and Happy the donkey. There was Lupin, the cow, and a small herd of heifers. There was Domino, the sheepdog who shepherded our geese, and Streaky, the pharaoh hound. We had laying hens with a cockerel, bantams, guinea fowl and two Muscovy ducks. It cost me my time for reflection, but provided a watertight excuse for not going to England.

In July though, Harriet went. She got me a stock of food and took Flora to Sussex for the summer. I had seven free weeks to myself. Sometimes it was wild and lonely and then the light would change. I'd be overwhelmed by the privilege of working to realise my dream in one of the most inspiring places on earth. In the tumbledown shed, I milked the cow. Then I sat back to gaze down the bay through a hole in the wall. I could see twenty miles of coastline and not another building in sight. It was as though humans hadn't yet ventured this far. In fact it was hard to believe that there was anyone else in the world. Then, along the bay, across the mountains and another sea, I'd visualise my mandala; Piccadilly Circus, teeming with people going round and around. Funny English policemen and a double-decker bus. It was good to know that it was there, and better to be so far away from it all. It kept me sane and it kept me here.

In September Harriet returned, exhausted from a summer with her family. She told me of an incident at the customs in Cork. She had some cuttings for the garden. Conscious of the law forbidding the importation of plants, but unaware that it didn't apply to unrooted stock, Harriet had devised a means of smuggling them in. She must have looked guilty. You could always see, in her face, everything that was going on. They made her unbutton her ankle-length coat. Tied from a belt round her waist were suspended three sponge bags full of moss and plant slips in water. Surrounded by the drug squad, she stammered the Latin names of the plants until, laughing, they told her to go.

A few days later we heard that Chairman Mao was dead. We'd tried not to remember the stories of his atrocities in Tibet. Of the Chinese hammering six-inch nails into the skulls of kneeling monks. Of the total destruction of the oldest intact culture on earth.

That night of 9 September, we invited some friends to our small house, such a long way from China. We drank to the death of the sinister chairman, the symbol of the absolute absence of freedom. In some ways it was the influence of people like Mao that had brought us to live on the outer rim of the mayhem. To hope to relax the power of those passions that make us all Mao in our moments. Hoping to open, as we struggle up the millennia, towards who we actually are.

Sometimes after dark, I sat Flora on my knee and made shapes on the wall with the shadow of my hands, from the paraffin lamp.

One night the last mantle broke and we'd run out of candles. Sitting in the darkness, we decided that it was time for electrics. Maybe Harriet would even agree to a washing machine. It would liberate her from the drudgery of scrubbing the clothes on a washboard.

We loved the soft light of the living flame and the magic that's lost in electric light. The mysterious empowerment of flickering candle and firelight. The dark corners and strange moving shapes that inspire the imagination to fly. Civilisation had cost us so much when it made night as bright as the day. The purpose of day is to make it all solid and ready for work. The whole point of night is to get it dancing again. To remind us that anything's possible because there's no such thing as a matter of fact.

We'd lost this balance when we cut down the trees. Now we visit lonely stone circles on wind-blasted moorland and wonder why they built shrines to the gods in such god-forsaken surroundings. We forgot that those sanctuaries were often at cross-paths, deep in the forests that covered the land and shuttered the sky. Silent and windless, warm in the torchlight; a stimulus to the spiritual life and the creative power of the mind.

That Christmas we stayed in Ireland. West Cork, being still poor, provided no outward display. No Christmas lights, no carols on the street and no presents for the children in the threadbare shops. We struggled to invoke the spirit. A shoal of home-smoked mackerel hung from the beams and steadily dripped oil onto newspaper beneath them. The room smelt of poverty, peat smoke and the past, and nobody came to the door.

One storm-torn night with Harriet and Flora asleep, I stood at the dormer window. Below, on the ocean, the light of a lone fishing boat was the one sign of life on the planet. As I watched the night swirl on a westerly gale, I saluted the bravery of those men on the ocean and wished that we'd learn to stop killing fish. And as I listened to the lonesome rattle of wind, I wondered what we were doing, so far from the rest of the world and its Christmas.

Although I no longer had to draw water each day, the pipeline brought its own problems. When the finane grass dried in the winter, it blew off the slopes and into the streams. It repeatedly blocked the filter and the water would fail at the house. It meant climbing to the source, getting into the pool, and clearing the filter, under the water.

It was less easy when there was a storm and the pipe was washed onto the bank. It meant slopping the stream into a funnel to get suction going again. Airlocks would result which might take all day to shake out in a January rain. When it was done I'd walk home, soaked to the skin, with crossed fingers. Had it worked? If water was flowing into the tank, I'd feel as good as ever I'd felt in my life, and I'd laugh for sheer joy that I lived in West Cork. If it wasn't, I'd clench my fists and tell myself how lucky I was not to be on the chemical mains, as I trudged back up the mountain and started again. By mid-January the frogs would be mating. The dawn mountain was alive to the sound of their croaking, as they writhed in the spawn-bulging ponds. And I'd clap my hands at this promise of spring, and rejoice that at least someone was having some fun. Then the sun would give birth to a field strewn with violets and the sea would lick open the eyes of the year. And there was nothing to want that I didn't have, and there was nowhere, anywhere, better to be.

I remembered my youth in the deep lanes of England where I first found the key to a grace that I couldn't define. I'd dropped that key while I marched around paradise trying to fix it. Now I stood on the cliff when the winter was over, and talked to myself about me.

I watched our pet seagull glide up the slope of a field to the house. The magic would surely return, but first I needed to work. I'd long ago sealed my fate with a crazy intention, now I just had to follow it through. Then, one day, others could share in the light of this land that we could never have kept for ourselves. I knew that there was no conflict in getting back to stillness by way of the action. If the action is inspired by an urgent inclination to help, it will itself begin to loosen the tethers of ego. If the journey is taken with others in mind, the destination is the stop beyond 'me'. And then I told myself that I might make up the words, but it was a long way from words to their meaning.

Some time after midnight we were woken by a banging on the door. Our neighbour, Vince, told me that the mountain was on fire. It was blowing towards our water pipes and the forest. I grabbed a shovel and we joined the men who were beating the flames.

Some farmers burnt part of their land at the start of each year to encourage new grass. Others said that the furze and the heather were best left unburnt because they provided shelter and forage. The experts said that generations of burning had ruined the soil. Because of the wildlife, there was an unenforced law that prohibited the practice from the beginning of March. It was almost always after that date that the burning took place.

By the end of that night we'd saved the pines but so many lives had been lost. There were nestlings of skylarks and stonechats and snipe. There were voles and frogs, lizards and insects. Millions of beings, each with precisely the same right to existence as the humans who'd burnt them to death. Of course, I didn't say this to our neighbours. If I had, after listening politely some would have agreed and others would have thought, 'bloody hippies'. But inside, everyone knows that we exist by courtesy of those few inches of soil and grass that we continuously burn with our greed. A fragile, life-support sliver of dirt that creates the atmosphere that allows us to breathe, as we sail round the sun, with thousands of miles of boiling iron under our feet and a frozen infinity of radioactive space, resting on top of our brains.

Harriet was finding life difficult, perched on the last rock between nowhere and now. They said that it was tougher for the women. For centuries, the girls had left first and the boys had followed to anywhere in the world that had work.

Where the track from the house met the old Allihies road, there was a gap between the tumbling hill and a cliff. The remains of a cart house huddled in the bracken and rocks. This melancholy place was haunted by a feeling of loss. I learnt that this was the parting place, where generations had said goodbye to their children. One by one, down the years, the mothers had walked their daughters and sons to this lonely spot, too far from the world for most to return. How quickly they'd grown, how briefly you'd known them, how swiftly the day had arrived. The men would know when the great liners were due to sail round the Mizen with their cargoes of children bound for New York. From small harbours of Beara, they'd row out onto the ocean, lean on an oar and wave goodbye to the child that they'd not see again.

Now there was food and transport, but still it wasn't easy. Harriet never complained. She had few friends although everyone liked her, being captivated by her innocent, impulsive nature, and by the way that she listened, completely.

Locally, women connected through church or by being related or simply having grown up together forever. One man I knew had thirty-four uncles and aunts and an inconceivable galaxy of cousins. It was strange, for a stranger, related to no one in a world where everyone else was related. You might see yourself as more on the outside than ever, or you might see it as a further extension of your natural path.

So three years had passed, inspired by Harriet's wish to live as a frontierswoman and mine to pursue a retreat. It seemed like a great combination, but isolation magnifies vague inclinations into titanic forces which accelerate evolution, if you're up to the strain.

Harriet and I talked about this. Our relationship was strong, though by no means a conventional one. We tried to live without attachment or judgement; without restrictions to hinder our right to be as free as the skylarks to sing our brief summer's song. We both understood that no one has a right to jurisdiction over anyone else. At best, you might claim a short-term authority over a handful of inanimate objects. But any attempt at ownership must ultimately fail. For who can draw up deeds of possession for something that's constantly changing its form? How futile to attempt to own anything that you cannot take with you, when all you take with you is what you have done.

I'd realised that happiness comes from requiring less. Fewer objects, less recognition, less love. Love is to be given and freely received, but it must never be sought. Wanting little, there's not much to covet, not much to protect, and the grip of emotion decreases. As accumulation gives way to continuous disposal, you are freed from envying what others might think they possess: flash houses and cars, flash husbands and wives, momentary good looks and talents. You recognise that envy is a chemical, released by the delusion of property rights. Covetousness gives way to compassion for those who are still possessed by their objects. Fine words, I said to myself. So difficult if you have many needs, but easy if you have few.

Harriet and I hoped that we might eventually achieve such a state. We also reminded ourselves that we were both humans. The emotional winds of millennia would continue to blow us down routes from which there is no escape, until we learn to relax and let go. Then we might catch a glimpse of the extent of the dream, and see that we make it all up. And if we make it all up, it's already ours, so the issue of grasping has ceased to arise.

It was late July, when things become a bit crazy; the summer steams up with flies, the heat, and tourists peering into the windows. Harriet said, 'To hell with evolution,' and got on a bus for England. She'd visit her parents and then find a place for the winter, maybe with Jenny from along the cliff, who was returning to Scotland.

17

History Grins

I sat in the late summer garden, listening to gorse pods explode in the heat. Flora's sandpit was empty, a small desert with two wooden spoons where she'd dropped them. Domino was growling at tourists who gazed at the well-tied gate with intent. Harriet and Flora had left on the ferry, the goats were sold, and the geese had flown off to the sea.

I was reading a large-printed letter that Harriet wrote on the ship. 'This is unbearable. Little Flora is sitting on the deck eating a sandwich. Thank God, she's too young to know what's happening and, thank God, her mother is too.'

I haunted our home for a few days, until there was a knock on the door from two strangers. 'We heard that you were selling up,' they said, as I faced them in disbelief. 'We heard that you had a refrigerator, and thought you might want to sell it.'

So the vultures were circling already. They enhanced the feeling of loss. I thought of how angry Harriet would have been, and that made me smile. Why should anyone understand what was going on here? Harriet would be back. I'd never give up on the dream which we'd hardly begun. It had just been too difficult trying to get started.

I reminded myself that each situation is there to be learnt from, and the vultures arose for a reason. With a new resolve, I set about finding homes for the rest of the livestock, except for the cattle which a neighbour would mind. Some friends arrived with an old van and a lift back to Samye Ling. I could stay with them until August was over and meet Harriet when she was revolted with Sussex. We took the long journey north to Larne, where I was glad to get on the ship. I spent the voyage in the bar. Then, walking along a dark passage, I fell down a twenty-step flight of invisible stairs. Lying in the hall at their foot I became aware of people leaning over me, to see if I was alive.

'Jesus, it's a rough crossing,' I said, by way of excuse.

'Aye,' said a peering Scot, 'except that we've been docked in Stranraer for ten minutes.'

Then, one day in early September, Harriet and Flora got out of our van at Samye Ling gate. We moved into Trungpa's old room in an empty Garwald House. Harriet began to relax and swim with the tide, instead of battling against it. She said that she always swam with the tide; it was just that the tide was usually going in the other direction.

At the end of September we returned to London. We'd been told that the next piece of coastline from us, along Bantry Bay, was for sale. I suggested to Harriet that we should buy it, to prevent development, before it came on the market. I'd been waiting to receive the address of the London-based vendor. One day, a note arrived saying, 'Meet me at the Black Lion on Wednesday at six.' There was no address and an illegible postmark. Finding, in the phone book, dozens of Black Lions in London, we narrowed it down to three, where there were Irish communities, and finally settled on Kilburn.

So it was to Kilburn that we went with a prayer and a map in my pocket. On the map there were just two words printed across the land to be sold. 'Dooneen Point' it read, where the western cliffs plunged into the ocean. As we opened the door of the pub, we were greeted by loud Irish music. It was Christy Moore singing a ballad, and the first words that we heard were '… the cliffs of Dooneen'. Harriet and I gave each other a 'here we go again' look. It was a recognition that we only had to go through the motions. Whatever part of our minds was running the show, it already had it all worked out and our role was to keep cool and watch.

By mid-October it was time for Harriet and Jenny to move to Perthshire, while I returned to Ireland. How strangely our ribbons of karma wave on the breeze of our life-streams and occasionally tangle together. Jenny had turned up, living half a mile from us in the same Irish townland. We were amazed to find ourselves neighbours. The last time that I'd heard of her was in Scotland at Heriot. It was where Amalie had taken Tara six years before. Now Jenny was moving back to another Scottish cottage and Harriet was taking Flora to live with her and Daisy, her daughter. History was grinning and thumbing its nose.

I arranged to meet Harriet at Christmas and returned to Ireland to work on the first retreat hut. Meanwhile, if I was to live alone, I'd need transport, maybe a moped, to ferry food from the town. In Cork, I stopped at the motorbike shop on Winthrop Street and came out with a shiny red Italian machine which I pushed to a small hotel. Then, in the morning, I walked it out of the city, got on it, and rode to the outskirts of Bandon.

The idea was to walk through the villages, and ride slowly the roads in between. The three-hour car trip would take me eight hours. I remembered that there was a fork at Bandon where the road took two routes to Bantry. The wrong one would take me to Clonakilty, and miles out of my way.

Gaining in confidence, I was no longer walking the bike, but riding the traffic-less streets. I could see signposts just fine, what was written on them was the problem. I rode right up to the one at the junction in Bandon. To my dismay, it was out of range over my head. I thought of resting my bike against the pole, and climbing on it to study the letters. That might look a bit odd, so I jumped as high as I could, to get closer. I waited for a car to pass and repeated the process. After several more jumps I worked it out, got on my bike and took the right fork to Dunmanway.

Now I was out in the country, on the Armageddon road to

West Cork. Potholes stretched in a fifty-mile string, half a metre out from the edge. Such detail wasn't available to me from the saddle. I had to concentrate on staying on the road by fixing my eyes on the verge ahead, and keeping my wheel half of a metre outside it. I went in and out of every pothole from Cork to Castletownbere. As it grew dark, I turned left at the cross of Garranes with a shout, a sore arse and a sigh of relief.

I mused on how to build the retreat. On how to offer the elemental surroundings as a base for the radiant teachings of Buddha. A free space where those of any persuasion could breathe again, after life in the airless solidity of sought-after status and objects.

I prepared wood for the retreat hut and panelled the farmhouse kitchen. I'd developed a technique of joinery that required a minimal use of the eyes. For example, I'd use a vinyl album cover as a square, drawing a mark with a fat felt pen on a plank to be cut. After the first few saw cuts, I'd bend down to see which side of my line I was drifting. I'd then make a few more cuts to correct the diversion, bend down and continue the process. If you checked each time after three or four cuts, you could zigzag your way along a straight line with barely a trace of a waver.

I met Harriet on a freezing December morning at Notting Hill Gate. She marched up without time for 'hello', and said, 'Please take those gloves off. I know it's peculiar but it freaks me out. Men in gloves look so sinister.' I felt a rush of affection for this girl who always surprised me. Besides, she was right about men dressed in gloves.

We stayed in her parents' attic at Phillimore Terrace. I avoided the pre-festival tension by taking Flora out to the streets, so vibrant with colour and Christmas. It seemed such a long way from my wild Irish rock, and my Scottish moorland before it. I remembered that here, a few years before, I'd chosen *Crime and Punishment* as my last book, and wondered what I'd done to sentence myself to such exile.

On Sunday mornings the pubs opened at twelve. As I made my escape, Harriet's mother called out to me at the door, 'Do try to be back around one-ish. I'm thinking of throwing a hunk of meat in the oven.' This was an English invitation to Sunday lunch, combined with an apology for actually planning an event so self-indulgent as eating.

Just before Christmas we drove down to Old Turks, the family's country house on Romney Marsh. Oliver got the Christmas fire going with the trunk of an apple tree, cut from the orchard. It protruded out of the fireplace, a metre over the carpet, to be kicked in day by day as it smouldered.

After New Year we returned to Kensington and telephoned Jenny. She'd been searching the papers and agents for a new place for her and Harriet near Comrie. She said that it was impossible; there was nothing to rent. I promised Harriet that I wouldn't return to Ireland until I'd found them somewhere to live. 'Ring Jenny and tell her that we're driving to Scotland tonight.' Harriet liked me to take charge of the situation. It was what our relationship had been about from the start. She also knew that I would succeed. She'd heard me say, too often, that it's only self-doubt that puts 'im' in front of the possible.

While we were talking it had started to snow. It was reported that roads to the north were closing. Harriet's parents said that we'd be crazy to go. Then I remembered that there'd once been an overnight car-train from Olympia to Perth. I rang and they said that it still existed but was filling up fast because of the snow. We threw some things in the van, raced to the station, and were the last car allowed on the wagons.

After a long, cold night we arrived at Perth. Smart cars were purring off into the snow. Our rusty Ford van wouldn't start. Behind us, a Rolls Royce was becoming impatient. It was a Sunday morning and there was no help, so I pushed the van from the train.

Next morning, it was time to outwit the system. Harriet dropped me around the corner from the smartest agents in town.

It was vital that they shouldn't see me getting out of a van. They were the same firm who'd told Jenny that they had nothing available. Although Harriet and Jenny would probably be the best tenants that they'd ever get, two hip-looking, unmarried mothers were not at all the sort to encourage, in the tweedy claustrophobia of Perthshire.

I was quite prepared to play their insidious game if it got the girls somewhere to live. So, I burst into the office, shook hands with the agent and said, 'Now, I don't know if you can help me, but you look like the sort of a chap that I can confide in ...' I had Mister Cartwright eating out of my hand as I told him the truth, which I polished and presented with certain omissions. Like the marriage status of his two future tenants, and the exact nature of the important business that had called their husbands abroad. After discussing the relative suitability of various properties that miraculously appeared on his books, he gave me the keys to the stable cottage on the Aberuchill Estate.

We took a few days to organise the house and Jenny joined us with Daisy. We kept putting off my return to Ireland until I could avoid it no longer. When I left, my little girl was playing with her friend in the snow. I'd no idea when I'd see her again, but it was no time to insult her morning with a grown-up 'goodbye'. So I said 'see you' and walked away, as though I was going to buy a packet of biscuits.

Harriet and I wandered in silence across a field to the road. With arms around each other we followed the tracks of a hare. It was leading us through a winter, towards a life that we couldn't foresee. I was wishing that this walk through the snow could go on forever, when Harriet said, 'I wish it was twenty-five miles to the station.' We tightened our grip and wondered what next. It was crazy to wish things would last. The snow, a short walk in the stillness, a meeting, a life. Everything as transient as the footprints that mark out our journey towards the radiant result that we hide from ourselves in each moment.

In Cork it had been raining all day and I sat, soaking wet, on the Allihies bus. Dismounting at the cross of Garranes, I walked home with the help of a near-full moon. The cattle were lying by the gate, where my neighbour had been giving them hay.

I opened the door of the house and stepped into inches of water. It was still pouring in from a hole in the wall. I found out later that rats had gnawed through the pipe. Our bright Indian rug was lying submerged, while water lapped the pedals of Harriet's piano. I disconnected the pipe outside, and slopped around lighting a fire. Most of the plants in our garden had been blown over, or out of the ground. The cattle had eaten the rest. I opened a tin of beans and stood it on the range to warm. I brushed most of the muddy water out into the night and ate the baked beans still cold, from the tin. I went upstairs and crawled into a moist bed, not quite sure that I was glad to be home.

I sat bolt upright, woken from a deep sleep by the sound of somebody playing the piano. I got up and went downstairs and there it was once again. Slowly, I pushed open the door. Brilliant moonlight streamed through the windows. There was nobody there, but the shades of a million dead moments.

'It's just too tough here,' I said. Then the piano played again, just a few random notes. I heard a scuttling and realised that the rats had found an ideal place for their nest. 'Welcome back to paradise,' I laughed to myself, to the rats and the moon.

I was thirty-five years old. Buddha was thirty-five when he realised his enlightenment. I wanted to speed up my quest, to at least show some sort of progress; something more than just sitting in my shrine room trying not to think. I'd found this perfect location beyond the noise of the world and now I needed to enter its stillness. I needed to re-ignite the awareness that I'd known, in those mountain days of my youth.

It was time to complete that first retreat hut. If Harriet didn't return, it would also be the last. I'd live in it and try to follow the way of meditation. If she did return, I'd continue the path of action; continue to build a retreat place for the inspiration of others. That made me feel strong again. Either way was a winner. Let Harriet and the wheels of our karma decide.

I cleaned up the house and went to work on the hut. It was along a track, above the bluebell hollow and wrapped all around by the ocean.

18

Back to Abnormal

I n the spring, Harriet wrote to say that she'd stay in Scotland, at least for the summer. Then, one morning, I was sawing timber for the roof of the hut. Any gloom that lurked in the shadows of winter had been dispelled by the advent of April. I looked up from my work to watch a sea mist unwrap and offer Ireland to the incoming light. Seagulls soared on currents of silence while wild flowers stitched possibilities into the raiment of day. Beara flirted with herself in her mirror of ocean and showed off to the Mizen and me.

Suddenly, the sound of a motor ploughed a furrow into the stillness. I walked to the end of the house and there was Harriet, bubbling with apologies for her sudden return.

So much for my plan to retreat. That would now have to wait. The die had been cast and I could only celebrate the return of Harriet and Flora. Now my world would be turned upside down again, while she threw open windows that I'd failed to notice were there.

At my Eskdalemuir house, Ram Dass had taught that every instant is a new life. Harriet proved this by dying at the end of each urgent expression, to be reborn into a present that was uninhibited by any obvious connection to what had just happened. Stability quivered and gave up the ghost, in the knowledge that her only constant was continuous flux. Change was the one thing that you could rely on. She was sometimes heavy, sometimes as light as a feather. She was playful, tearful, tyrannical and submissive, all in the same string of out-of-breath moments. She would paw at the ground of your being, until you answered the unanswerable question with words that she put in your mouth.

Apart from a couple of huddles of scrub oak, carved head-high by the wind, there was just one struggling tree on the land. Only fuchsia and hazel seemed to thrive in pockets of shelter. I'd tried to grow all kinds, but even pine trees were blown from the ground. I'd been sure that they'd grow because I'd found massive pine stumps in the bog, high up the mountain. Next spring I'd try again, using the furze for its shelter.

Harriet took Flora to her parents in July and I started, again, the retreat hut. It was inspiring work, that summer, making the little house above the sparkling water. By late August I'd nearly finished. Its hidden location meant that I'd avoided most of the tourists. Only the most determined got through, drawn by the sound of my hammer.

As the work was completed, Bernadine Freud came to stay with her daughters, Bella and Esther. I hitched to Allihies with Bella, who was beautiful, fifteen, and alight with youthful alertness. I talked about Rimbaud and Rilke and the absorption of splendour when you roll back assumption and let rise the light. About the secret world that so easily slips past you unnoticed. The glimpses that come to everyone and last for no more than a wink. If you catch them, in the season of the opening of days, they'll last you forever. If you miss them, time and convention will order your thinking and lamely force you to grow up.

In the pub, the animation in her eyes was probably reflected in mine as I talked of the magic. I was woken again by this sparkling girl who enticed from me the inspiration that I'd mortgaged through striving. The landlord came over, collecting the glasses, and pointedly asked if Harriet was well. I laughed at the crooked presumption of a world that failed to recognise the innocent flight of the spirit.

Then, when the summer was gone, we settled into the routine of exhilarating uncertainty that was everyday life with Harriet. Going to town, she'd forget some vital ingredient like Marmite, which we'd then be without for a week. I was told that my suggestion of a shopping list just proved how bourgeois I was. I thought that she might accept some old-fashioned sort of solution; something to match the cast-iron coffee-grinder on the wall; the wooden butter-churn and the strings of overhead onions.

I bought a box of chalks, found an old roof-slate and framed it with pine. I hung it by the range, saying that she might chalk up items as they came to her mind. Harriet admired my ingenuity, dismissed the concept with a toss of her head, and handed the slate to Flora. 'Nice try, Peter,' I said to myself, 'and anyway, who gives a damn about Marmite. Or salt. Or tea bags. Or butter.'

'Let's get me pregnant,' said Harriet, one day in early '79. I checked the calendar. If conception was delayed for six weeks, we'd get a Sagittarian, like Harriet and me. With Flora a Leo, we'd have a house full of fire signs, whatever that meant. Flying the flag of infinite possibility, I was neither convinced nor dismissive of astrology. In a world where nothing is ultimately real, everything is potentially valid. Harriet asked why should forces from space not influence the tides of the mind, when the moon lifts the tides of the oceans? We got her pregnant and the baby was due in December.

Next, we ordered a telephone and Allihies 32 was its number. For five years we'd walked miles to make calls. Now there was a large battery under our stairs and, just like in old movies, a black box with a handle to wind. So we'd wind and wait for Eily at Allihies post office shop to finish serving a customer. On asking her for a number, she might tell us that they'd gone to Cork for the day. It was an intimate and well-connected world into which we'd wired and wound ourselves up. I'd need to speak to the sawmills at Lauragh, a few miles across the peninsula. I'd wind my handle to get Allihies to the west. They'd connect me to Bantry, back past us to the east. Bantry would telephone across to Kenmare who'd, in turn, ring the Lauragh exchange, who'd connect me to the number. With the words going through plugs in so many switchboards, you could hear almost nothing by the time you eventually got there. However, you felt obliged to converse with the static because everyone had been to such trouble. The best thing about the Irish telephone system was that it was turned off for the night at nine o'clock, to allow the operator to sleep and the world to calm down.

One evening, at dusk, Harriet burst into the farmhouse and poured out her story. She'd been driving home, having drunk two glasses of porter. At Dunboy, the police were manning a roadblock. They asked her to return to the station and walk a white line. Harriet did that with ease and then, to really prove herself sober, she stood on her head.

It was impossible to be exasperated with this exasperating girl. If you tried anger she'd disarm you with total submission. If you tried sarcasm, she'd smile sweetly and say, 'Sarcasm killed the cat.'

They took her licence away for six months. Being pregnant, it was awkward enough without transport, but at least she'd get it back just in time to drive to Cork for the birth. So from then on, we hitched to town, which was easy. Most of the time there was no need even to stick out your thumb. In those days, people just stopped and asked if you needed a ride.

On my birthday, 24 November, we drove to Bantry and got married. The baby was due on 7 December, which was Harriet's birthday. In Cork we found a guest house with an owner who was very maternal, treated us like strays, and kept bringing us food. She also kept telling us how brave we were to be wandering around sounding English, in spite of the tension and the IRA bombing campaign. I told her that we were both eligible to play for the Irish team, but that didn't work. We told ourselves that the anguish of the times underlined the relevance of Garranes as a refuge for all. A place where people could remind themselves that all life is sacred, and we shouldn't be deceived by the outer shell which conceals our innate perfection.

On 12 December Harriet gave birth to a nine and a half pound redheaded boy who, I swear, was born smiling. After three days we flew to England for Christmas, where Harriet's mother was delighted with her first grandson who we called Tom.

'But I cannot imagine why on earth you bothered to marry,' she said.

'We did it for you,' I teased her, 'so that you can start talking again, to your gin-swilling bags of East Sussex.'

Back in Ireland, winter storms skidded across the Atlantic, rattled our door and insisted that I should establish some shelter. I'd poked cuttings of fuchsia into the bank beside the incoming track. It was a wild spot with views west to Dursey Island and the open Atlantic. I dreamt of transforming it into a leafy old Irish boreen. Harriet said that this was the perfect example of my 'optimism stupide'. Each spring I'd planted the slips. Each winter the winds had swivelled them around and ripped off their roots.

My sheep fence ran on top of this bank. After six years of failure, I planted a new row of three hundred cuttings. This time I tied each stick, top and bottom, to the fence with a blue baler twine bow. I could hear neighbours taking the piss. 'Jesus, what's next? First it's bells on the cows, now it's bows on the bushes.' But they said nothing, perhaps knowing that I gave not a damn what anyone thought so long as it worked.

With fifty acres of coast to be fenced, we needed a grant, and for a grant we needed a farm plan. With a government advisor it was decided to establish a three-quarter bred Charolais herd. By mid-May I was feeding milk replacer to fourteen half-bred Charolais calves from Skibbereen mart.

Next I needed a house for the bull. An agricultural building would be exempt from planning permission. I decided to build it north–south, as a windbreak, across the end of the meadow. It would fit into a hollow, slung between two ridges of rock, where the wind whipped through and laid waste to our vegetable garden. On top of the bull house, I'd build a first floor whose south wall of glass would have views over Bantry Bay.

Of course, it would start life as a bull house. That never excluded the possibility that, at some future date, it might evolve. With its 'million-dollar views', it could even turn into a retreat house. I decided to build it to a very high specification, looking old and strong, with walls that were two feet thick.

At that time, they were demolishing many fine buildings in Cork. I bought a lorry load of antique wood from a brewery. An entire floor of pitch pine, four inches thick, a massive twenty-five foot beam and various other large chunks of timber. We dragged the beam from the road with a tractor, lying astride it as it swung out over the bog on the hairpins. Then we lifted it with levers and blocks to the ceiling. By autumn we'd completed the slate roof of a pedigree house for a pedigree bull. The government inspector said it was the only cowshed he'd seen with a smart teak front door and double-glazed windows. Within a week it was in the press. 'Enterprising immigrants build the most luxurious bull house in Europe ... but is it really a bull house?'

It wasn't long before the planning department arrived. An irate fellow argued about its agricultural credentials.

'And what's worse is that this building is sky-lining,' the young official objected.

'Oh, perfect,' I replied, 'I've been searching for a name. You've just got it. Brilliant. We'll call it the Skyliner.' So, 'The Skyliner' it became, and has remained ever since. And luckily, the young man had the strength of character to laugh. He told me that I should plant some trees to hide it, and apply to the council for 'retention'. He became quite friendly when I showed him the lengths to which we had gone. He liked the thick walls, the rounded corners, the old beams and the chunky slabs of the ledges and lintels.

I wanted to explain that my idea of planning was to somehow encourage the natural evolution that cannot be planned. Designed by necessity slowly, it grows from the landscape in rhythmic chaos; a haphazard huddle of dreams that gave birth to Dingle and Pylos. The role of the planner should be to ban right angles, straight lines and levels. To stimulate the disorganised magic that's not measured with rules or rulers, but with footsteps and teardrops and time. Then they'll go to sleep in the suburbs but will dream of Eyeries and Oia.

I told him none of these things and we parted as friends. Meanwhile, the irony of the situation was that, although no one believed it, my bull house was really a bull house. Or at least it would be until the first retreatant arrived.

At the foot of the cliffs there's a hidden world. It's dangerous to get to and thereby protected from humans. Being south-facing and sheltered, it's a few degrees warmer than everywhere else. I loved to climb down to this realm of the sea, entranced by its silence, reborn by the roar of the surf.

There are sea flowers and samphire and the salt scent of the rolling-in ocean. It washes your consciousness and carries you back to before you thought you began. Life and its tides flow in and out of the rock pools, in a dance that has lasted for ever. Alone on the shore you can learn from the sea, that there's no beginning or ending. The 'you' that you know is a progress of moments in space. Constantly changing, a stroke of the brush of awareness that has painted this life from its palette of galaxy dust.

One day, when it was time to go, I decided to take a new route up the cliff. There seemed to be a possible way that I'd not noticed before. It was just about vertical but there were handholds and foot holes, so I'd give it a try.

I got almost to the top quite quickly. My toes were on outcrops of rock about half the size of my feet. My fingers were in fissures above me. What looked like the clifftop was a foot above that.

Far below were the jagged black rocks of a ravine into which the ocean was boiling. I couldn't move. There was no possibility of going down, other than falling to a certain death. The top of the cliff was just out of reach.

Thoughts came to me about potholing at school, when I was wedged in a dark funnel, and going to die. This time, no one knew where I was, and within a couple of hours I would tire and fall. How we take this thread of current existence for granted. Why don't we realise how precious it is until we're woken by the cries of the flesh-tearing ravens?

I'd been there for a long time and I was beginning to weaken. On top of the cliff was a rock jutting out. If I let go with my hands, bent my knees and jumped, I might grab it and scramble up, if this was really the top. The trouble was that I couldn't touch it until I jumped. I'd no idea whether it was part of the cliff or just a loose stone that would come away in my hand. I'd have only one go; my life was in the hands of that leap for the top.

I'd become totally calm. I looked down at the rocks below and knew that it'd be quick. The light was beginning to fade, but it was too hard to say, 'now'. I prayed to the Buddhas of the Four Times, and made all kinds of promises about my future behaviour. Then I emptied the dustbin of thoughts and I jumped.

My hand reached the rock and it held. I clambered up and lay in the sweetest smelling grass on any clifftop, in all of the impossible planets of heaven. I stood up and moved a few paces in from the edge and lay down again. 'You have a purpose to fulfil in this place,' I said to myself and the tut-tutting shades of my evening mind. 'Maybe it won't be achieved by a half-blind man climbing up and down cliffs in a selfish pursuit of outer perfection.'

19

Gelignite

The plan was to press on with the retreat centre by building cottages and letting them temporarily to tourists. First we'd need to blast a road with gelignite and use the rock to build a new causeway over the bog. Due to the troubles, it was hard to get explosives. The exact amount had to be escorted from the city by police, who'd stay to see it all used.

We spent two weeks with neighbour Vince, drilling deep holes into the rocks at the hairpin bends. When the day came, the gelignite arrived late, with two uniformed policemen. Now it was a race against the light as well as the weather, which was closing in fast. The slightest rain would result in the job being abandoned. It might cause a short in the network of cables and we'd all be blown into orbit.

Beneath a leaden sky, we used broom handles to ram gelignite into the dozens of boreholes. Vince inserted the detonators and connected wires. I was conscious of our lack of expertise. Instruction for everything that we were doing had come by word of mouth.

Half of the job was ready when the drizzle started. The police said that it was far too dangerous to continue. Vince, who'd never quit on anything, threw broomsticks at the law, and told them to get stuffing. The light was fading as he finished the connections.

Harriet took Tom to the cross of Garranes, while Flora and

I went to the Skyliner basement to shelter. Vince pressed the plunger at the bridge. There was a spectacular flash, a shower of rocks and a shock wave that broke a window in the room above us. Then we had to connect the cables for the next explosion. It was dark by the time that we'd finished.

The digger came and, within a week, we could finally drive to the house. Now we were half as remote, which was good, and twice as close to the world, which surely was not. To make the track look ancient again, I built sod and stone banks, and planted some pines.

For the next stage I'd need permission. It surely should be granted because the houses would be visible to no one but the dolphins that played in the bay. And even the dolphins would have trouble trying to find them. Built against the mountain with thick walls faced with rocks and sods, they'd have turf roofs to blend into the background.

I applied and permission was refused. The designs were too radical for bureaucrats of the eighties. All the innovation of the sixties had curdled to a crust of dull conformity. Inspiration threatened a past that was revered. I took a deep breath and told myself that this was *my* dream, and it couldn't be infiltrated by others who were asleep in a different bed.

Padraig Murphy, the son of Peter who'd sold us the farm, was an engineer in Bandon. Like all the Murphy family of Garranes, he'd been amazingly supportive. He said that you could achieve nothing in Ireland without having someone in power to lobby for you. So I met a local county councillor in Herbie's Bar in Allihies village, to explain how my project would benefit the community. On 15 April, a phone call advised me that, should I apply for permission to build three traditional Irish cottages, permission would be forthcoming. I sent a bottle of Veuve Clicquot to Allihies.

Things were beginning to speed up. There was less time to sit and calm the mind. Less time to relax and let go of the misleading trip of daily perception, or wonder what I was doing on this peculiar planet. As moments of stillness grew rarer, they intensified through being unsought. When they did come, I threw down the shovel and sat on a rock and let myself swim in the vastness. Forgetting everything then, I was part of the great sanity that can't be described. I could catch the faint roar that starts in the stars, like the gasp of a child who's not yet resigned to the splendour.

Each time that I entered the Skyliner I was shocked by the view. It seemed such a waste not to make the upstairs available, so I started to finish and furnish it. It was already different, and I wanted to make it the more so. I painted Celtic motifs on the beams, and a mandala on the internal, open gable of the roof. It tired my eyes to try painting again, but I managed. In June we took our first booking from an ex-pat Irish nurse called Kath O'Hara. This, I hoped, was the start that would eventually lead to a spiritual oasis for those who needed a break from life as a competitive consumer.

In April I went to Cork to buy some coloured inks. A young girl knelt to get them from a shelf. As she stood up, her face passed close to mine and she gave a radiant smile. I think that this was the first time that I saw the spontaneous smile of a stranger. It flooded through me like a collision between immeasurable joy and the suffering of the aeons.

People ask me what I miss from not seeing the world as they do. I ask them if they miss not seeing as much as a peregrine falcon. Sometimes they ask what it's like never to see the face of another. I tell them that, if there's no face, there's no mask with which to be fooled by, or flattered. Then I think of the smile of that unknown girl one morning in springtime. I think of how happy people must be, constantly swapping smiles in random encounters. My God, you'd die if someone gave you a wink. Then, I saw that all of this smiling has made little difference. We get used to what is, take it for granted, and the magic is lost.

If we could allow ourselves to open, be continuously caught unawares by each moment, our sudden clarity would shatter the glass between us and our shining potential. Like a flash from the lamp of a timeless lighthouse, the smile of that girl still fills me with life, across all of the years in between us.

In the autumn we moved into the Skyliner. It was an attempt to ditch the dark past for the bright lights of what was to come. On Christmas Day, with the family in England, I sat in the sun with a gin and tonic. Below me, the grass sloped to a sparkling sea. I thought, 'The only thing that's missing is trees.' The neighbours, and even the foresters, had told us that they'd never survive here. On my second gin and tonic I recalled the tree-clad mountains that plunge into the sea at Amalfi. On my third I promised to cover the land in woods, except to the south where the view was. I never had the fourth drink. It was Christmas Day. No Christmas tree. No snowflakes. In four days I'd not seen a soul but, hey, the sun was warm, with no breath of wind, and there was a spade in the cowshed. What better time to start turning Garranes back to woodland? In May, much of the land is covered with bluebells, which indicates the ancient coverage of trees. Even the name, Garranes, is translated as 'place of the trees'.

That spring, Harriet and I had gathered the cones from a Kilcrohane pine. We'd stuck them behind the range to open and give up their seeds. Flora had helped me to plant those seeds, and now we had pots full of saplings. So, on a warm Christmas Day in 1981, alone on my rock, I found myself singing gin-inspired, out-of-tune carols to myself and the sun. Planting Monterey pines on Skyliner Hill, I felt as content as the lizards who came from the darkness to bask on the slopes of December. It was the start of a project that was to take decades, to reclaim the windswept mountain for the wildlife and its woodland.

After Christmas, I had to decide about a road to the planned retreat houses. Harriet left decisions to me. Plans, she said, were dangerous. They tempted providence by assuming that you'd be around to fulfil them. So, I sat in the Skyliner window gazing at the impossible drop. How would we ever get materials to the terraces below? All I could see was an inland cliff, steep angled fields and a three-hundred-foot plunge to the water. I talked to Oliver who'd helped make the dynamite road to the farmhouse. He had a reputation for preferring the dangerous jobs. He said that it could be done, but we'd have to find some wild Kerry men with lorries and nerves of tranquilised steel.

The fill would be tipped from a cliff, onto a steep sloping field, against the rise of the mountain. Oliver offered us the hill that was next to his house, on the coast road to Garnish. With his digger, he'd bucket it into three lorries, which would haul it the few miles to us.

After the first twenty loads it started to rain. One of the three drivers quit, saying that it was too dangerous. The lorries were turning on a thumbnail and sliding, in reverse, downhill to the edge. One false move and they'd be gone, somersaulting into the ocean.

By the second day, we'd dumped ninety loads. Now they could drive across the new fill, onto the terrace, and turn below. The wind had risen to storm force with a driving rain. I watched them spinning and snaking along the edge of that vertical drop. Tipping their stuff as they snarled up the hill, they left the lorry backs raised, to put weight on the axles. This made them unstable, as they rocked with the strength of the storm.

There was something primeval about working out there, all mixed up, muddy and drenched with the elements' fury. The roar of the earth tipping out of the trucks; the air in your teeth; the fire of the engines, and the water lashing into your eyes. You were completely involved with the swirling dance of the force that had made us. You felt part of the way that the planet was formed from the stars, but the thrill was tinged with a sadness. In trying to help, you were helping to violate one of the last sacred places. Ploughing the sublime with the arrogance of humans, who swagger and swarm through perfection, riding their crazy machines.

Conscious of living far out on the edge of a place that

belonged to the seabirds, we felt that the integrity of our intent had been tested again. Somehow we seemed to get through. It took one hundred and forty-five loads, or nearly three thousand tons, to do what they said was not do-able. As the last lorry left, the storm suddenly died, and the maelstrom settled back into order. We *can* live in harmony with all that exists, but first we must open our minds. I prayed that this place might inspire all who arrive here to respect their brief resting place on this planet called Earth. As an offering, to appease the spirits of my own unease, I planted five hundred trees.

At the back of the mountain, the dry-stone key wall that held up the causeway had been intended for no more than a horse and a cart. Now it was bulging from all of the traffic, and slipping into the valley below. I spent most of that summer building it back.

Having let the Skyliner, we moved back to the farmhouse. It was the start of a series of moves that would make us itinerants on our own land. Each time that a building was roofed, we'd move into the half-finished shell and rent out the place we'd vacated.

Against the barn we'd built a studio that we'd let for the summer, although it was still only half finished. We started working late into the nights. Finally, one Friday evening in early July, I sat on the floor in six inches of wood shavings, with the bathroom to tile. The tenants were already on the night ferry and would arrive in the morning. So I stayed up all night and got the work done. I'd dug up ferns and put them in pots to camouflage gaps in the fabric. I had oriental rugs, bedspreads, and Tibetan teapots to divert the eye from slight imperfections. I just hoped that the tenants would be cool, or too tired to care. When they arrived, they were both. They were young and thrilled with the place, and didn't give a damn that the door wouldn't lock, or that they could see through into the barn.

I spent the next winter scraping soil from the bedrock on which to lay foundations for four retreat houses. Then, in the spring, I asked Jimmy from Allihies to come and start laying the blocks.

He was a quiet and genuine young man who politely accepted my crazy ideas and got the job done without fuss. Although his previous experience had been limited to a cowshed or two, he knew a lot more than I did. He was great company as we worked on the wind-blasted edge of the bay.

Jimmy often kept his radio playing and I heard my first new music for a decade. I learnt that, through the isolation of my Scottish and Irish retreats, I'd entirely missed the reaction to the sixties by an era of something called 'Punk'.

While Jimmy laid blocks, I built a crush for the cattle. I was fed up with chasing them around the yard in order to dose them. Catching each one by her nostrils. Pushing a bottle of worm-dose between her clenched teeth. Holding her head up high until she had swallowed. And all of the time they were bucking and rearing and stampeding in circles together. If you let go before she'd swallowed, she'd spray the creamy chemicals into your face. There were only fifteen, but that was enough, because you had to remember which ones you'd done so that no one got more than one dose.

In November I became forty. Already blessed with good health, this Atlantic existence had blasted well-being into my airways. I felt as alive as I'd been at twenty, but was still uneasy about tethering my spirit to the pursuit of an external goal. So I wrote to the Buddhist Society in Eccleston Square. They sent me tapes of various teachers. I was thrilled again with the profundity that's missing from life on the surface. I started to sit for an hour in the evenings as well as the mornings. I felt that a phase in my life was coming slowly towards a beginning.

We had few tools and no cement mixer, but a shovel and a bucket and trowel. In spite of the lack of equipment, the houses were built to high standards. They all had the same double-thick walls, substantial timbers and open pine ceilings. Rather than chemical stains, I used a peat fire, alight in an old cast-iron pot, to fill the buildings with smoke. After some weeks, the white pine was tinted to antique gold.

On Easter morning, Flora, Tom and the children of friends set off on the annual Easter egg hunt. I'd laid a trail with paper and clues, via the barn to the meadow and down the celandine slopes. The eggs were concealed on a mossy bank, surrounded by ferns, while the ocean sparkled below with the incoming light of the spring.

Harriet's father had taken to coming for Easter. 'Better that he's hunting Easter eggs in Ireland than wild duck in Sussex,' she said.

'Grandpa, why d'you hate ducks?' Tom had asked him, when he was four.

'I think I actually rather like ducks,' his grandfather replied.

'Then why d'you shoot them?' Tom said.

On one of these visits, Harriet's father provided me with a perfect display of the stiff upper lip of the Brits. We'd gone into Bewley's for coffee. He picked up two packets of sugar, which we stirred into our drinks. Oliver drank while I waited for mine to cool down. With my first sip, I nearly choked. It had been ground black pepper in those packets of sugar. Oliver had already drunk half of his. He apologised for being so careless. I said that I'd take the drinks back and get them replaced. 'No, no, Peter really, actually I think it's rather delicious.' As I realised that he was going to finish his toxic concoction, I thought, 'What the hell,' and I did the same.

With the next cottage almost complete, we let it from the beginning of June. I was a bit behind schedule again. The guests turned up while I was still tiling the floor. Harriet kept them talking on the terrace for two hours, with stories and continuous tea. She said that she'd got her husband to do his share of the cleaning at last, and he was a little bit slow. I laid the last few tiles, grouted them, and welcomed the visitors onto the wet kitchen floor.

At the same time, cottage three was finished except for the interior. We had to move in for the summer because we needed the cash from letting the others. The walls were un-plastered and there was no kitchen, bathroom or electrics. The floor had yet to be laid, so there were bare joists above a six-foot drop to the rock. I rested a handful of planks on the joists, and on these I balanced a table and our old iron bedstead. Most of the floor was still missing. The children became quite adept at walking the joists as they balanced their way to a mealtime. They delighted in 'accidentally' dropping teddy bears, spoons, and bits of Monopoly into the abyss, and then descending a ladder into the darkness to get them. With the adaptability of our species, we quickly got used to living on slats.

Harriet cooked on a large yellow gas bottle with a single ring attached to the top. Things were good, although we were a bit tired of having cement in our hair, sand in the bed and pulling on concreted socks. We accepted it all as the price that you pay for having a crazy goal. For the children it was just life, made easy by a beautiful summer, through which they ran barefoot and free as the breeze. And nobody fell through the floor.

We'd been so long without rain that the wells had run dry. Neighbours were coming to the Garranes River to fill dustbins with water, and then the river dried up. By July, the supply that I'd piped from the mountain was failing, and we had four houses of tourists. I bought two rolls of pipe and hauled them a thousand feet further up, to where the water still flowed.

With enough retreat rooms for now, we needed a Centre House. I started to draw up plans with a large felt pen on rolls of ceiling paper nailed to a door. The ideal site was where the original cow house stood. I'd already decided to get out of farming and sell the cows when I could find them a decent home. Their shed and hay barn were on a terrace where the land dropped most steeply into the bay. We'd have to knock them down to construct the large main room with two sides of glass. Building down the slope, it would take a lot of block work even to get up to ground level. This would result in a view with no foreground, only the ocean and its seabirds so far below that you would think you were flying.

I sat on a rock and gazed at the vast expanse of luminous space. In such a light, the ocean merges with sky and the radiance begins at your feet. I addressed myself and imaginary minds of the morning.

'All right, so your reasoning mind asks for proof that it's all a reflection, but perhaps we've got further to go before our science can prove it. Or maybe that which transcends the grasping of ordinary mind can never be proven. We'll see. Meanwhile, we might investigate the proposition and enjoy its profound implications. Like, when we begin to see the environment, and everyone in it, as the display of this mind, there's no longer an 'other' to blame; no scapegoats to resent or attack. Instead, we're stopped in our tracks by the vast perspective of items at play in the mirror. When we see that every event is an aspect of some remote or immediate part of our nature, we cease to react. It puts us in total command of ourselves and our future, and hands us the key to our freedom. If I create my version of you and you do likewise with me, we're tangled together with increasing affection for all of us beings adrift in the infinite dance.'

I put down my hammer and picked up a feather, and thought. 'Words are like hammers and feathers are silence, and it's on silence that we can fly.' But my thoughts refused to let go. I continued to talk, secure in the knowledge that I had a long way to grow before I could realise what I was saying.

'But if your mind created all this, then you must be God,' said a seagull.

'Well that's right, God, or a Buddha. The only big deal about being God is if you are the only god. Actually, we're all God in our essence, and failed gods in this outer existence. Failed for sure, because no worthwhile god would perpetrate something like *this*. We go cruising around, creating ourselves, and everything else with our ordinary mind-stream. Each spinning a world into flimsy solidity, convinced by our own vast production of pleasure and pain. Forgetting our inbuilt option to wake up and see through the artwork.

'Then, one day, we're startled back to awareness by this recognition that it's all a reflection. That glimpse makes us laugh at the utter simplicity of this dance of timeless perfection. And that glimpse lets us shed the concept of needing to prove it. It would be like trying to prove music.'

20

Surviving Public Opinion

I had to cut away this shelf of rock with a sledgehammer and wedges, but it was easier to sit and let thoughts trickle like sand through my fingers. I loved this place that I found myself in; the blue planes of emptiness with the coastline scribbled across them, etched by storms of the ages. It was the realisation of a dream of childhood and a doorway to the path that leads beyond wanting. And yet, in spite of that, it was sometimes still not sufficient. I missed the fragrant evenings of summers long gone. I tried, each year, to grow plants that had scent. When my favourite wallflowers failed, I tried sweet peas, nicotiana and night-scented stocks.

When I'd grown enough shelter to keep them in the ground, still they flowered with no fragrance. I complained to the seedsmen that, these days, they bred flowers for colour, size, and the number of florets per stem, with no regard for their scent. Then I remembered that we form our worlds from bubbles of thought, and float around inside them with eyes closed. Out in the stream of interactivity, these bubbles are burst by arrows of incoming thinking. But here, in seclusion from the world, they just grow bigger and more opaque. You have to learn this, and burst your own bubbles for fun. It's part of the sport of solitary evolution.

It took me a long time to burst my bubble of the missing scent with a sharp little realisation. Wanting someone to blame, I'd clung on to my theory, but it was nothing to do with the breeders of plants. It was simply the continuous movement of air that takes place on a clifftop, and blows the fragrance away before it gets to your nose.

I laughed at myself, remembering. People say that if one sense is diminished, another increases. I'd tell them that, for me, it was a vaguely enhanced sense of smell. Then I go live on a mountain. 'If you want scent,' I told myself, 'go back to the motionless air of the valleys of people. If you want clarity, stay on your rock where senses are stripped and, instead of flowers, awareness grows, unseduced by sensual diversion.'

So I reasoned with myself, in order to stop mourning the lost fragrance of wallflowers in May. And sometimes it worked and sometimes it failed. Then I teased myself that I wanted it all, though my goal was to learn to want nothing.

In late '83 we began Centre House. I'd drawn it with two storeys, in cruciform shape, with a three-storey tower and a six-foot circular window for a shrine room in the roof. There was a restaurant and library, a reception-office-shop, and a four-bedroom apartment for us.

At this time, Tom befriended a stray cat, who he called John. John was emaciated and sick and the vet said that he'd best be put down. There were those, at that time, who claimed that all animals apart from us have no feelings. John, who was an extraordinary teacher, taught us that beings trapped in a non-human body still feel compassion. Tom sat on the sofa, crying. John ran in from the kitchen, jumped on Tom's lap, put one paw on each shoulder and nuzzled his neck until he cheered up. He did this each time that Tom cried, over many months, until our respect for everything that lives, was completed.

There was a boggy hollow halfway along my attempt at a West Cork boreen. I dug it out to make a lily pond. Maybe they were right to laugh. Why would you think that water lilies would survive on the side of a mountain?

Harriet gazed from our eyrie and said that the world was a bog pond. Everyone submerged, not conscious of even the surface. Someone would stir and struggle upwards with an idea or a dream. Immediately a thousand arms from the black bog of convention would enwrap them and suck them back down. To get anything done, you had to be crazy, protected by blinkers, or propelled by some force that you couldn't explain.

By the summer of '84, there were lush hedgerows where my gale-torn twigs had been lashed to the fence with blue baler twine. There were bees sucking nectar from star-drops of fuchsia on either side of the lane. Spires of foxgloves stood proud in the deep grass verge, and there was stillness where a wind had been, and 'barren' had become 'boreen'.

Halfway along this was a lily pond. The old bog hole had transformed itself with water mint and flags of wild iris. Its surface was of lily pads, with cup-shaped flowers rejoicing in stationary grace. They say that from confusion arises perfection, and the bog-pit is there to nourish its bloom. It was how the world had evolved, and how each of us actually is. I'd done nothing more than shuffle a few transient phenomena, and then stood back to allow it. Maybe that's all that we have to do.

Meanwhile, two wings of Centre House were complete with roof-tiles and skylights. The flat roof of the tower would take a lorry load of concrete, dumped on the track and hauled to the top in buckets.

We installed the insulation on the tower, cut and wired together reinforcing rods to form a double grid of steel and covered it with plastic, held in place with concrete blocks. But then, in the night, a storm got under the polythene. I was awoken as it threw off several blocks and crashed them into a skylight. The sheet was flying like a kite and snapping at the house. In the dark, I could see nothing as I felt my way along the wind towards the ladder, praying that the flapping shroud wouldn't dump more blocks on my head.

As I climbed to the roof, the sky must have cleared because I could see the flash of the Sheep's Head lighthouse and, far below, the white surf. The wind roared in the flying sheet as I crawled along the apex and up onto the top. I lay on the plastic and hauled it in, stuffing it underneath me. Then, one by one, I rolled off the blocks and let it sail away into the darkness.

I felt my way back to the house. How invigorating they are, those moments that force you to wake. Next day, the storm had abated and the day wore a wicked smile, as if it were saying, 'Who, me?' I told it to behave because the concrete was coming.

Vince, as always, offered his help. He arranged for six neighbours to assist us. This was the most daunting task that I'd attempted so far. Before it or the sun set, we had to haul twenty tons of liquid concrete up onto the tower in buckets. We made a dam of blocks to hold the mix on the sloping road. Pouring from the lorry, it started to slurp downhill, pushing our dam before it. We finally held it with a panic of blocks, before it got too far away.

Two men barrowed concrete to the tower. I and another man shovelled it into buckets, and four men hauled them up. Within an hour there was blood on the ropes so Harriet drove to town to buy eight pairs of gloves. The concrete was hardening fast and it was growing dark as the last bucket went up. To make it waterproof, we vibrated it and finished as the sun sank into the ocean.

I was enjoying the small challenges presented by the building of the Centre. Nonetheless, I was still weary of the endless immersion in material things and isolation from spiritual inspiration. So I contacted Samye Ling and learnt that some Westerners were already fluent in Tibetan, and meaningful translations were appearing. Trungpa had written best-selling books and great teachers were starting to visit the West.

I reminded myself that life itself is the path and I only needed to follow it, calmly. Needed to remember that these vast empty planes of sea and sky are mirrors of clarity in which answers, already inscribed in the mind, will arise if we can let go to allow them.

Ordering recorded lectures by Tai Situpa, I remembered sitting in my Scottish wilderness, gazing at pages that I couldn't read. Now the wisdom of ancient Tibet was available in English, and only the push of one button away from my brain.

With my thinking mind I knew nothing. With my innate awareness I knew everything, but it was hidden from realisation. In spite of my searching I'd merely brushed against the odd possibility; encountered vague intimations of openings, a glimpse here and there in the stillness. Trungpa had brought all of this into focus and then I'd wandered away. Now listening to those teachings was like dancing with rainbows in the spray of a sunlit surf. They reminded me that everything is available, behind a translucent curtain of conceptual droplets that ripples in the breezes of thought.

The most important thing is the question. Once you have the question, the answer is inevitable in time. And the question is simple, and there's only one. How do we access the wisdom that's shining inside, but is obscured by this process of thinking? What's for sure is that you need a certain humility, but humility arises spontaneously when you open to the continuous flow of instruction that comes from all that surrounds us. When you recognise the vastness of the infinite array, in just one sliver of which you're skimming around on the surface. When the heart opens to the suffering of all that struggles for light, and you find that you don't matter so much anymore.

From Tai Situpa, I received further encouragement. While discussing geomancy, he described the perfect site that would be sought for a mountain retreat in Tibet. Built on the edge of a drop facing south, there'd be mountain behind it, closing the north. Open to the east, the road should arrive with the rising sun; with moonrise, star-rise and incoming light. The view should be closed to the west, which signifies death. To the south there must be a plain of space, with a distant cluster of hills, from which a river should come with its waves flowing always towards you. It should pass away under the foot of the mountain, so as never to be seen flowing away.

It seemed as though this might have been written by some Tibetan who'd come to Garranes in the ancient times, so closely did the description fit this place on the cliffs of the west. We had the mountain behind us and the east was open, where the road came all of the way from the world. The west was closed by Skyliner Hill and in the south was the vast plain of the ocean, with the far-off hills of Sheep's Head and the Mizen.

I sat in a window of the new Centre House and trained binoculars on the edge of the cliff. Behind close-up tussocks of grass, far below and beyond, was the continuous surging towards us of waves, from the hills of the headlands. To Tibetans, this represents the ongoing accumulation of the positive that ultimately leads to enlightenment. It was rolling in from stores of the radiant, to fill the Centre with light. On an outer level, it represents a guarantee that the necessary resources will always show up.

How did all of this happen? What really inspired me was not the perfect match of this place to a Tibetan retreat, without anyone having heard of the rules. It was that, long before I saw Garranes, I had it all in my head. How could that be? I was satisfied that it was neither a miracle nor a coincidence. It was also doubtful that it was some pre-ordained plan that was pulling the strings from afar. At first I thought that we all carry these archetypes in our mind-streams and the Tibetans had merely learnt to let them arise, and then had written them down. I still think that applies, but have gone a bit further. Is it not that, when you pursue a powerful ideal with the right motivation, the energy generated will manifest the required phenomena? The realisation of this dream was dependent upon the perfect location, so the perfect location arose. This makes complete sense if you believe that the whole thing is a dream, which you project into life as you go.

And there's nothing surprising about perfection, when perfection is already our nature. We'd find ourselves in the perfect environment all of the time, if we could stop puzzling and allow pure awareness to flow. When that time arrives, you need neither mountains nor oceans, because everywhere is always all right. But until then, like me now, you need landscapes and teachings and all of the props you can manage to muster.

Now Centre House was finished and that was enough building for now. The first stage of establishing the retreat was complete.

When I told people what we were doing, they usually asked the same question. 'Oh yeah? And who's going to play teacher, you?' I'd laugh and tell them that I'd never fall into that trap. It would make it all one more rip-off. What? Build a centre, grow a beard, and set yourself up as its guru? My aspirations for the place were so much higher than that. Besides, there was the simple truth that I was ill-educated, un-read, and completely unqualified to teach anything. I'd merely clutched at the occasional straw, while ignorance swept me along. As I clung on, I saw the immense ocean that I still had to cross. All that I desired was to keep myself in the current, pointing in roughly the right direction, with my only business being to enjoy the adventure.

Another reason for keeping in the background was my attitude to authority. If, in this life, you become so unfortunate as to find yourself in a position of power, you need to keep super-critical of each of your moves. Your actions must be as fine as grains of pollen that drift through Beara on a summer's breeze. In no way was I wise enough for that. I was just about wise enough to see that, as power increases, integrity shuffles away, until finally, you betray yourself, your friends and all your ideals. That's why I shun power. That's why I prayed each day, for years, that I'd never be powerful, until I was realised enough to use the power only to benefit others. Then, one day I awoke and saw that it was too late. We're already all in positions of terrifying power, due to our habit of breathing.

So I told them that, when the time was right, a Tibetan lama would appear. They laughed, of course, which in itself was a great incentive. 'Yeah, right. You think you're actually going to get a Tibetan lama to visit West Cork?' In those days, with few lamas in the West, many people hadn't even heard of Tibet, and Allihies was an unlikely destination at the end of an unlikely road. But the wheels had turned and the time had almost arrived. A letter came to say that Sogyal Rinpoche, a young lama of the Nyingma School, was to teach on 'Death and Dying' at Trinity College in Dublin.

It was unexpected and completely unsurprising. Ten years had passed since we'd moved to Ireland to build its first Buddhist retreat. Though not quite ready to invite a lama, it was time to make a connection, and overcome my few reservations. One of which was the potential invasion of 'helpers' who'd come to watch us work, as they'd done in Scotland. The second and worse threat was the possibility of a sect developing; a closed and inward-looking, pseudo-spiritual clique of groupies, who had proof that only they were correct. When the time came, could I ensure that such cultish in-groups, which are entirely opposed to the philosophy of Buddhism, could *never* take over control?

In spite of this, it was with joy that I attended the seminar at Trinity College. I was amazed to find that this lama was able to transmit the ancient wisdom in near perfect English. That alone represented a major step in the right direction. The talks were inspiring and, in a tea break, I gave Sogyal Rinpoche a brief resume of our work. I left Dublin, content that the first seeds had been sown.

One day, Michael Joe Lynch came to see me. He had inherited the farm next to ours and would sell it to us for seventy thousand pounds. We'd spent all that we had on building the Centre, living simply, keeping the cash for the project. Now we had nothing left. Since the horse and cart, we'd owned mostly half-wrecked, second-hand vans. We wore old clothes, ate basic foods and almost never went out. Apart from catching the bus to Harriet's parents, we'd been a decade without a holiday. We couldn't raise the cash, but we had to purchase the farm. The house was within an ass's roar of the Centre, and its land was part of this other world that lay hidden in the hem of the ocean.

Michael Joe's agent gave us a deadline, after which he'd put the farm on the market. We knew that it'd be sold within days. With no cash, I stalled for time by making a tentative offer. If they left out thirty acres of mountain, would they accept fifty-five thousand for the house and the land on the coast? While waiting to hear from them, out of the blue, a young relative died in an accident and left enough for us to purchase the farm. While Harriet was upset, she consoled herself with the thought that it was good for him that his wealth should be spent on a spiritual project to benefit others.

Most of the windows in Centre House stared at the vastness of sky and ocean. Though always inspiring, in some lights it could seem a bit harsh. To balance this, I'd designed the building with a north-facing glass wall which looked at a close-up, moss-covered bank. I wanted to re-create the soft, green moistness of the Ireland that we'd encountered when we arrived. A reminder of a world that was commercialising itself out of its magic and slowly passing away. I planted the bank so that all you could see from the window was a lush glade of maidenhair ferns and mosses. A trickle of water fell into a pool, where a statue of Buddha was illuminated by butter-lamp light.

We heard that Sogyal Rinpoche was returning to Ireland for St Patrick's weekend, to teach at Kilfinane in Limerick. I'd go and, when I showed him the photos, I was sure he'd come to Garranes. If that didn't work, in a while, a different lama would appear.

I'd kept the cows for as long as I could, but now it was time to stop farming. I needed to put all of my energy into the Centre. I was going to miss Sulky, Shammy and co. Feeding them, dosing them, staying up all night while they calved, I knew each of them like a child, and they were so tame that they followed me around. I saw them as noble beings, trapped for a while in an animal's shell and unable to express what they felt. Just like the rest of us, only more so.

I knew a farmer who was looking for Charolais cows and who'd treat them with the respect they deserved. It was time to plant twenty-five acres of trees, sponsored by the cow sale and aided by a government grant.

We'd keep unplanted all of the fields with the dazzling views. We'd plant the rest to shelter the future, to shelter my dream of a temple. In twenty years they'd have grown to a height that would hide an inspiring building. A sanctuary for all, wrapped safely in trees, to protect it from planning objections and weather.

Ten thousand trees arrived and were stored in the farmhouse bathroom. We'd start to plant when the cold east wind had abated. Meanwhile, I was off for St Patrick's weekend. It was time to invite the ancient wisdom to Beara. It was the moment that had led like a lamp through this forest of challenge and mad aspiration.

21

First Retreat

I had a lift to Kilfinane where the three-day retreat was at a tumble-down hall in the town. With no food supplied, Harriet had packed me a loaf of bread and margarine and a packet of biscuits. I'd been allotted a place in a house full of people who wanted to talk.

A shrine had been assembled in the hall with various statues and sacred objects from Tibet. I wanted to sleep right there, to receive inspiration and avoid the chatter. This was more than a short retreat for me; I was about to ask a stranger to join the dream, to guide it with compassion and wisdom. I gazed at the shrine. How cold it had been in those northern hills and on the cliffs of the west. Trying to practise meditation, not sure of what to do next. Waiting for an outer display of the light that's hidden within, not realising that it already surrounds us.

While lost in these thoughts I was approached by Martin Leonard, the jovial Irishman who'd organised the event. He told me he couldn't find anyone to mind the sacred images, some of which were from the time of Padmasambhava, and would I sleep in the hall?

The teachings and stories of Tibet cascaded like rivers of sunlight into caverns of a grateful mind. I shivered with anticipation at the prospect of what lay beyond this latest door that was slowly opening. Sogyal Rinpoche was quoting the

Bodhicitta Prayer; the deep aspiration to benefit others through your practice and your example:

'Mesmerised by the sheer variety of perceptions, that are like the illusory reflections of the moon in water, beings wander endlessly astray in Samsara's vicious cycle. In order that they may find comfort and ease, in the luminosity, and all-pervading space of the true nature of their minds, I generate the immeasurable love, immeasurable joy, immeasurable compassion and immeasurable equanimity of the awakened mind.'

This song of commitment to benefit others by encouraging the realisation that, in their essence all beings are perfect, seemed to express the whole purpose of our project at Garranes.

Keeping away from the good-humoured chat I stayed alone in the hall for three nights, in a state of heightened awareness. I tried to talk to Sogyal Rinpoche but each time he was busy. I asked Martin to arrange a meeting. Then, on St Patrick's Day, Harriet arrived with the children who joined the crèche. On the last morning, I knocked for a third time on the lama's door and, again was told, 'later'.

I reminded myself that 'Difficulty at the Beginning' is an auspicious omen. You push to a certain point, and then let go completely, just before you turn into a sucker. Was I banging on the wrong door, or were we acting out some sort of a ritual?

At the final session Sogyal Rinpoche discussed the creation of a conducive environment for practice. He went on to describe, in uncanny detail, the moss and waterfall shrine that I'd spent that winter creating. Then he said that he was cutting back on his travel, and it might be a few years before he'd return to Ireland. I let go, relaxed and gave up. Immediately he said, 'Wasn't there someone from West Cork who wanted to see me?'

I showed him the photographs of Garranes while talking of my plans and inviting him to come and teach. He told the audience that it looked as though he might, after all, be back in

Ireland quite soon. I watched the dream race into daylight and dance. Of course, I'd never doubted it for an instant. Well. Not for a moment more than a decade or two.

Talking to Harriet, it seemed that she felt the same. We knew that we'd have to give up ownership, make the place a charity, and that would be tough. Harriet said that she was ready for anything, as long as it had nothing to do with her health. I told her that she was amazing and marvelled at how I'd been dealt such a radiant consort in my quest for the realisation of a dream. She said that she wished she could say the same about me.

Now the weather changed and we started planting the trees. The forestry inspector said that the land was too near the salt storms of the ocean with too many rocks. He told us that he was legally obliged to allow us a grant, but the trees would never succeed.

In late March, I heard that my father had suffered a minor stroke. He was in a Plymouth hospital called Freedom Fields, with his new wife and bevy of sisters. I flew to see him and returned to paint the houses for Easter, to finish planting the trees, and to hold the first meditation group of a dozen people. I worried that we were too remote, both physically and in our philosophy, from most of the inhabitants of the eighties in Ireland.

Martin Leonard visited from Limerick and answered questions about the Nyingma School of Buddhism in Tibet. Then, another student, Christine Whiteside arrived. They were both good people who were later to make great contributions, but they were still *people*. As others turned up, I knew that each person would arrive with their own agenda. I needed help but I could already see the potential for conflict. This was going to be tough. Friends insisted that we were insane, inviting all of the hungry ghosts from the shadows, to come and pick our bones clean. I told them that that sort of talk wasn't helpful. I said that our lesson would be to let go completely, and we were going to have to learn it.

While I was working on the courtyard garden, Harriet brought me a bag of dahlia tubers. Dahlias. I couldn't believe it.

In Scotland, she'd quoted, 'Hurrah, it's the first frost, the dahlias are dead.' As for myself, I loved them, these starbursts of radiant colour that lit the late summer gloom. If you want subtlety, go to the hedgerows, I'd teased her. Now Harriet's conversion was the result of the first law of Garranes: make use of whatever you find in your hands, or, if it will grow, then bloody well grow it. Living on the fringes of space, you learn to make deals with the wind, and cut through the tethers of concepts like 'taste' and the vulgarity of the dahlia. If there are people, enjoy them. If there's food, be grateful. If the sun shines, the rain rains, or a flower blooms, rejoice. If you allow it, geography and the climate slowly will grow you, until one day, before you know it, Harriet might even bring you a *tulip*.

For some time I'd been having trouble with a knee. It was the consequence of chasing livestock across rough land that I couldn't see. The cartilage would flick out causing intense pain for an instant, before it slipped back into place. At first it happened rarely, but soon it was every few days. The joint was swollen and, suddenly, I was on crutches. The consultant said that it was incurable and they should cut it out.

I'd been doing prostrations; a yogic exercise that entails certain visualisations and the throwing of yourself, full-length, onto the ground. It's a practice to open you, unblock the dam of assumptions and allow the stream of innate instruction to flow. A side effect is that it makes you physically fit. It's suggested that you complete one hundred thousand prostrations. I thought that I'd have to give up, but I found that, if I laid down the crutches and moved without twisting, I could continue, slowly. I was soon doing three hundred a day. Within weeks, I discarded the crutches and in months the knee was mended for good. The consultant might have said that it was the constant flexing that had cured the incurable. For me, it was both that and the spiritual power of the practice, and there was no difference between them.

At this time I heard of a machine that would enable me to read for the first time in a couple of decades. It was a camera, mounted beneath a monitor which would magnify text to whatever size I required. What a difference that would make to my life. Like, not having to ask people to read my letters, and re-opening the whole world of books. The only trouble was two thousand pounds. I soon forgot the idea when, in reply to my invitation, I heard that, at the end of July, a Tibetan lama would come to teach at Garranes.

That was the good news. The bad news was that all of the houses were let for the summer. There was nowhere to put him, no large shrine room yet, and no money. Still, those things were details. The main thing was that the sacred word would come to the mountain, and a light would settle amongst the rocks of the west.

In mid-June I heard that my father had died of a further stroke. An American woman had been staying. She was motherly, kind and Californian, and was distributing a text that she'd written, entitled 'After enlightenment, what next?' I felt slightly sick, and wondered if there was any point in what we were doing.

She offered me a lift to Cork on my way to my father's funeral. Driving fast out of Castletownbere, she overtook a car, around a blind bend. 'You're perfectly safe,' she assured me, 'I'm psychic. I can tell if anything's coming. I don't need to see.' This incident emphasised how vital it was to ensure that Garranes never went down this road to new-age confusion. It stressed the importance of appropriate discrimination, while keeping an open mind. After all, we did get to Cork in one piece. I was as grateful to Serina for the lesson, as I was for the lack of traffic on the roads of West Cork.

The family gathered at my father's new house. On the walls were the oil paintings that had been part of my youth. One was of a Scottish loch with misted, blue mountains, autumn trees and a shingle beach. It had hung by my bed throughout my childhood, inviting me into its silence. A secret world, where none of this mattered at all; where there was no success and no failure; no school, no rules; no one but yourself to let down or live up to.

It was politely suggested that I might sit down, so as not to get in the way of the grown-ups. I was handed a gin and tonic without any gin, while they grouped around a cousin called Charles. A chief advisor to the Bank of England, he was their stand-in for God. Inside, these people were fine. It was just that they'd never questioned the status quo, and so the issue of freedom had failed to arise. Their answer to my question about the ultimate meaning of existence was, 'family'. They'd long since given up on me when I'd told them that 'family' included us all; rabbits and racists, songbirds and maggots, bankers and rapists and the rest of us animals, crazily hunting for supper and love.

My father, in reaction to his pompous father, taught us to avoid pomposity and the delusion of self-importance, which leads to the disastrous conclusion that we are correct. For his funeral, he'd chosen a passage from St Paul's first epistle to the Corinthians in the King James Bible. After the advice of Diogenes on simplicity, it was my second reminder from Corinth. It was his last word to me, and I saluted his humour in delivering it through this particular preacher.

We walked to the small country church in brilliant sunshine, without a blemish on the clear summer sky. When we were settled, the parson made his entrance, upright and very slow moving. He was so full of himself that he had to walk slowly, to prevent himself from spilling. Now, with his first words, there came a distant mutter of thunder. Was this elaborate churchman ready for a direct intervention from Dad?

Throughout the first hymn, the heavens kept silent. Then the parson, in exquisite English, started to deliver Dad's message.

'Knowledge puffeth up, but compassion edifieth. And if any man knoweth any thing, he knoweth nothing yet,' and 'Though I have the gift of prophecy, and understand all mysteries and yet have no compassion, I am nothing.'

As the vicar continued, there was a massive explosion. The rest of his words were lost in the crack of lightning and simultaneous roar of its thunder. The church actually seemed to be shaking. The lights kept fizzing on and off, until they finally spluttered and died. We were left in a livid twilight that filtered in from a violet sky.

The storm seemed to be centred on the church, but the vicar kept going, his words unheard in the uproar. I imagined that my father was up in the tower, getting rid of resentment at a childhood of bourgeois repression. He was delivering his final teaching to these devotees of the Bank of England. The storm had lasted for most of the service, and when it was over, we walked from the church, into a breathless day of June sunshine.

My father had already told me his will. He'd left us some cash and the house in trust until his new wife, Muriel, died. I could afford the reading machine. Was it possible? I felt a surge of excitement. Wow. I'd be independent again. I could read and write and find Garranes on a map. I could consult Longchenpa and discover exactly what it was that Diogenes said. I could pluck a bluebell from the splendour of May and see it clearly for the first time; or a shell from Ballydonegan Strand, or a dead fritillary's wing.

When I calmed down, I realised that there were other calls on the cash. There'd barely be enough to prepare the place for the coming retreat. That was the dream and anything else was a self-indulgent diversion. I couldn't afford that reading machine, and so I forgot it. The cash would have to be spent on building the shrine room. We had six weeks in which to complete the impossible, and this was no time to dream about reading.

The lama would have to use Lynch's. It had no water or electricity, missing doors, broken windows and the plaster was hanging from walls. It was now worse than when we had lived there. A bathroom would have to be built on the back, drains dug and a septic tank made.

The weather was rough and, as usual, our remoteness slowed everything down. I worked on the shrine room, while a group of lads slogged, night and day, to renovate the house. Jimmy built the bathroom and somehow, in spite of continuous rain, it all got completed.

Harriet said, 'I just hope we've got the right teacher.'

I said, 'We've got what we need. If he's wise, we'll learn from his wisdom. If he's wild, we'll learn from the tumult. We'll learn how to be and how not to be, and it's all up to us and nobody else.'

On the night before his arrival, we lit a fire in the fireplace that we'd re-built in the lama's house. We stoked it all night to dry the wet plaster, while the rain that couldn't rain any harder, rained harder.

The next morning, a surprise summer's day had dawned on the mountain. We bought bales of straw and spread a gold carpet on the mud between houses. I thought of the scriptures that describe the 'Five Perfections' that enable the truth to unfold in the mind.

Had I really arrived at the point in time that I'd chased for so long in my dreaming? Had intent, at last, overlapped with the shifting shapes of the actual? Incessant rain had purified the land, the morning was still, and this was surely the 'Perfect Time'.

With the crystal air washed clean, the sun dressed the fields in the clarity of a mind on its way to its nature. Bright colours of the shrine were backed by the dazzling ocean, as phenomena fizzled with light to lay out the 'Perfect Location'.

From the ancient world, a messenger had come. Not a self-assigned, new-age purveyor of pledges, but a bearer of the wisdom that had been waiting for us to evolve. Was this not the 'Perfect Teacher' come to offer the 'Perfect Instruction'?

And forty people took part in that first retreat, urgent, in search of the route to fulfilment and freedom. In the house at the end of all 'that', they came to rest for a moment in 'this', and their 'Perfect Assembly' completed the five-fold perfection.

I was filled with a sense of great peace. Everything had begun to take place. A Tibetan lama *had* come to Beara to teach. A spiritual terrace was established on the side of the mountain that gazed at the vast expanse.

I prayed that all who come to this place would encounter the daylight of concept-less seeing. That they'd soon reach the realm of radiant light, whose colours wipe out the false gloom of conditioned perception. I prayed that, in opening their minds, they'd inspire the beings of all the dominions of space, to find their way home to their nature.

22

Flicker, Flicker

It had rained all summer. Healy Pass was white with waterfalls and floods had closed the road to Kenmare. Then, in September, the sun came out. Spring orchids opened and Albertine flowered on the farmhouse wall. We heard that the lama could come to teach from a sacred text in November.

And then Dark Matter turned up. She came to remind us that what had happened, so far, was the easy bit. Disguised as the last of the Dharma bums, she sniffed us out as she moved around various centres, exploiting support and leaving a backwash of debris behind her. Having used up all the goodwill in America, she was now preying on Europe. She'd been thrown out of hell by some despairing demon who could no longer stand the disruption. Or was she a Buddha, come to warn us to keep our eyes open, come to warn us to be kind. And to remind us that, the brighter the light, the deeper the darkness around it.

Before Dark Matter, another woman had arrived. A genuine practitioner, we let her stay in return for help with the Centre. With the spiritual side, that is, she made clear. She wouldn't help with the business because business didn't mix with a spiritual life. I could see her point, but lacked her faith to give up work and wait for manna to descend from the heavens.

Then another stranger, Victoria, arrived and explained that she had a condition which prevented her from helping. Had nothing changed since the seventies? We needed people if we were to establish a charity, but it was all going to take a great deal of patience, which was something I lacked and obviously needed to practise. The moment that I realised that, the two ghostly Buddhas departed and we were never again blessed by such shades from the past.

The woman who was helping with the spiritual side was promoting her agenda that the place should be run as a commune by workers' committees. I said that a Buddhist retreat had no requirement for contrived ideologies from Karl Marx and co. Having no ambition to accumulate status or wealth, we aspired to the ideal of putting others before ourselves. That was the only doctrine you needed to cover all that Marxism offered. It seemed to me that respect was the key. You could respect even the rulers, as long as you didn't obey them. I told her of the motto that I'd thought up at school, when ordered to salute the tyrants that headed the system. 'Respect all, except all who expect respect,' I'd written on the covers of each of my schoolbooks.

Sogyal Rinpoche came and taught on 'Turning Suffering and Happiness into Enlightenment'. Concern gave way to joy as this teaching from the Land of Snows was transmitted in the southwest of Ireland. But of course, as humans, we failed to live up to our ideals. As more people joined us a committee was formed and battle commenced, with each person fighting for personal versions of our future.

Harriet was angry with the committee for causing negativity, and with me for letting it happen. Sometimes agreeing with me, sometimes with the others, her honesty precluded any suggestion of loyalty. I often wondered, who *was* this sparkling spirit of unreason who kept switching the lights on and off? Sometimes we danced, sometimes we jousted, and I never knew quite which was which. If I assumed her support, she'd whip the rug from under my feet and insist that she did it for me. And I knew that she was so much better for me than a subservient 'yes-girl' who'd sweetly stir gelatine into my ego. I tried to persuade her to attend the meetings but, 'I have no inclination to get my head stuck in that particular set of banisters,' she said.

The year of Halley's Comet was drawing to a close, its display in the heavens eclipsed by terrestrial fireworks. For a while, it had seemed that the very fabric of Garranes was hot-wired to the national grid. As tension fizzled and flared, we told ourselves that a traumatic birth implied a robust and radiant future.

At Christmas, Harriet decided not to go to her parents until the New Year, so on Christmas Eve I prepared the food for the following day. Then, during Christmas Day the wind dropped to a whisper, emphasising the peace that had descended with all of the residents gone. I enjoyed cooking the family dinner and spent most of the day in the kitchen. In the evening, I stood outside Centre House by the arch that I'd built on the cliff-edge. We'd named it 'Hangover Corner' when we first came to Garranes because, the morning after a serious night in the village, it would sort out our heads with its constant salt breeze.

It was just dark. There were stars above Bantry Bay as its waves lapped at the rocks far below. Surprising warm air added to a sense of well-being, with Christmas night calling me back through the lights and excitement, to the magic that hides but never is lost.

I went to the kitchen to pour a slug from the bottle of Irish offered by a grateful supplier. I'd earned my first drink of the holiday. The previous week we'd agreed not to drink again, until this birth of the Centre was over. But hey, it was Christmas Day and resolutions could wait for New Year. I went back outside to raise my glass to the stars.

I heard Harriet coming. Oh-oh. She was in her wrathful manifestation, storming full tilt from the house. She must have seen that I'd opened the whiskey. In a silent fury, she emptied the entire bottle over my head and Hangover Corner. I was laughing to keep it all light. It seemed likely that such a dramatic baptism must represent an initiation into some new way of thinking. It was the perfect finale to a perfect day, at the end of the year of the comet.

And Harriet was right about alcohol. It had taken her intervention to impress me that we shouldn't drink. Actually we didn't normally keep drink in the house. We only drank when we went out and we almost never went out. That's how the work got done. Now we needed meditation to keep our heads cool, and alcohol and meditation don't mix.

With Harriet and the children gone to England, it was a chance to take stock. In that year, my father had died and I'd found a new teacher. We'd completed the first stage of building and planted ten thousand trees for the future. The dream had got out of bed and dressed itself in the illusory cloak of the real. I watched the flurry of events stirred up by promises I'd made to the stars. There was a picture that was perfect, though I was too blind as yet to perceive its perfection.

The way ahead was now being confused by the thinking of others. Should I walk away and let it take care of itself? The professionals say that those who create are rarely equipped to stay on and run their creation. Perhaps that was the source of the conflict. But how could I abandon ship and watch others sail it away in a different direction? It was not yet time for me to go into retreat, so I'd better continue the day-job. To create an environment in which others could make the journey whose destination is reached without moving.

I thought about the universal legend of a past golden age that was surely based on our innate inner light. It is said that there was a time beyond time, when everything was all right. When wisdom and its energy, compassion, prevailed. When the daylight of pristine awareness flooded the plains of the mind. This time passed from our world, but traces remain. It lingers on the outskirts of inspiration, to startle the receptive with occasional outbreaks of light.

The practices needed to unlock this light were preserved in the esoteric teachings of various philosophies and religions. When

Buddhism was driven from India, its profound practices had already been preserved for the future. They were frozen in time on the Tibetan plateau, beyond the ice wall of the mountains. Not as academic curiosities, but as a living tradition passed from teacher to student, along the lifeline that connects this morning with the Buddha. Then, as with all the establishments of humankind, the Tibetan system corrupted itself and reaped its inevitable karma. The Chinese invaded and the lifeline was flung out of history and into a world that was drowning. Trungpa and others extended it far to the west. Now the first centres were being established for the preservation and practice of this pathway to ourselves and beyond. Right here, amidst the ruins of this little planet, whose dominant species has nicknamed it 'The Earth' in honour of that species' tireless attempts to reduce its splendour to dust.

On this last day of the year I had lost my way, for a moment, in fog. I stood at the gates of the institution that I was loath to establish. I wondered if things would be any different this time. Or does our greed, sooner or later, always almost snuff out the flame? It is institutions, hierarchies, political movements, churches and so on, that stir up ambition and make us corrupt as we fight one another for power. That's why I was building a place for individuals to consider all this, alone in retreat. But I could see no way to pursue that goal other than through the creation of organisation. I would just have to trust my conviction that we can never entirely extinguish the flame. It is our innate nature. In each of us, it will eventually ignite a new golden age to expel the gloom of a personal era of grasping.

I'd developed a cold. I never caught colds. Perhaps it was caused by the shock of opening my secret retreat to the world. On such a day, it would be typical if the water went off, so it did. I renewed my commitment to build a supply from one of the springs of the mountain. Meanwhile, I spent the morning in and out of the icy stream, brought back to health by the fresh air and strength of the mountain. On the last night of that year I carried a candle to the window in the tower, for all of those who'd ever come to this place while searching for light.

I'd agreed to an interview with a girl from the *Southern Star*.
She asked questions like, 'who created the universe?' I wanted to
tell her that she did; that she created hers and I created mine, on
an ongoing basis. But she gave me the feeling that it was best to
respond with an answer that left less room for debate. So I gave
her the equally valid response that Buddha might have taught to
reporters. He said that, if we learn how to follow the path, we'll
find it all out when we're ready. Until that time, the absolute
truth is beyond the scope of the ordinary mind.

Meanwhile, the conflict increased. The group had split into
two. The communists, who were trying to take over, and the
capitalists who said that I should quit the engine room and return
to the bridge. I knew that neither extreme was the way, and told
myself to be patient. Outsiders put pressure on Harriet and me to
give up, saying that we were both victims of our single-minded,
Sagittarian determination to persist.

I turned to the 'I Ching', which I hadn't consulted for years.
I got hexagram 44, changing to 18. Hexagram 44 is 'Coming
to Meet'. It said, 'The principle of darkness, after having been
eliminated, furtively returns. An unfavourable and dangerous
situation.' Hexagram 18 was, 'Work on What has been Spoiled'.
'The wind blows low on the mountain. Decay. A bowl in whose
contents worms are breeding. Stagnation. It has come about
because gentle indifference has met rigid inertia. We must see
that the new way is safely entered upon. Then there is supreme
success.'

The mirror of the 'I Ching' had given a precise reflection
as always. I had no option but to continue, encouraged, though
money was ever more tight. Bookings for the holiday houses had
fallen by half since the committee took over. Retreat fees made
up for some of the loss, but Harriet and I still had to cover the
shortfall. The committee wanted us to change, overnight, from
holidays to retreats, but who in Ireland would ever take part? We

were almost a day's drive from Dublin with the whole spiritual side sewn up by a dominant church. We were on our own, apart from a few in Dublin, Galway and Limerick. And that lone Tipperary farmer's son, who'd once been inspired by an Indian trip.

I received word to call Sogyal Rinpoche in India. He could come, for his third visit in eight months, to teach at St Patrick's weekend. On arrival, he spent hours cleaning and adjusting the shrine, to create an auspicious environment, and then he taught Dzogchen. Its radiance filled the gap that had existed since Trungpa had left for the States. Dzogchen, ultimately untranslatable, because it represents a state beyond words and the ordinary mind, is provisionally labelled the 'Great Perfection'. It's the goal; the state of innate awareness which pervades us all but is blocked by confusion, caused by this process of thinking.

I'd been searching for a name for the Centre. A few times I'd asked Sogyal Rinpoche, but now he was about to leave for the airport again. I decided that a slightly dramatic approach was required to create the conditions for a name to arise.

Longchenpa is renowned as the great fourteenth-century exponent of Dzogchen. Longchen means 'vast expanse', which is the view from Garranes. I wanted a name which would link this saint and scholar to Ireland; would link Dzogchen to this place on the Beara Peninsula. So, I drew a map of the five peninsulas of the south-west and marked ours as Beara. On the top I wrote. 'Rinpoche, we need a name. How about Longchen Beara?'

Rinpoche was giving a press interview and there was barely enough time to get to the airport. Luckily, Ashley was driving him in his Saab, but he'd almost run out of petrol. It was Sunday and filling stations were closed. I rang the garage at Waterfall, a few miles east of the town, and said that we'd a VIP rushing to catch a plane. Would they mind opening? I explained that the lama had been commenting on the slowness of life in Ireland. Could they do me a favour and, when I next rang, go and stand at the pump, holding the hose? As the Saab screeched to a halt, could they fill the tank and wave them away, shouting that there was nothing to pay. Then I would settle up later.

I thought, 'That should unblock things a bit.' I'd never met the man at the garage but he readily agreed to my whim. It was a further example of how everything in Ireland was still transacted on trust. As the Saab roared up the hill, out of Garranes, I flagged the car down. Rinpoche lowered his window an inch. I yelled to Ashley that there was petrol at Waterfall, posted my request for a name through the window and the car raced away.

Later, Martin Leonard returned from the airport and handed me the paper with the map and the name. Rinpoche had drawn a line through the 'Long' of 'Longchen' and scrawled the syllable, 'Dzog'. So it was that we earned a name so prestigious that I wouldn't have presumed to request it. From that day we became 'Dzogchen Beara'.

Now I started a series of meetings with Patrick Gaffney. The closest student of Sogyal Rinpoche, his wisdom was delivered with a great sense of humour, as he devoted his life to the well-being of others. Harriet and I were trusting this man with our lives and we never had cause to regret it.

We set out to define the future of Dzogchen Beara. I explained that we wished to establish an independent charitable trust to preserve the teachings and practice of Buddhism in general, and particularly those of the Nyingma School of Tibet. It was also to provide a place of retreat for people of all traditions and none, and thereby never succumb to the risk of becoming a closed sect or cult. A board of trustees would be chosen to safeguard and promote these ideals.

I'd asked Sogyal Rinpoche to be spiritual director for his lifetime. His role was to nourish the spiritual development of the place and its people. After him, future spiritual directors were to be carefully selected and, if necessary, changed by the trustees. The trustees would be accountable to the people of Ireland and the world, to whom we'd given the place. All of these points were eventually enshrined in the Deed of Trust.

I explained that I'd planted so many saplings to provide shelter, when they became trees, for a small and traditional temple. At the same time, I stressed the importance of developing the site with the utmost respect for this sacred place, where the stillness of meditation would radiate peace to the planet.

Before Patrick left, I suggested breakfast with Harriet, to go over what we'd discussed. With her dislike of plans, she said that she'd rather leave it to me. I had to persuade her, on the grounds that what we were doing would have profound implications for the family. We were creating a charity that would be under the control of others, and then bequeathing it almost all that we owned. Patrick assured Harriet that, with solicitors, we'd create an unbreakable trust that would preserve our objectives into the future. This was the only ground on which we'd proceed and was of the utmost importance.

Over the years I'd had many vivid dreams about Trungpa. On the night of 4 April 1987 pictures of him kept breaking my sleep. Finally, I was back, seventeen years earlier, in his room at Samye Ling. He'd given me his hand at Monopoly and gone to sit on his mattress on the floor. Suddenly, in the dream, I became aware that he was no longer with us. Everything else was exactly the same as the moment before, but Trungpa was missing and I realised that we wouldn't see him again. That realisation woke me with a jolt. I got up, lit a candle and practised. Then, I went downstairs and, as I got to the bottom step, the telephone rang. It was Sean Duggan ringing from Dublin to say that Trungpa had died.

In the following period I had many crystal clear dreams of this extraordinary being. My view of him was simple. It had been an inconceivable honour to be on the same planet as him, and in the same time. We may or may not have received his teaching by direct transmission, but hundreds of thousands have listened. He offered himself as a signpost to the hidden path that leads beyond birth and death. When we break loose from the prison cell of the judgemental mind, we may catch a glimpse of where he was pointing.

Harriet drove to Cork and returned with two English architects, Giles Oliver and Jack the Baker. They were students of Sogyal Rinpoche, coming to help draw the future. I, who'd done everything myself, now had to sit on my hands and be grateful. The professionals had arrived. I felt slightly sick. I could no longer draw my dreams with my magic marker.

We sat talking until dawn for two nights. By day, we sheared the sheep, and I showed sites to the boys. We projected and deliberated until I just wanted to sit down and gaze at the patterns that need no designers to draw them.

Harriet and Giles were talking. There was a shriek when she realised that this stranger, Giles, was the little Giles next door. It was his parents who had had the house next to theirs at Littlestone, Kent, in those summers when they were both small. Though we mused on the strange strings of karma that tie us together, this eerie connection did nothing to reassure Harriet. She was unsettled by the boy next door, wandering our land with his briefcase.

In each of us, two approaches struggled for dominance. On the one hand, there was a fizzing expansion into dangerous light, a blind leap at a brilliant tomorrow. On the other hand, a turning back to the soil and its slow promise of sanity. It was poems and dreams of a contemplative life versus sweat and muscle and mud. I was grounded and determined to fly, while Harriet soared like an angel and searched for the earth. I milked the cows and built houses, while she read Padmasambhava and Jung. Then she grew vegetables and babies, while I worked on gazing at the colours of space. This was the reason that we were together. I put on my boots and showed her around the ordinary world, trying hard to sound like I meant it. When things got a bit hot, I rushed to stamp out the fire, so she taught me to dance in the sparks.

23

Power

I continued to remind myself that difficulties are born from our own confusion. When we realise that it's our personal blindness that makes the world seem dark, the darkness will lose its threat and be dispelled by growing gleams of light.

Like when I first met Dilgo Khyentse. He was in London, breaking his journey from Kathmandu to Trungpa's cremation in the States. Trungpa had told me about this gentle, wise old giant who was his own teacher; told me that, if I wanted to meet the Buddha in person, I should go to see Khyentse. His face and broad forehead reminded me of a young Marlon Brando, with every trace of tension transformed into kindness.

He was staying, with various tulkus, in the Rigpa Fellowship shrine room in Camden Town. And somehow I managed to be there. In the midsummer city, he taught us with words that flowed like a spring of fresh nectar, direct from his wisdom mind. Later, I stood in the courtyard looking up at the lighted windows. The sound of Tibetan ritual music was subjugating the uproar of London. Hours after we'd left him, this wise old lama from the mountains of Earth went on practising into the night.

For the public, he gave a talk at the Friends Meeting House on Marylebone Road. It was a formal lecture hall in stuffy old, wood-panelled England, as far as you could imagine yourself from the Buddha fields of colour and light. Some of us were asked to sit, facing the audience, to the side of the stage. We could see along the corridor through which Khyentse would come. The smart city crowd was hushed in anticipation. Then suddenly Khyentse appeared at the end of the passage. Tibetan clarinets played and the audience stirred, although they couldn't yet see him. He looked like a mountain, vast without fat, as he came towards us, supported on each side by a lama. As he stepped into the hall, the crowd gave a great gasp. The gasp of that moment was the expression of 'liberation upon seeing', in sound.

Naked, except for a little pink skirt, he was the colour of evening sunlight filling a windowless room. But it wasn't this that made the world gasp and go silent. It was some indescribable peace that pervaded the hall and quietly put paid to your thinking. It left you receptive, full to the brim, and empty of anything other than love.

And so such days illuminated my progress towards the temporary goal of my dream. Difficulty was irrelevant then, or relevant as the background hum of phenomena emitting their teaching. Everything was worthwhile and possible. I'd grown certain that the way to happiness was to want almost nothing. I knew that you had to unclench your fist, to see that what you were grasping was nothing but the sparkling void of imagined existence.

Khyentse was leaving for the airport. We were watching, through the window, while Sogyal Rinpoche showed him the photographs that I'd taken of Dzogchen Beara. The others urged me to go in, but I was held back by my distaste for the New World doctrine of self-assertion. Besides, I had to live up to my belief that, once you relax and stop chasing, everything falls into place.

Concealed in the roar of the world shouting 'sucker', I heard the voice of the sages. 'Humility, with strength and dignity,' they whispered into my ear. Humility that derives from seeing the sheer scale of the vast expanse; strength of the truth beyond words, and the dignity that sets its silent example. I dreamt of, one day, beginning to live up to that.

Then the door opened, Rinpoche was calling me in, and Khyentse was laying his giant hands on my head. Gone was my mistrust of the powerful. I saw a man who'd only given up his mountain retreat because people had begged him to come out and teach them. I saw only goodness and I saw that power, in the right hands, can be handled.

It was time to meet Tara for the first time in a decade. She'd moved to California while flying back to Summerhill School for each term. Born while we were at Samye Ling, with Buddhist grandparents, parents, and her Irish-Buddhist name, Tara had grown up immersed in the dharma. So I arranged to meet her at a talk by a lama in London.

I sat on the floor at the front and asked the ushers to direct her to me when she came. The packed room was silent because the lama was already seated. Then suddenly a beautiful young woman was settling on the cushion beside me and the lama started to speak. We sat for two hours in silence, while serenity placed its cloak on our shoulders, and a decade became an instant in the vastness of the time that our traces had tangled together.

The moment that the teaching ended, Tara's grandmother, Dora, was upon us. She was now one of Britain's more famous painters. She was saying, 'Oh, wow, too much, they haven't seen each other for ten years, what a trip. Don't you think she's beautiful, Peter?'

Tara and I arranged to meet in Holland Park the following day. In the lavender garden, where I'd kissed her mother when she too was seventeen, and a peacock had flown up to watch from the wisteria wall.

This time, the early garden was draped in mist and deserted. I saw a slim figure in white, on a bench. I sat down beside Tara and, as she turned, I saw that she had been crying. I put my arm round her and asked what was wrong. She said that she was sad because she'd left school. She loved Summerhill and it was unbearable to think that she'd never return. I thought of how sad it is that the rest of our petty, competitive system still teaches our children to look upon others as rivals. How wrong that it forces them into the obedient queue, to be threatened by debt until they forget about freedom. In Tara's school, the kids make the rules, and they only work when they want to. I wanted to cry with her for a society that still teaches that happiness comes from the accumulation of fame, objects, facts and the rest of the fiction. Tara made me a daisy chain coronet, placed it on my head, and I wore it for the rest of the day.

I had dinner that night with Giles and Ros Oliver, in their garden in Hackney. I sat by candlelight in the warm night, lulled by wine and the scent of their roses. I'd missed this life since leaving for Scotland, almost two decades before. Since I'd decided that, to follow my path, I had to live in the uplands. I missed the company, and the ease of life with the world at your elbow. I missed the false security that comes from living in clusters. But I only missed them because I had missed them. Yes, there was the genetic longing for the ancient caress of soft summer nights, but I loved the wilderness more. I saluted the pounding sound of an ocean that keeps you awake and alive. The turbulent elements and the blast of salt air, for what is the wind but freedom in motion?

Tara and I got on Slattery's bus to Cork, and she stayed for a week. Harriet welcomed her with genuine affection and Flora and Tom were delighted to discover a sister.

And all the while I was growing more frustrated with the inertia of the committee. There was a photograph that I'd taken with Harriet's mother's Minolta, set to infinity and pointed in roughly the right direction. Harriet called it my 'Zen photography' and somehow it worked. It was Dzogchen Beara in late summer, with the ocean licking the cliffs. I took it from amongst the young trees on Skyliner Hill, having stuffed blue agapanthus into the foreground. Everyone who saw it said, 'Wow. Where is *that*?' I suggested that we made it a postcard to advertise the place and raise funds. The issue was still under discussion by the committee, six months after I'd given up. How would we ever get a temple conceived if we couldn't give birth to a postcard?

It was twenty years since I'd been in France. No holidays, when all of our cash had to go to the Centre. Now I had a lift to a place called Les Ages for a summer retreat. We received teachings from Sogyal Rinpoche and various lamas. A Bohemian-looking one, with long beard and a topknot, was a great yogi and artist. He had a powerful voice which, like curlews in April, was wired direct to your soul. His chanting flew you to secret valleys of the ancient lands, where everything that had ever concerned you dissolved like fire-sparks in space. I played a recording of this voice as I travelled, and it turned the world into a shrine where sacred syllables lit unknown pathways into the fabric. It was to be twelve more years before I was sufficiently open to receive its owner, Chagdud Tulku, as my teacher.

Back at Dzogchen Beara I told myself that, sometimes, no progress can be progress itself. I often lied to myself when things got tough, but I never believed me.

The heating and phone bills had gone berserk, so we sold the car to pay them. We replaced it with a derelict Datsun, an enormous old bus that Harriet loved. Now we had nothing left to sell, so we had to trust that future cash really would roll in with those waves.

At Halloween, Sogyal Rinpoche's older students from Europe came on retreat. They fell in love with the place and the place responded with a spectacular display. On the first night there was a violent welcoming storm. This transformed into days of warm sunshine without a whisper of wind. Sometimes Dzogchen Beara did that. It was like a petulant child, angry at an influx of strangers. It stamped its foot and smashed a few things, before it began to enjoy the attention. Then it started to show off its toys.

At this time, with the dream coming to life, and immersed in the vast profundity of the words of the Buddha, I lived in a state of somewhat heightened awareness. I had many vivid dreams and insights, but they say it's not good to talk of these things.

It lessens the integrity of the experience, might put others off, is egotistical and probably boring. However, because it was such a part of the story, I'll risk the inclusion of just one minor incident here.

One night, in my room in the tower, I fell asleep listening to a recording of the Dzogchen Lineage Prayer being chanted in Tibetan by the lama of the mesmeric voice. I became aware again sometime before dawn. Half asleep, half awake, I watched my dreams from a great distance inside and beyond them. Then suddenly, a Tibetan voice shouted a loud exclamation. I was instantly, utterly awake. The space before me had folded into segments which were overlapping and opening to reveal faces, one after the other.

The format was like that of the series of blue pictures that I'd painted a long time before. The difference was the intense clarity, insubstantiality and inconceivable depth. I recognised that the faces were those of past masters of the lineage of Dzogchen. With the serenity of Buddhas, they appeared in a slow waxing light, remained for a moment and folded away in the segments of space. The light grew and waned in regular waves with each face's appearance, like the beat of the pulse of existence.

It went on and on. A state of enhanced perception had torn through the veils, and startled me into life. After a while, a thought chugged by, like a tractor that ploughs a furrow in a field of silk. 'Would this continue if I opened my eyes?' I didn't dare do so, in case I was dragged from this sacred dimension. I let the thought go, but it hovered like the orphaned intention of an impudent child. So, slowly I opened my eyes and it made no difference at all. The lineage continued as before, or even a little bit brighter. Another thought told me to pinch myself, but that was a joke, because I was so wide awake that it almost hurt. I gave up and gazed on in awe.

Then, as suddenly as it had begun, it was gone. New thoughts came tom-fooling along, like a troupe of players, juggling and tumbling down the main street of the mind. They were calling out newly out-of-date questions that would have staked the immaculate to the terrestrial field, had I honoured them with attention. Instead, I lay there, while the first waves of light lapped at the shores of upcoming day. Later, a cock crowed. I stirred and became conscious of gratitude. After all of my immersion in material things, I could still steal a glimpse of that radiance that shines beyond the shutters of reason.

For some time, I'd been trying to decide where to build a retreat hut. My first one was now part of the Centre. I needed a place to escape from the politics and keep myself sane. There was no cash, but if the intention was right, that would come. One site was a sheltered slope quite close to the Centre. The other was a wild and secret fold in the tumbled rock. Aware that this was becoming a pattern, I chose the wilderness because actually there was no choice. I just had to let go of the easy option, with no thought of purposely choosing the difficult one.

One day I was made aware that, if my head was occasionally in the clouds, my feet were firm on the good earth of Ireland. The postman was delivering the mail. 'I hear you had a bit of an accident yesterday,' I said. He and Rachel had collided on one of our bends. 'Oh God, it was nothing,' he replied. 'Nothing. No damage done. Cosmetic. Purely cosmetic.' So saying, he jumped into his van and roared away amidst a series of violent explosions. The front bumper was hanging off and the exhaust pipe clanked on the ground.

The postman had delivered a package for which I'd been waiting. Although the Centre's bills had taken most of the cash that my father had left, I wanted to invest a little in something sacred for him. I'd ordered two Tibetan scroll paintings from a well-known artist in Kalimpong. They were of wrathful deities, painted in gold on black; powerful images used in the practice of cutting through our inner obstacles to realisation.

They'd been sent in a steel tube, sealed at both ends with soldered-on metal caps. Customs, unable to gain access, had bent the tube into a right angle. I saw immediately that the paintings would be cut at the kink, and ruined. I took the tube to Andrew in the farmhouse hostel. We straightened it as best we could, but it remained in a shallow v-shape. We spent an unsuccessful hour with knives, and a hammer, trying to remove the steel caps. Then we gave up until morning. I placed the still-sealed tube on the shrine for the night, practised, and lay down to sleep.

Next day, after my morning practice, I lifted the tube from the shrine. It became perfectly straight in my hands, without any pressure at all. There wasn't even a trace of a kink. One metal cap fell off and I removed the scrolls which were intact and undamaged. However I looked at it, I couldn't explain it through reason. Maybe it seems trivial. Maybe even to record it reduces my credibility with those, like me, whose minds are still trapped in the concrete reality which we're so busy projecting. But I cannot help that. For me, maybe it was a sign of the power of the practice. Certainly, it was one more indication of the fluidity of mist-like phenomena. Of the dance that continuously eludes us, as we turn it to stone with our thinking.

Meanwhile, the turbulent inertia of the committee continued. At the height of the negativity there came a storm such as we'd never seen. We watched from the glass wall of the kitchen. The wind had increased all morning, until sheets of sea-spray were blowing through the sky. A stream that ran off the cliffs of Pulleen was turned back by the wind, and billowed like smoke on the mountain. We watched sheet lightning at play on the fields between us and the water. The children were excited and scared. Though it was the middle of the day, it was almost dark. The sky was a crazy purple, where you could distinguish it from the ocean that was on the boil in space.

We'd never seen lightning like that. It was all over the ground, snaking, rippling in blue flashes over the sodden grass. Once it climbed the wall and exploded in a stream of sparks from a socket beside the window.

For a while, we were living on a different planet from the

normal one that time and perception had harvested out of experience. Everything was insubstantial, alive and dangerous. We were watching lightning playing at our feet, not in a flash but in the electric menace of its dance. It took us and our little games and showed us the power with which we were messing. The power from whence we had arisen, and the power that will soon take us back again.

24

Symbolic Fish

The young Dzogchen Rinpoche came to our summer retreat and more than eighty attended. It began to look as though it would work, if we could sort out the structure. Through sleepless nights I searched for a different approach but, planning for generations to come, I could see no alternative to majority rule. I just had to stand back, let others make decisions and hope that we'd all grow up.

I walked into our old room, in the farmhouse, to find that the committee had painted it cream. I'd painted the interiors brilliant white, with bright-coloured curtains, lampshades and rugs, in honour of pristine awareness. Now room by room, slowly my dream was faded to a colour invented for an institution by a committee. Eventually, even my inspiring, temple-red shrine room succumbed. Its yellow silk curtains were removed, its bright rugs were replaced by a carpet of inspirational beige and its walls de-mystified with a dollop of cream. Now we had a shrine to the pigment of police stations, public lavatories and schools. Safe and polite and boringly nice, cream is the shade of the blanket that society stuffs into the throat of initiative. It's an insult to the scintillating light of the truth. I asked if they could imagine anyone having a religious experience in a room that was painted in cream. They said that white was too dazzling. I said that the whole point of this place was to dazzle.

In the sixties, we'd rejected this bourgeois non-colour because it dulled the excitement. Society reacted, re-invented it, called it 'Magnolia' and went back to sleep. Now it was being smeared all over tomorrow, in the name of an out-dated concept called 'taste'. It was hard to accept that those to whom I was entrusting my dream were still limited by concepts like taste. Bound in strait-jackets of borrowed perception, we insist that this one goes well with that. Instead of allowing the natural perfection of whatever turns up on the screen. Instead of realising that, if you relax, nothing will clash and we'll see phenomena as shimmering projections in temporary juxtaposition, arising and fading without beginning or ending.

We'd thought that the future would be like that; a continuous leap from the past into radiant white and its rainbow refractions. But our world wasn't ready. It was still run by its lineage of dingy institutions, terrified that the vitality of light would show up the mess that it was creating to hide in.

So I dreamt of Dzogchen Beara as the antidote to cream: a far-away world of colour and light that exists, unseen, such a short distance into our eyes. A radiant realm for people to enter; to encounter the world as it is; like the child who wanders wide-eyed in the temple without any notion of grasping. It was why we'd searched for that turning off the road to the west. To establish the opportunity for direct perception, so that I too could deal with my personal concepts; could learn to stop ranting and take cream as a part of my training; trusting that, one day, I'd evolve enough to see even cream as perfection.

Then there was the day when I came home to find that they'd demolished two walls that I'd built, years before. At that time, and later, when I found a strange German with a rock-breaker in my beautiful garden, I reminded myself that it's all just a dream, and all dreams come to dust before long. Reminded myself that all that remains is what we carry around in our hearts, and it's there that we need the rock-breakers. And I knew that, ahead of me, were innumerable episodes that would nudge me and knead me, until I accepted them all as part of this path of the slow letting go.

Harriet, busy being a brilliant mother, was also struggling with the tension of the place, which was taking its toll on our relationship. Never depressed, she said she was too busy analysing what was coming in under the radar. We often discussed our theories about being open to whatever arose and our theories were soon to be tested.

I'd been working on the mountain and was walking home, when Harriet screeched the car to a halt beside me. 'I've got myself in a terrible mess. Please, I need you to help me.' As she continued, her words came tumbling and scrambling to catch up with her thoughts. This was Harriet as I'd first known her, vulnerable, trusting, needing help and needing it now. She was open, uncertain, and at her most loveable. Harriet was always herself, but this was a magnified version. She explained that she'd fallen in love. That it was unbearable, impossible, completely overwhelming, one-sided and what should she do? I wondered how anyone could not be in love with Harriet.

As always, we were immediately dealing with titanic forces that made up her larger-than-life-sized existence. They rendered irrelevant any vague feelings that might be lurking in me. There was no time for 'me' to arise, when we were dealing with Harriet. So, there was no feeling of rejection at this. Quite the opposite, in fact. Harriet was including me, depending entirely on me. It was an honour to support this enchanting being, as she danced, barefoot, on the rim of her own volcano.

We drove out to Adrigole while Harriet told me her story. For the next few weeks there was an intense discussion between Harriet, Padmasambhava, Carl Jung and me.

She said that it was easy for me because I couldn't be beguiled by the sparkling eyes of another. I reminded her that I'd been no angel and that there was no need to see eyes. You could get lost without trace in the toss of a head or a chuckle. Everything is in the control of our ordinary mind, it's just that we cannot control it. The only way is to relax, enjoy the sensation and watch it drift off into space with a giggle. She said that was fine, but she needed a more conceptual antidote to attraction. I suggested that she might try to view us as an alien might. See us, fleshy and hairless, stumbling around this chunk of old space-rock, perched on hind legs, trapped inside these tottering towers of meat. She said that it wasn't the meat that interested her, but what was happening inside it.

On 12 June, we were sitting on the farmhouse wall in the mist. The silence was enhanced by the echo of waves at the gates of Puleen and the distant boom of the foghorn from the Bull Rock. Harriet pulled the wedding ring from her finger. 'Here. Perhaps you should take this,' she said. 'It seems such an inappropriate emblem of freedom right now. Maybe we should sell it, and use the cash for the Centre.'

I heard the dog barking and slipped the ring into my pocket. It was Eileen of the Murphys, back from fishing, and carrying an enormous pollack. She said that it was to thank us for making people so welcome for all of these years. I told her how, in the early days, we used to hide in the cowshed on Sundays. But I was thinking of this woman's appearance, out of the mist, at that precise moment, to hand me an exaggerated symbol of the spiritual life. Did the perfect timing of this latest move of the dance suggest that it was time for me to live and practise alone? Harriet said, 'I need you near, but I also need my own space.'

One evening the group was talking in the kitchen. I said to the others that I'd had enough of juggling concepts with the committee; to hell with the dream and the building. I wanted to go into retreat. They said that it was a 'cop-out'. On the floor was a basket of old '45' records that I'd found in the roof. There were fifty discs that I'd not seen since I'd removed them from my jukebox in the Birmingham club. I reached down into the basket, saying that I'd do a divination. The title of the song would dictate the course that I'd take. I pulled a disc from the pack and handed it to Rachel to read the words on the label. It was an Elvis track, and its title was 'Follow That Dream'.

Divinations always work. If sometimes they surprise us, it just shows how little we knew our own minds.

An old friend, Tessa Heron, came to our June retreat. An attractive character with a wicked sense of humour, she was just right to cheer up Harriet. Someone told her how I'd given up the reading machine to spend the cash on the shrine room. She offered to buy one. I was touched and excited and unsure. Did I really want to start reading the concepts of others again? I rejoiced in my particular path, and to change it now seemed sort of ungrateful.

I had a lift to the summer retreat at Brunissard in the Alps. Half of the people had already arrived and were listening to Rinpoche in the marquee. I was always a bit apprehensive about approaching a gathering that I couldn't see. I hoped to slip in unnoticed and sit at the back.

I found the entrance because of hundreds of shoes outside it. I took a deep breath and pushed in the flap. On the far side I could see a blur that would be two hundred people sitting cross-legged on carpets. Unable to see the lama, or a gap in the crowd to slip into, I sat on my own in the empty half of the tent, facing the voice of the lama. So much for being unnoticed. As my eyes grew accustomed to the light, I became aware of my predicament. I was sitting, in dramatic isolation, with my back to the teacher, facing the opposite way to everyone else, gazing towards a loudspeaker, to which I'd just done three prostrations.

'Oh fuck. They must think I'm weird,' I thought. Then my loyal sense of humour giggled and said, 'You could just die, or let go of the ego that cares what anyone thinks.' I decided to live and let go and be happy that I was back in the mountains of France. In Ireland, my mountain was a near-fatal accident of rocks that lunged at the shoreline. Here, in the Alps, it was distant peaks and a meadow of green, a thousand breaths nearer the sky. Listening to the timeless wisdom, I felt entirely alive. Phrases were woven in tingling air, from threads left in space by the ancients. I was listening to time-proof songs of a truth beyond the outposts of thought-addled mind. I was at peace, untouchable, picking my way across the astonishing field, free of limitations imposed by requirement.

There was a day when I sat on a rug in the tent of words, whose side flaps were raised to the light of the view. The green of the slopes and the blue of the peaks were enhanced by a red prayer banner that rippled and rode on the air-streams of morning. The haunting song of Chagdud Tulku called out to Padmasambhava in the high pastures of lost Tibet. It cut a sliver from the circle of time, invited you in, and then put the sliver back again.

I was drifting past low-flying images to gaze at planes of the sky. It was then that I noticed that a new piece of my sight had gone missing. It had been stable since school. They'd said that I'd never go blind. The lama's voice became distant, and his words were a cascade of sound beyond meaning. They had said that I'd never go blind. They had said. They had said ...

For an instant, I was gripped by a rush of panic, but then, straight away, there arose a bewildering kindness. A slow poignancy spread through my being, as though I was perfectly in love with no one and everyone that ever there was. It rose, peaceful and infinite, above the turmoil of ordinary feelings; beyond here or there, with no good or bad to bewitch it and bitch it with judgement. A pristine intimacy with all that is breathing and with its fragile container. The purest, uncluttered joy, like I felt as a boy, when alone in the light of the magic.

Then thoughts came trundling back, like a wagon-train raising dust on a distant plain. 'It'd be all right if death was like that. No thoughts, just a vast expanse of perfection. How precious all of this is. How sad to see us drifting along, dribbling our time down the drains of dissatisfaction. I must work harder at what I must do, and stop as often as I can.'

A few minutes later there came another surprise. Sogyal Rinpoche started to talk about how it's through suffering that we learn, if we let go and open. How sometimes, in the moment of despair, there arises a pristine and unfathomable sensation of bliss. He went on to describe my mysterious experience of minutes before. It was the first time that I'd heard of such a state arising from panic or fear. It was further proof that there's so much going on that our workaday mind can't explain, or that, when something breaks through our outer protection, the radiant core is revealed.

So then, back in the factory of practical mind, I reminded myself that it's all just a part of the process. As my sight changes, it will push me further into the practice. If I go blind, I'll do a dark retreat. How wonderful. 'Would-be seers don't need to see with their ordinary eyes,' I teased myself. Those eyes are mostly engaged with distraction.

I rejoiced in the sight that had kept me alert and apart; that had shown me a glimpse that you miss when disturbed or delighted by detail. It had led me into surprise situations whose humour rattled the bars of our prison. Situations whose humour still makes me laugh, like the story of Mary Noonan.

She was an Irish girl at the retreat. Nine months pregnant, she and Brian had made arrangements with the French doctors to have the baby in France.

Some of us would rise in the Alpine dawn, to do prostrations in the marquee before breakfast. I'd finished mine when I noticed Mary prostrating, a short way away in the tent. How could she throw herself full-length at the ground when she was nine months gone? When she finished, and was standing up, I walked over. It wasn't until I was close that I realised my eyes were at it again. It wasn't pregnant Mary at all. It was a stranger; a very large and very fierce-looking, red-faced American woman. But it was too late. I'd already spoken. 'My God, you're amazing,' I'd said. 'I can't believe you can do prostrations with a belly like that.'

That afternoon, Rinpoche offered to hold a three-month retreat at Dzogchen Beara. He asked how many would attend and four hundred people said 'me' This would establish Dzogchen

Beara as a permanent retreat, of real benefit to the people of Ireland and Earth.

I arrived back from France in time for the weekly meditation group. After the session I gave the committee the inspiring news. It was greeted with groans. 'Too much work,' they said, 'we must ensure that it happens elsewhere.' Once more the committee had smothered the spark, in case it should ignite a fire of initiative which they couldn't control. When I suggested that this was 'poverty mentality', they replied that they thought I was into poverty. I said, 'Poverty without the mentality, yes.'

I reacted by agreeing to Tessa's reading machine. I'd build my hut in the rocks and give up this struggle against the tide of missed chances, to study and practise instead. Unwrapping the machine, I remembered. The last book that I'd read was *Crime and Punishment*, some twenty years before. Now I reached for the first book that came to hand, and put it under the camera. Its title appeared, magnified on the screen. It was *The Wish-Fulfilling Jewel*, by Dilgo Khyentse. Could it be that this set of the dance was completed? Could it be that my years of hard labour, breaking rock in exile, were over? Had I paid off some of the crimes of my selfishness, to arrive at the next shining door?

Not quite. Over the following days, I found that still I couldn't read books. It was too slow and tough on my eyes. I could, however, see short texts such as poems and what I'd just written, and those bluebells and how quickly my fingers were ageing.

In the autumn of '88 I started work on my hut. It was hidden from all of the hundred and fifty acres which we were giving to the charity. I'd chosen a place with no view, in order that there were no viewers.

Two tons of cement were delivered and stored in my bedroom in the Skyliner basement. Across the mountain each morning I barrowed, one at a time, two hundredweight bags of the stuff. A bag and a barrow weighed as much as my body. There was no track, so I dragged the load up a rock-strewn slope, through a chaos of gorse and heather and bog. I made, by hand, a one-bag mix in the mornings and another one after noon. I built with rocks that I'd gathered the evening before. So determined was I to make my retreat, that I worked in all weathers and loved it. Out there alone with the wind and my shovel, I mixed joy with the elements again. Able and easy, I was one with the earth, the sea and the sky.

In November I got on the London bus. A great lama, Penor Rinpoche, was giving the empowerments of the Nyingtik Yabshyi. It was a privilege beyond ordinary measure to receive these Dzogchen teachings. Although I was neither open nor aware enough to be there, I was thrilled to be tangling with the truth to which I'd devoted my life.

I was staying in Hackney with Giles and Ros. The talks were at the YWCA off Tottenham Court Road, in the evenings. I needed to leave early to get there because I couldn't see much in the dark. One afternoon things got a bit late. It was dark by the time that I started the long walk up Mile End Road to the tube. Then it started to rain. Car headlights dazzled in a spatter of raindrops on each of my lenses. Everything beyond was a shadowy blackness in which figures were running for shelter. I had to slow down and wish that I'd remembered my coat. A bicycle whizzed past while I dealt with a lamp post and bus stop. Soon everyone had gone from the streets and I was alone with the swishing of traffic.

I laughed, recalling something I'd heard that morning. 'You should do one thing each day that terrifies you.' I wondered, does it count if you celebrate the storm while you tremble? Perhaps this was the point of my eyesight. When each step is a step into the unseen, it's the perfect incentive to keep you awake. I joked with myself, 'If people really want to see a bit more, they might try a walk up Mile End Road in the rain with their eyes closed. Or go home each night, without seeing their feet, on a cliff-edge path in the dark.' The trouble is that it's not enough to be threatened like that. We have to learn to be threatened and completely relaxed.

I wasn't relaxed, and then I came to the main road which ran at right angles to mine. From daylight, I remembered a four or six-lane nightmare of traffic. I had to cross that road. I could see nothing, and there was no one left in the city to help.

Normally I'd have listened for a gap in the roar of the rush-hour, but the swish of wet tyres on wet tarmac filled up the night and my senses. I stood there in the driving rain, praying for a stray human. Then I spoke aloud to the wet wall of noise. 'I can't go back, I never go back, and I've got to get to the teaching.' Actually, I had no key and probably wouldn't have found the house if I'd tried. I stood for a long time, letting my mind flush out. Then I stepped off the kerb and slowly walked into the hissing of lights. There were cars all around, moving just fast enough to actually kill me. I could see nothing but dazzle and darkness, split open with splinters of rain. But there was no squealing of brakes, no shouting, not even a honking of horns. It was as though my body had ceased to exist. I gained the far pavement and continued the quest for the tube.

Back in Beara, I worked through the winter building my hut. Before dawn, I practised Rigdzin Dupa in my room, and then went to the shrine room to practise with whoever turned up. One night, I awoke to an immediate and intense awakeness, like the time that I'd seen the Dzogchen Lineage. With eyes open, I watched shifting images, layer upon layer of moving shapes, sliding one over the other within a vast and varied perspective. Out of this would emerge locations, portraits and fragments of various events. It was like scanning the files of a multi-dimensional memory store in super-high definition.

It seemed to be the factory within which the fabric of 'reality' is assembled. Created from prototypes evolved from juggled experience, it was the library of ordinary mind, in unbound volumes of everything that I'd ever known. Something had led me backstage for a glimpse of what's normally concealed by the safety curtain. Shuffling the traces from which I'd invented a person, I was showing me the blue-prints of my ordinary self, to remind me that nothing is lost. That every circumstance that we've encountered has a part to play in each succeeding occurrence.

It was shortly after this that I received another lesson from a teacher of the animal realm. A rat had been stealing offering-rice, and now had taken, from the shrine, a small crystal image of Buddha. I went to find the cat, to put him in the roof-space. Of course, I wouldn't kill anyone myself, but somehow I'd worked out that I could let others do my killing for me.

The cat was a placid ginger tom that my son had named 'Biker'. He used to sleep in a basket, curled up with his paws around our Tibetan spaniel. I picked him up to carry him to Centre House, to do my dirty work. He lashed out, striking again and again in a frenzy. Spitting and snarling, he slashed his way up my clothes and onto my head, where he buried his claws in my scalp. I tried to lift him but the claws were under my skin. Finally, my only option was to kneel on the ground, as though in penance, to let him jump off and run.

It was quite a lesson that he'd taught me. I'd picked him up a hundred times. This time he put me somewhat in the position of the rat. Except that the cat would have to be five times bigger than me, and would have torn my eyes out, slowly. Shocked at myself, I promised never to practise such hypocrisy in the future.

We caught the rat in a humane trap and let him go on the mountain. Biker lived to be one hundred cat years old, and I never again saw him do anything other than purr.

The Cornish family in 1948. The author at the bottom left.

The author in 1963.

With Norma in 1964.

Amalie (top left) with her parents, Dora and George, and her sisters, Hermione and Hepzibah. Tushielaw, 1969.

The family cow. Garranes, 1976.

Before the trees. The newly built Dzogchen Beara, in 1986.

View from Centre House.

Flora (left), Tom and Tara in 1987.

With Harriet in Castletownbere in 1987.

Harriet, above the beehive huts. Skelligs, 1992.

Harriet with Sogyal Rinpoche in 1992.

With HH Dalai Lama. Dublin, 1991.

Dodrupchen Rinpoche at Dzogchen Beara with Alak Zenkar Rinpoche in 1991.

From left: Ringu Tulku, Sogyal Rinpoche and Ato Rinpoche, on the occasion of Dzogchen Beara becoming a charity. August 1992.

At Great Stupa in Boudhanath, Nepal, in 2001.

Mature woods at Dzogchen Beara.

25

Streams of Ancient Wisdom

By the summer of '89 things were coming to a head. Could Dzogchen Beara, by 1992, host a three-month retreat for four hundred people, with all that it would mean for its development as a centre? There was to be a meeting at the French retreat, at which Giles would present his proposals.

While enthusiastically supporting the project, Harriet saw Giles' plans as a threat to the integrity of the land entrusted to our care. Factions had formed and campaigns were fought, by the English to keep their lama in London, and the French who wanted the focus on France, while Ireland was regarded as an impudent upstart. I saw my dream on a knife-edge. Saddened by the politics, I slowly realised that, however lofty might be our ideals, we remain human and subject to human reactions. We may talk of putting others before ourselves, but it's a long journey from the thought to its actualisation.

Shortly before the meeting, I was told that my wife was in a feisty mood in the bar, but there was no way that I could intervene, once Harriet's battle tanks were rolling. Besides, as the natural protector of Dzogchen Beara, her views were to be respected.

I arrived at the meeting of about forty people from various national groups. Harriet was in the front row. Giles was standing at a blackboard with a pointer, having pinned up a large-scale map of our mountain. With my life's work in the hands of others, a feeling of calm detachment pervaded my mind-stream. I wondered how Harriet would behave. She'd have no plans. The only certainty was that she'd be spontaneous and fearless.

Giles called the meeting to order and started to talk. Harriet interrupted him before he'd finished a sentence. Each time that he got going, she stopped him again. 'Absolute nonsense,' she retorted to each proposition. 'On whose authority are you empowered to desecrate this sacred place with your fantasies?' The meeting broke up in disarray. Brian McMahon from Ireland came over to me. '1992? More like 2092,' he said.

Back in Cork I bought a bowl of goldfish and liberated them into the lily pond. I'd contacted Ato Rinpoche who I'd last met twenty years before when I'd made dinner for him and Trungpa in Scotland. In late August, he came to Dzogchen Beara to teach. He was wise and kind and lit up the world with his laughter, which made everyone warm again for a while.

I worked on my hut to keep the flame burning. Each fingertip was bleeding from stuffing cement between rocks. I wrapped them in lavatory paper, stuck it on with sticky tape, and kept building. Sometimes, in the storms, I tied a rope round my waist so that I could work on the corbelled roof. I shrugged off my fear that we'd blown our one chance. We'd not come this far to turn back. I'd proceed on my own if I had to, but there was a hollow feeling inside. Then Patrick Gaffney arrived to tell us what I'd suspected. They'd pulled the plug. They'd bought land in France, the three-month retreat would be there, and we wouldn't develop in the foreseeable future. Now I felt completely alone.

The reason they gave was the Irish weather. Too risky, they said, to sleep a few hundred in tents. I told myself that it's dangerous to mix your dream with the dreams of others. Especially when they prefer talking to action. We needed a great feast of manifestation, but the committee wasn't qualified to visualise breakfast.

In spite of it all, I found it difficult to successfully achieve any anger. I was too aware that you can't claim the dream and absolve yourself of the nightmare. How could I blame the committee when everything was my projection, and therefore my fault? It was all no more than my mundane mind, busily trying to teach me. I wanted to blame the strange beings that kept popping up with obstructions, but if everything's a self-portrait, who can you blame but the painter?

So what could I do but give up, laugh and continue? In that case, I thought, shouldn't I go and hug each member of that bloody committee? I didn't have to think about that. I was neither advanced nor Californian enough. Rather, I'd be compassionate to these negative reflections of my character, and spend less time in their presence in future.

In those days the children were the best part of Dzogchen Beara. There were seven living on site, and more would hassle their parents to come to the practice. They'd watch a film downstairs, while we went up to the shrine room. They'd wait until we'd settled and then throw golf balls at the wooden ceiling, above which we sat in dignified silence.

Sometimes, a crack in the gloom would open, to reveal the humour that's always within, and is occasionally released by my eyesight. Like once in Cork when I was renting films for the kids. I gave the assistant a list of various titles. She read it, gave me an old-fashioned look, as though I were asking for porn, and went off to search through the shelves. She finally returned, apologising for having not one of the titles in stock. I looked at the list that she handed back. I'd given her the wrong one. It was the list for the garden centre, and it read: 'Large, scented lily, natural fertiliser and rake with steel teeth.'

In the storm days of winter, another Tibetan lama, Ringu Tulku, came to teach us to be joyful, compassionate and open. He sat in the window watching waves roll in, having seen an ocean for the first time in Ireland. He was to come back each year, right up to the present, and become a true spiritual friend, a long-burning beacon of inspiration to us all.

The winter passed and, before you knew it, bluebells were draping the slopes of May with their rags of ancient blue. I'd run out of rocks, so I devised a new method of building. I bought fifty plastic washing-up basins in which to manufacture blocks. I oiled them and filled them with cement and the rubble that we'd dug from the mountain. It was a great way to keep a man from a meeting. And down there in the rocks, high on the mountain, through all of the joy and the conflict, there ran the silver stream of the ancient wisdom. It kept waking you, washing you out of your shallows and waving you on.

Sogyal Rinpoche invited Dilgo Khyentse to teach at Prapoutel, above Grenoble. He set about demonstrating how the auspicious conditions should be created, to allow the teaching to arise. A great marquee was pitched on the edge of the mountain. It looked towards a panorama of Alps, and down on the misted city, asleep in the sun far below. Fifteen hundred students were expected, including many of Trungpa's from the States.

Along the cliff, a second tent was erected to become the luminous domain of Khyentse. Yellow silk draped the roof and the sides, so that the sun shining through turned the air into gold. Someone was sent to India for thangkas of deities to be hung on the translucent walls. Tibetan carpets were borrowed from Switzerland and brilliant red shrines and tables were made. The lama was waving the wand of devotion to clear a path for the light.

One side of the tent was open, onto a lawn freshly laid on the tarmac and planted with rose bushes brought up from Grenoble. From inside you could see, past a foreground of flowers, a cloudless sky and the violet mountains beyond. The lama had juggled the elements of confused perception to present an alternative view; a pure land, to transport the old master back to his youth in Tibet.

Hoses sprayed over the tent to cool it and enhance the Alpine stillness with the falling of water. Finally, four wheels were fitted to the throne that carpenter students had built for Khyentse to live on and teach from. Requiring only the utmost simplicity, Khyentse would never have allowed such a fuss, but in this way, the old giant could be wheeled from his tent, along the cliff and into the great marquee. He usually walked with the help of aides because of his age, and his stiffness from years of retreat. It was inspiring for us to observe this manipulation of phenomena to transform the mundane into a sacred domain.

On the day of Khyentse's arrival, I saw the kind-looking yogi lama who I'd heard teach at Les Ages. Chagdud Tulku was drawing the eight auspicious symbols, in white, on the black page of the tarmac. It was part of the traditional preparation for the arrival of a great master. This tulku was one of the foremost exponents of Dzogchen, and the lama of the powerful chant. He was an artist who painted and sculpted and wrote sacred verse, and he looked it. But it was something less tangible than his long beard, his topknot and unconventional clothing that made me feel an immediate connection.

I saw him once more, later that day, and then not again for a decade. Little did I realise then that, ten years later, when I was ready, I was to do a five-month retreat under his guidance in a bare little cubicle in the Brazilian jungle. Or foresee that, during the first hours of daylight, in an old waterfront house in Rio, I would receive, one-to-one from him, the empowerment that would make 25 May in the year 2000 the most significant day of my life.

Meanwhile, in the French Alps, he'd finished that day's practice of Rigdzin Dupa. I was waiting for the lift in a darkened hall of the apartment block in which I was staying. Fresh from the practice, I stood in a state of quietened mind in the afternoon silence. Suddenly, the lift-doors slid open in a blaze of light to reveal the old yogi standing before me. He beckoned me to join him, but I indicated that he should carry on up. The doors closed, the vision was gone, and I was back in the darkness. I wondered why I'd declined such a dramatic invitation to travel on up with a Buddha. I took it to mean that there was still work to be done. I was not yet open enough to receive his message of light.

Over the next days, Khyentse taught and gave empowerments for the most profound teachings of the Nyingma School of Tibet. He also gave individual blessings to everyone there. The most affected were those who'd doubted the value of receiving the blessing of a stranger. Through simply being, he opened the hearts of the world.

Marshals had been enlisted to stream people into the tent. On the first day, I joined the crowd pouring in. I turned towards the front, in order to be able to see. A man who I'd met in London, ushered me to the back. 'The privileged get no special treatment here, Cornish,' he said. I was surprised because he knew that I couldn't see. There had been jealousy amongst some of the English. Although a relative newcomer, I'd received preferential treatment from Rinpoche, over some of his older students. Who the hell did I think I was? I'd been aware of the potential pitfalls from the start. In London, on my first visit, Rinpoche had offered me his private room at the Centre in Camden Town. I declined and slept on the floor of the shrine room with others, to avoid the possibility of arousing resentment.

Now I could easily have made a stand against this display of the tyranny induced by a faint whiff of power. Instead, I said to myself, 'Actually, I don't need to see. Let go and accept it. Besides, if you sit at the back, someone else gets to sit at the front.' And that was partly a lie for a start. Wasn't it the truth that I was also too proud to argue or beg? Anyway I turned to the back, knowing that I was committing myself to ten days in that tent with a Buddha, probably without seeing him once, and, hey, that was all right, I could hear.

It was my belief in the power of acceptance that made it all right. Once you learn to accept, you have no fear of the tyranny. You disarm the tyrant by making him your agent of progress. Slowly you let go of everything except your awareness, and the smile that comes from knowing that you cannot be beaten. Each time that you do that, effortlessly everything falls into place.

So it was on that day. Suddenly everyone was standing up. They must have seen Khyentse at some entrance to the vast arena. I gazed at what was going to be a ten-day panorama of the backs of strange heads. The next moment, a space was opening where I was standing and his throne was about to be pushed by, directly before my eyes. I would see him after all, and much closer than if I was sitting up front. I said to myself, 'With what amazing precision things align themselves, once you stop grasping and simply allow them to happen.'

Then the brilliant red and gold throne, pushed by young lamas, was coming my way. It had a high back and the back was towards me. Khyentse passed by within inches, without me catching a glimpse. 'There's one for your smugness,' I laughed at myself.

The next day I positioned myself on the opposite side of the corridor of people. This time I would see him. The throne approached, but they'd turned it around so that again its back was towards me. I wasn't sure whether to laugh or to cry. A conspiracy of events was teasing me, was plucking its tune on the strings of my ego. I realised that it was all the display of this greatest teacher on Earth, and ultimately it was all the work of my mind. I was still grasping. I was still grasping to see him. It was up to me to give up. I said it aloud, 'Give up.'

At that moment, as if in slow-motion, the young lamas swung the throne through one hundred and eighty degrees. Furthermore, they left it there and walked across the marquee to fix the way to the stage. Khyentse Rinpoche was facing me, a giant golden Buddha, two metres away. The crowd surged forward with a gasp, pushing me until I was pressed against the front of the throne. I'd been tightly positioned by the light-dance of phenomena, exactly in front of him, with his face half a metre from mine. It was precisely the distance that I needed to be, in order to see him.

It was an incident outside the reach of this ordinary time of the sun. Some far-away note from a single-chord song of antiquity hummed in the vastness of now. Aeons of uncertainties shimmered in space, and flashed away like a shoal of fish, caught in the light of the moonrise. Gone was all doubt, gone were my thoughts and the tight little bundles that bound me. The very moment that I gave up on seeing the Buddha, I saw him.

Then a number of times in the following days, Sogyal Rinpoche arranged for me to be with the master. I sat in his personal tent while the young tulkus practised with him in the evening. Tibetan chanting was ebbing and flowing, like prayer streamers blown on a breeze. The syllables swung in from unknown horizons to wipe out stray fragments of you. They washed away residual resistance and gave you a ride through luminous space, beyond this limited sliver of humdrum perception, and brought you to rest in the yellow silk tent of the Buddha.

I was in the place beyond the harsh floodlight of thinking that bounces around projected objects to give the illusion of seeing. It was not good, for being good there would, somewhere, have to be badness. Good and bad were too gross for the subtle domain of this realm that had opened. Butter lamps flickered, incense smoke curled and there was nothing to want and nothing to fear. Being was simply a matter of breathing, or ceasing to breathe, and there was no difference or need to discuss it. In that mountain retreat with Khyentse, he showed us the flash of a crystal in starlight that had escaped, long ago, from the golden age of Tibet.

After Khyentse had left, a tsok feast offering was prepared. We practised all day and, when it was over, people headed for the tables of food. You took something and sat in the evening sun. Not caring for the scramble, I was usually one of the first to leave. On this occasion, I was overtaken by Brian McMahon. With a wicked grin, he flashed a bottle that had come from the feast, which was fine as long as he shared it. He said, 'It's Chartreuse; made in these mountains and coloured green for the Irish.'

Brian was accompanied by three happy men from the island.

We found a table and he poured five generous slugs into five paper cups. Unfortunately, the English turned up, to ruin the party again. This time it was Gilbert. 'This stuff is not for you bloody Irish to get drunk on,' he said. 'It's to be shared around, a small taste for everyone here.' So saying, he produced thirty paper cups in a tube and dramatically slapped them down, one at a time, on the table. Taking our five cups, he splashed their contents into the thirty that he'd laid out. The Irish looked on in dismay. There was a miserable smear of green in the bottom of every container. 'Does he think we're bloody homeopaths?' one of the Irish enquired. Gilbert walked away, satisfied that he'd taught the rabble how to behave. We split the cups into five groups of six, and each poured our six into one. 'Why do the English always make everything so complicated?' asked Brian as we drank.

On the last day of the retreat, a young lama called Dzigar Kongtrul gave an inspiring address. This lama became a good friend of Dzogchen Beara and still comes to teach us almost each year.

Back in West Cork, I was working in my hole in the cliff when a figure appeared, high against the sky on the hillside above me.

'You're a brave man, Peter Cornish.' The voice told me that this was Jack, one of the architects who'd drawn up our plans before the plug had been pulled. He'd now moved to Lerab Ling, the new centre in France.

'Oh yeah?' I replied politely, trying not to disguise my disdain.

'Because you're still working away,' he said. 'You must know that Dzogchen Beara is yesterday's news. Nothing will happen here now, and yet you keep working.'

I didn't reply, not wishing to encourage the prophet. Had I told him that, if necessary, I'd continue to do it all on my own, he'd only have laughed. So I ignored him, but it was a moment that I wouldn't forget. Perhaps no one had put it so bluntly before.

He turned away, unaware that there were no words that could have encouraged me more.

And so I worked through the wildest of autumns. Storms hammered the mountain, but compared to the negativity of people, mere weather was a piece of cake.

It was at this time that Harriet found a lump in her breast. She went to her doctor and was greatly relieved when he said that it was merely hormonal. She relaxed and enjoyed the children and we found time, each day, to practise together.

For me, awareness of a level beyond the mundane continuously made everything possible. More than ever, the ups and downs and blown-away dreams were events taking place at arm's length. If I stood far enough off I could view, with little attachment, the dramas that shrunk in importance with distance.

As I worked, homeless thoughts hopped about like hares of the cliff tops. Illusory reality hovered like a mist-shrouded moon and waned as the evidence mounted. Experience had, long since, disproved the solidity of all that is taken for granted, as I'd followed the clues that dissolve the images' limits.

It seemed to me that ephemeral projections arise in the mirror of mind. We inhabit a dream that seems so real to the dream dreamers that dream it. All that we see is no more than a product of the eternal housework of the senses; tidying and polishing traces left over from yesterday's party.

In this way, we project the ordinary world with our ordinary mind, and believe it. That dingy realm is a lie dictated by need. The cataracts of necessity have clouded our eyes to the radiant truth. It would be unproductive to wander our spaces, seeing things as they are. We need to build shelters, produce food, and spawn the new generation. So we navigate with no more than a shorthand plan for survival. This is the reality that we have created. Every time we get punched in the face, we *know* that it's real. So solid have we made our world that it actually hurts.

So, round we go, glimpsing no more than a glimmer of what's going on. In order to cope, we've invented a rigid environment to replace the dazzling array. The dream is so strong and we're so soundly asleep that we're lost without trace in the mischief.

I sat on the slopes washed by tides of light from the vast expanse. To slip from the tethers of reason I'd need to relax like this great milk ocean in movement. Then I'd know that it's not a matter of ordinary mind versus somewhere else better to get to. Not two separate states called samsara and nirvana, mundane perception versus innate awareness, or relative and absolute truth. Not really a matter of dark and a light in the darkness. It's only like that in the everyday state, when you're blinded by concepts and thinking. Which means of course, from where I'm standing immersed in words, it's exactly like that. But from the point of view of intrinsic awareness it's all one in the great perfection which is our nature. The wise masters explained that to me, but I'm much too unaware to truly perceive the non-duality of awareness and all of this, its radiant display.

26

Letting Go

Harriet moved out of our home at Centre House, prior to our handing it over. She and the children moved into Lynch's, while I continued to live in the Skyliner basement. The charity would receive the original farm of a hundred and fifty acres, the farmhouse, the five new cottages and Centre House, each with all of its contents. There were many items that we couldn't afford to replace: our library of philosophical, spiritual and self-sufficiency books, and my sound equipment which would be required to amplify talks. The Centre even needed our vacuum cleaner, so I bought us a broom.

Harriet worried constantly that her lump might be cancer. She went again to the doctor who ordered no tests but assured her that it was benign.

In spring I went to see the Dalai Lama in Dublin and later received some exciting news. A revered and realised master, Dodrupchen Rinpoche, who'd spent many years in retreat, was soon to visit the West. I'd asked that he should teach at Dzogchen Beara, and now we heard that he could come in July. Of course, the committee said 'no'. It wasn't enough notice, the houses were full and the air fares were too much. I said that Dodrupchen was one of the greatest living lamas of Tibet, and 'no' was no option. Living simply in Sikkim, he now devoted his life to supporting his monastery of hundreds of monks. There was no money there, the paint was peeling, there were no shiny artefacts, without even a throne he sat on the floor to teach. His simplicity set the perfect example.

We should take a leaf from the Dodrupchen book, and have faith. Secretly, I too was concerned. While Buddhist teachers received no fee, the custom was for each centre to pay the incoming air fares. And it wasn't just him. He'd come with Sogyal Rinpoche, another great lama called Alak Zenkar Rinpoche, and an attendant.

But of course, as happens in dreams, everything fell into place. A week before they were due to arrive, one cottage booking was cancelled. Another two of the houses had been rented by a French yoga group. On hearing that a great teacher was coming, they offered to squeeze into one house and sleep on the floor, to free the other for us.

And the cash appeared, as it always did, just enough for our needs with nothing left over. Dodrupchen Rinpoche walked the land and stood on the western cliffs at the place called Dooneen Point. He said that Dzogchen Beara manifested all of the signs for a special site of samadhi meditation, and was an extension of one of the twenty-four sacred places.

As we practised Rigdzin Dupa, Tibetan ritual music pounded out over the ocean. It blew open the turnstiles where you pay for each moment with the out-of-date coinage of previous thinking. It urged you to let go of all of that stuff of the human condition; waving goodbye, like the unconcerned child, with no concept of goodbye or tomorrow. It kept shaking you, waking you up to the carefree responsibility that comes with the knowledge that there's no one to blame, because *you* are the person that bore you.

Inspired by stories from the Land of Snows, I longed again to practise alone in silent retreat. It seemed so appropriate and obvious for me to do that. Empowered by that longing, my mind surfed on ripples that spread from implosions of handed-down concepts. I was filled with relief that I'd done enough practical stuff. Others could take on the physical dream and the political anguish of pushing it into existence. I wanted one thing in the world. To go to my hut, sit down, and practise in front of a candle.

On Dodrupchen's last night in Ireland, I had a high-definition dream that put paid to all that. It handed me a shovel, blew out the candle and ordered the next years of my life.

I dreamt that I walked to my hut to start my retreat. I found that it had spread out over the mountain, into a large, flat-roofed, Tibetan-style building. It was on the very edge of the cliff, like the Tiger's Nest in Bhutan. Stepping stones led across a pool of water lilies to a door in the rock, and a dark tunnel. A second door opened into an explosion of light from an inner garden. It seemed to represent the emergence from the womb of delusion into a new life of awakening mind.

The garden was green and moist, in a rock-scape of mosses and ferns. There was a cliff, over which a waterfall fell to a pond of wild iris and goldfish. It was a place for individual retreats, full of flowers and birdsong that echoed the distant sound of some sacred refrain. Someone who I couldn't see was talking to me.

'First do this for others. You're not ready yet for retreat.' There was an exquisite scent in the air, and a calm that had halted the passage of time.

I awoke from the dream knowing that I wasn't strong enough to really put others before me. At the same time, I knew that I could no longer keep my secret hut to myself. The dream made it clear that I'd have to start building all over again. I spent half an hour shouting half-hearted 'nos' at the morning, while plans were already evolving. At least the new place would be built on the land that we'd kept aside from the charity, so that it couldn't be stopped in its tracks by a contemptuous committee. I struggled for a few more days and then I gave up. I had no option but to delay my aspiration to retire into spiritual practice, and start to build what I'd seen in the dream.

Of course there was no money, nor any doubt that the money

would come. I'd always been provided with just enough cash, in the same way that I'd been provided with just enough eyesight. If I'd received a surfeit of either, I'd have got lost in distraction.

The making of blocks in plastic washing-up bowls had been all right for my hut, as had my dragging bags of cement up the mountain. The new building, however, would need a track for the delivery of ready-made concrete blocks. So, in the summer of '91, I hired a digger to cut a new route through the rocks. Dick and Ann, a couple from England, came over to help and we started work.

Harriet was happy that she'd moved into Lynch's. She enjoyed the comparative seclusion, after five years of sharing our home with anyone passing through. She was worried because her lump had grown larger. In December, she decided to risk a third trip to the doctor and, this time, he told her that it was probably cancer.

Harriet had the operation and was recovering in hospital. On visiting one day, I found that they'd moved her into a private room. I asked her how she'd arranged it. With a coy smile, she said that they considered her a little disruptive.

'Oh God, Hatsie, come on, what did you do?'

'The surgeon came in like God, with a gaggle of students,' she said. I'd met this man who'd learnt his bedside manner from a textbook on self-satisfaction.

'He *told* me to undo my nightdress and show these children the scar where my breast had been. I asked him if he was totally insensitive. Didn't he think that he might have the courtesy to ask my permission, before making an exhibit of me?'

'What did he say?' I could hear my smile as I asked her.

'He told me to behave myself. I couldn't believe the patronising arrogance of the man.'

'Oh oh. Then what happened?' I asked.

'I told him to fuck off and take his poor students with him. He could set them a bad example at some other victim's expense, and come back when he'd learnt a few manners.'

I thought, 'That's my girl,' and, 'That's what you get from

failing to recognise the radiance of such a free spirit as Harriet.'
She dared to say what the rest of the world was thinking. Her
behaviour was perfect, especially considering her treatment
at the hands of the medicine men. She couldn't tolerate the
ignorance that deluded anyone into believing that they mattered
more than anyone else. I said that it was a great way of getting
a room to yourself. She told me that she'd try to behave because
she disliked solitary confinement and would rather be back in the
public ward.

With the initial trauma behind her, Harriet handled the
situation with grace. She got through the chemotherapy and
then it was spring. She practised at her shrine and worked in the
garden. I continued to build the conservatory, around which
the new retreat rooms would grow when the cash came to hand.
People asked how I built walls without being able to see the
bubble in a spirit-level. I told them that the only gadgets you
need are a plumb-line and a horizon. All of the land had a clear
view of the ocean. I worked with my back to the north and laid
blocks against the line where the sky meets the water. It was free,
it was easy, and I got some interesting effects when the sea-mist
blew in.

When I wasn't building, or helping Harriet, I was trying to
get the solicitor to work on the charitable trust. It had been on his
desk for four years. Again and again I rang him, and each time
he promised to have it completed forthwith. I was determined
to have the charity set up by midsummer and he was equally
determined that I should not. To my nagging, his brilliant
response was worthy of a Tibetan sage, and it silenced my cry of
despair. 'We have a saying around here,' said the lawyer. 'If you
wait long enough, everything becomes irrelevant.' How could I
argue with that? I began to have dreams about chaining myself
to the railings in Ely Place. In the interests of my credibility, I
refrained from telling him that I wanted the work completed for
the tenth day of the monkey month of the monkey year. Or that
this was the most auspicious day in the Tibetan calendar and came

only once in twelve years. So I gave him the equally obscure but recognised version that came out of Africa, via a Pope, and was called 8 August 1992.

Meanwhile, at Lerab Ling on its plateau in the South of France, the three-month retreat had started in June. I thought of the obstacles that had prevented it from happening at Dzogchen Beara. The groan of the committee when I'd announced it, Harriet's intervention and the official excuse of rain in an Irish summer.

Reports began to filter through that it was pouring in France. Rain and more rain, and orders being placed for hot water bottles for those stuck in the mud of the tents. It had been raining non-stop for five weeks and we were exhausted from trying not to smile.

I had to telephone Ato Rinpoche who was coming to Dzogchen Beara for our summer retreat. His wife, Alethea, picked up the telephone in Cambridge. The lamas said that she was like Harriet. They'd both attended the same Kensington primary school.

'How is the retreat going in the South of France?' Alethea knew the whole story.

'It's been lashing with rain for five weeks,' I replied.

'And how is the weather in Ireland?'

'There's a drought. Not a cloud in the sky for a month. We're having a heat-wave.'

Alethea chuckled. She was aware of my disappointment that the retreat had gone to France, although it had been intended for Dzogchen Beara. She responded, in her emphatic and beautifully enunciated Kensington English.

'Now Peter. You know *exactly* what you must do. You must look most *terribly* dignified and say *absolutely* nothing at all.'

Harriet noticed a small dark patch in her field of vision and knew that the cancer had spread. She went for laser treatment in Cork and more chemotherapy. She continued to work in her garden, listen to Mozart and follow her spiritual practice. In between, we were up and down to Cork for hospital visits. A good friend, Andrew Warr, who was running the hostel, drove us and helped, with never a thought for himself.

Harriet said that dying was no problem but she was damned if she was going to go bald. 'It's hard enough trying to play the tragic heroine without an appreciative audience,' she said, 'never mind doing so without any hair.' And throughout the various chemotherapy sessions, she kept all of her long dark locks.

After continual phone calls to Dublin and the passing of numerous deadlines, the solicitor finally dispatched the deeds of the Dzogchen Beara Trust. We just had to sign them and the dream would become a reality-dream. A clearing in time, where others might use our arena of uncluttered elements to stand on the edge and take a deep breath. To see that we're possessed by our desire to possess, though there's nothing to possess but a dream. I signed the Deed of Trust and gave it to Harriet. She knew that it meant the giving away of almost all that we owned. Everything that we'd worked for. The houses and roads that we'd built and the woods that we'd planted. Our peace, our dream, and our stewardship of a few free acres of Ireland.

People often asked what it was like, watching others take over and re-direct your work of a lifetime. I said that it would happen anyway, once you had died, and I was just letting go early. Meanwhile, it was like giving up your baby for adoption, and then having to go and live with the adoptive parents.

Harriet read the document, kept it for a while and signed it. And so it was that, on 8 August 1992, Dzogchen Beara became a registered charity. It was the fruition of the first stage of the project that, almost twenty years earlier, had led us to the Beara Peninsula.

A large gathering heard three Tibetan lamas teach in a tent on a Bantry Bay field. I rolled the Deed of Trust, tied it with a ribbon of red silk and handed it over for the trustees to sign it. Harriet spoke to Sogyal Rinpoche, Ato Rinpoche and Ringu Tulku. She said that she was happy and ready to die.

We both felt that the sanctity of the place was assured by the Deed of Trust. I was impressed by the fact that Sogyal Rinpoche, as spiritual director, had always encouraged me to invite other teachers of any tradition. It was vital that the place should remain open, relaxed and accessible to all.

It had been one of those days with the sun at a dance on the ocean. We practised in the prolonged lack of difference between the radiant day and inner light breaking free. In the evening, we celebrated with a tsok-offering feast, and lit one thousand and eighty candles. Later, I walked back through the dusk to the tent. The large crowd of people had dispersed and left the evening alone and for me. Prayer flags hung limp on their poles, with all their work done, and the rose-coloured bay was a mirror of silence. A long journey was over, and the world was at rest in the space at the end of the action.

In the warm summer twilight, I lifted a flap of the tent and sat by the glow of the thousand candles. A fluster of events, like startled pigeons, clattered away to the past and a door clicked shut in the sky behind them. What had to be done was all done. There was no joy or sorrow, no hope or regret. There was only the all-pervading peace which is there in our nature, once we slow down and let everything trickle away. I sat there at ease on the plain that pans out beyond the cliff-edge of emotion; beyond the relief that arises when wind of weeks past has abated, and agitation is subsumed in the stillness.

It was time to move from the Skyliner basement and return to Lynch's, the better to take care of Harriet. At Christmas she took to her bed, having accepted that she was to die. She was usually in good spirits as she continued the slow letting go. She covered the walls by her bed with cards from admirers and friends, and practised in front of her shrine. She had many visitors but was clear about who she would see. She said that she'd settled her mind-stream and didn't want it ruffled by sightseers. Strong, resolute, coming up trumps in a crisis, she was better at handling her death than her life. She said, 'So-called reality is a piece of cake, it's the rest of it that catches you out.'

Each morning, I took her breakfast in bed and we talked until she grew tired. We pulled on our waterproofs and went wading about in our lives, pointing out flashes of silver. We saluted influences that had brought us to play out our charade on a clifftop in Beara. We talked of poets and karma and Padmasambhava, and what to do once you are dead.

At some point, Harriet might have to move to the hospice in Cork. She disliked the Victorian institution where people were dying, in rows, to piped music and a televised football match. It robbed them of dignity and stole their last rights to serenity at this most important moment of all. However, the nurses were angels of grace, and Doctor O'Brien reassured Harriet with his warm-hearted awareness. He asked what we could do to enable her to move into the hospice. I said that we'd need a single room with no television. We'd remove any gloomy old furnishings, hang Tibetan thangkas, put down rugs, and play sacred music at no more than a whisper. Furthermore, we'd want her left undisturbed for several hours after she'd died. I explained that we'd try to create a sacred environment of colour and light, because it's said that what's in your mind-stream as you die will influence what happens to you next. The good doctor agreed to all of our many conditions.

Meanwhile, Harriet was back and forth to the hospital and the children were boarding in Waterford. Tom had just started and Flora was about to sit her final exams. They came to Cork for the first weekend in June. We stayed at a friend's house in Montenotte and Harriet joined us on Sunday. Flora was swotting for the exams which she'd start the following week. I bought some food that I could cook for lunch, but Harriet insisted on cooking it all herself. She knew that this would be the last time that she'd take care of her children.

Back in Beara the nursing became more difficult, but friends gathered round and we coped. Finally, it became impossible for

Harriet to swallow her pills. I met with the district nurse and our friend, Doctor Geraldine Osborne. It was with sadness that we decided that we had to move her to Cork but, as it turned out, Harriet's death in that hospice was to be her last gift for the benefit of others.

On calling for the ambulance, I was told that, due to insurance restrictions, no husbands or wives were permitted to travel with the patients. I was able to overcome this inhumane nonsense with quiet insistence. It was easy in Ireland, where people still came before rules. Had I not been there, Harriet would have felt completely abandoned, as she rode alone to her death. As it was, I knelt for almost a hundred miles on the floor by Harriet's side, because the barbaric system allowed no seat for the next-of-kin.

On arrival at the hospice we were shown to a room, through double doors, at the end of a passage. Our friends, Bernadette and Penny, had followed us up with Harriet's things. We set about transforming the room. Removing the furniture, we spread oriental rugs and cushions on the floor. We hung brocade-framed paintings of Buddhas on the walls, and yellow curtains in the window for the light to shine through and turn the grey walls to gold. In the gap between them, we hung cut-glass spheres to fill the room with rainbow light. We lit candles and incense, assembled her shrine, and surrounded it with vases of lilies and roses. The dingy grey room had become a celestial realm.

When all was prepared and Harriet slept, Bernadette and Penny sat in silence on the rugs. Over the next days there was always someone sitting quietly in practice. I spent the nights on the floor, and each night the kindly old matron would look in and, thinking that I slept, tiptoe over to blow out the candles.

It was early morning when the doctor told me that Harriet had only a few hours to live. Bernadette and Penny returned and sat quietly on the rugs in practice. We'd made a tape of Harriet's favourite Tibetan chants. It included the Dalai Lama, Karmapa and other great masters. This played softly over and over. A great peace had settled on the room. Even the incense smoke, as it curled through the roses, seemed to say that it was all right. Friends came in without speaking, sat in silence and left. Sometimes the nurses would come and stand by the bed to whisper a prayer.

Then someone came to get me from the telephone, saying that Harriet's breathing had changed. I knelt by the bed and placed my mala in her hand.

The whole room felt so sacred that 'practice' seemed irrelevant, almost irreverent. I united my breathing with hers. In a timeless space beyond sorrow or pain, thoughts rose and subsided without meaning. Small events splashed like drops of rain on a far-away windowpane. The Dalai Lama started to chant the mandala offering. This seemed so perfectly appropriate at that moment. Harriet's whole life was an offering for the preservation of the ancient wisdom and now, so too was her death. Then the sun came out to shine through the crystals that stirred in a summer breeze. It spread dancing showers of rainbow light around Harriet's head on the pillow. Time lapped without passing on the limitless shores of existence. In the silence of a peace beyond words, there had settled a stillness within which the whole universe had come slowly to rest. Harriet gave three long and gentle out-breaths. Her final out-breath coincided exactly with the last long syllable and the chanting ceased.

All of that day, people came and went, bringing flowers and sitting in silence. Sometimes the nurses would join us. It all seemed so natural and right. Alone with Harriet, that night, I thought of how far we'd gone wrong with our denial of dying. We'd developed a culture where possessions are everything, and losing has become a disgrace. To lose even the body that you live in is the final humiliation. Such a failure has no place in the American Dream that has so distorted our thinking.

We have to change things, I thought, as the matron came in to blow out the candles. We have to begin to see death as the successful end of our latest instruction. Later, we'll see the ultimate purity and perfection of everything, which is but a reflection of our inner nature. At that time, it won't matter where we are or what happens to us. But until that time, environment is vital. Having created this sacred space for Harriet and ourselves, the practice almost practised itself. How sad and lonely we would have felt, had Harriet died in a cold grey ward, had a sheet pulled quickly over her face and been wheeled away to the fridge.

All of the staff came to me, at various intervals, some of them with tears in their eyes, all of them saying that they couldn't believe the sense of peace in that room. They thanked us for allowing them to be there. They said that the warmth seemed to spread out to the whole of the hospice. They found that they kept making excuses to come in, and they hoped that they hadn't disturbed us. Disturbed us? Oh yes, they'd disturbed us all right. They'd disturbed us with their serenity, with their loving kindness and compassion. They'd taken our hearts and wrapped them in grace. They'd reminded us of the deep-down goodness of all who exist.

27

Into the Vast Expanse

In a shrinking world it had seemed right to build on a remote shore of the western ocean. Now Harriet's death made me wonder again, had we strayed too far from the world? Everything began to feel pointless. Those facile arguments about the shape of tomorrow with good people whose main fault was no more than a different view. I was exhausted by our intransigence as we preached flexibility but refused to budge even an inch. It seemed that my ego-dream had contributed nothing but a little more suffering.

I needed to stop digging the mountain and allow the dust to settle. It's the busy-ness that makes us stare too hard at the fluorescing panorama that our staring keeps turning to stone. If we wish to see, we must learn to gaze without looking. As I unwound my mala from Harriet's cold fingers, I felt that I needed to cut the string and let the beads fly in their own directions.

It is said that, after death, you remain in the 'bardo' for a while before your propensities coalesce into a different form. This state has no fixed duration, but traditionally is said to last for forty-nine Earth-days. Practices are performed for the dead, until the last day, when a concluding ceremony takes place.

Harriet's forty-ninth day fell on the date of the birth of Padmasambhava, and the first anniversary of Dzogchen Beara becoming a charity. Two days later was Flora's eighteenth birthday. She, Tom and I decided to go to the Skellig Islands. We invited her friend, Daisy, and Andrew Warr. It would be a pilgrimage to a place in Harriet's heart. It entailed a three-hour drive to western-most Kerry and a boat trip out into the ocean.

The visit to that holy island of Skellig Michael became a spiritual experience which inspired me to continue the work. It answered my question about the necessity of being so remote. Seeing where the early Christians had built *their* retreat, on a shard of slate, took my petty issues and dumped them into the waves.

We carried a cake with eighteen candles to celebrate the coming of age of a radiant girl, and as an offering of homage to a secret door in the fabric.

The fisherman said that the sea was too rough but, because we'd travelled so far, he would risk it. It was a dangerous crossing in a small wooden boat and no one else would go out in that swell, so we'd have the island to ourselves.

A stiff breeze with a drizzle blew us out of the harbour. Heading up the coast, it took a while to reach the open ocean and when we did, we knew it. The skipper gave us a tarpaulin because spume from the crests was blowing into the open boat. The girls clung to the rail and the birthday cake, as the land slipped away in the mist. Each time that a giant wave approached, the skipper cut back the engine and turned the boat to face it. We'd ride the wave and then head on to nowhere in the now driving rain. We saw a storm petrel flying along a trough, but knew that this bird has no need for land. Then, Tom pointed out a vertical black triangle in the wave-scape beyond the bow.

We pulled in to a sort of jetty, on the lee side of Skellig Michael. It was above our heads at one moment, and below our knees the next. Each time the shore came level with the deck, the skipper shouted 'Jump'. And as we jumped, the sun split the clouds and we passed through today, into a different dimension. We'd leapt from the cold grey world of our mourning, onto an island set like a diamond, in the clasp of an ocean of darkness.

The fisherman laid off from the rocks and left us in the stillness of a wind stripped of its motion by a suddenly radiant day.

A flight of seven hundred steps led up the rock to the old retreat huts perched on a shelf in the sky. Sea campions covered the island, like a summertime dusting of snow. All kinds of seabirds crowded the ledges with their young, and everywhere, eye-deep in flowers, were puffins tamed by centuries of an absence of humans with guns.

We climbed to the beehive huts; a retreat centre built in the West of Ireland at about the time that Buddhism arrived in Tibet. Those heroic builders were well aware of the vital role of the stillness. They'd left us their inspirational buildings as a sign; still standing after fifteen hundred years in the teeth of the North Atlantic.

So calm was the day now, that we sat on the doorstep of one of the huts and lit the eighteen candles. It was a momentary link in the chain of aspiration that races like quicksilver through the arteries of the ages.

I couldn't express the profound effect of that place. I caught a glimpse of the garden from which we've banished ourselves with our greed. I witnessed a serene display of the harmony that is everywhere, until we humans start meddling. It was a turning point and I laughed at its split-second timing. It seemed a typical miracle that we'd found the isle at that moment. How the sun had come flashing through as we jumped into the magic. How we'd been offered the whole place to ourselves. The island had appeared at the moment that I had the thought of giving up. It inspired me to continue. To stop questioning the validity of our new retreat, a few miles and fifteen centuries along the coast from this display of intrinsic perfection.

On our return trip to Portmagee, we passed a flotilla of visitors headed for the rock, now that the sun was shining.

A few weeks later Flora received the results of the seven exams that she'd sat on either side of her mother's funeral. She'd achieved such high grades that she could do anything. She chose psychology and, at the end of that long sad summer, she started at Trinity, while Tom went back to school. I sorted through Harriet's things in Lynch's, alone in the room where, two decades before, we'd slept with the rain blowing onto the bed, while we burnished our dreams of a world set free from its grasping.

Harriet had left few possessions. Before she died she'd even sent back the ring that Aunt Jean had given her for her twenty-first birthday. It was an exquisite gold-mounted scarab from the tomb of King Tutankhamun. It had been auctioned to help pay for the expedition. She'd never worn it because it had made her uneasy. 'Sod the curse of the Pharaohs,' she'd said. 'It's uncool to wear something that was stolen from somebody's grave.' Her unoffended aunt re-auctioned the ring and gave the proceeds to charity.

After a while I reminded myself that Harriet had moved on. Having discarded her body she'd become free to fly. Fly from this tiny island of thought, in the out-flung arm of a spiral of stars that spins for a moment in space. Fly, to re-arise somewhere in the infinite arena of time-scapes of the mind that, on arrival, instantly turns into home. I reminded myself that this clifftop, where she once touched down for a while, had been blessed by her presence, and was already no more than some station that flashed by on her journey.

Now I had time to assess my position. How far I'd travelled; how little I'd learnt on the way. At least I'd learnt that the absolute cannot be realised through exertions of mind in its fairy-tale realm of conditioned perception. I'd learnt that the ultimate role for ordinary mind is to be receptive and still.

As a child, I'd gazed on Gauguin's painting of the three questions. I was drawn to its mystery, filled with resolve to find out.

'Where do we come from?' the artist asked first. I sat on the cliff catching stray thoughts, blown on the breeze of a lifetime's reflection. It might be said that these flickering structures of carbon-based being have evolved along links of luminous chains in the vast expanse of our cells. We trace them back past our slither from a primal sea; back through the star-dust of long-gone galaxies that revolve in the mirror of mind. As we struggle to identify some sort of beginning, we're teased by the elusive display that recedes as we chase it. It's only the ordinary mind that requires a beginning. And it's the refined labours of this ordinary mind that deliver the answer that our self-conceived forms are continuously born from the womb of our ongoing action. That's the ordinary and obvious conclusion. The real answer lies beyond thought and our concept of successive events, and is only approached through absolute stillness.

'Who are we?' Gauguin asked next. Having recognised it all as a dream, I'd accepted the ancient assertion that we've imagined this self and its playground. Research and various insights convinced me that we are intrinsically perfect, but have strayed away to confusion. In this realm of confusion we are, at any given moment, the sum total of all that we've ever spoken or done, or dreamt with our wandering mind-stream. This ordinary mind and its manifested body represent the temporary result, which we change with every new thought, word and action. In this state of continuous flux, we flutter about in search of the person who comes to life only when we give up looking and settle completely.

'And whither do we go?' came the painter's third question, as I watched the morning star fade into light. It appeared to me that we lurch along an infinite variety of individual routes to perfection. Our personal past has intimately tailored a self for our needs. Everything that occurs is our guru. If we react against instructive phenomena, we move down one grade to learn the lesson again. If we accept and learn, we move on, eventually to unite with the light like that star of the morning. Acceptance of everything that happens, as a teaching, is the thought that flicks the negative switch onto positive. It imbues even our suffering with purpose and lessens the pain. This acceptance is not the resentful acceptance of our lot; the partial acceptance which leads to enslavement. It is absolute acceptance, even of slavery, which guarantees freedom from these tyrants of ours, that roam the days of the dream.

I sat and watched dawn fling streamers of possibility into the lightening sky. As surely as light spreads westwards into the darkness, confusion is dispelled by the slow letting go. I watched the flotsam of mental events wash in and out of the caverns of mind. I might fish out a few flapping solutions, but the real answer swims in clarity beyond the ebb and the flow. It comes into focus as tension departs and we relax into luminous stillness.

The artist didn't include the fourth question, which is surely, 'How do we get there?' We might need a teacher for that. I can only mutter with the ignorance of one who's passed decades without reading a book. Whose thoughts must be judged as unqualified interpretations of the words of various masters. As meagre gleanings from fragments of experience, and a few whispers picked up from the wind.

As a schoolboy, on watch by the hedgerows of dawn, I'd learnt that you cannot traverse the gossamer field with your boots on. Beyond the day-to-day bluster of survival mind, there had to be a subtler way.

Perhaps the first step is to ascertain that there's actually somewhere to get to. For me, early hints of a hidden reality made me aware that something was missing from life on the surface. Unable to join the games of my schooldays, I stood outside and gazed at the wild charade. Then, drifting alone in the unpeopled places, I came across corridors into the magic. Slowly I learnt that they led, not to some alternative haven, but straight to the heart of each new perception.

I saw that there are no realms other than this one. No hidden heavens or hells underground. No innumerable dimensions or different realities to aim for or run from. There's actually only one reality; one reality per person. It's just that we perceive no more than the slightest sliver of a wafer-thin wedge of its wealth.

It was this realisation that convinced me that there *is* somewhere to get to, that that 'somewhere' is our true nature, and that we're already there, once we totally open our minds.

And all of the while, events kept flexing assumptions until I queried it all. A lesson from a primary school teacher was underlined by the Buddha who told us to take *nothing* for granted. To question even his words, until we make them our own. By questioning each supposition, we slowly dismantle the stuffy museum and plough the field where it stood. The first seeds of awareness can then take root in the open ground, from which we've cleared the debris of handed-down concepts.

How futile is our constant manipulation of phenomena for personal gain when they don't exist, except in a state of perpetual decomposition. How foolish our attempts to create solid structures in the dance of the flickering network. We need to stand back and allow the initial glimpses to stretch like these ribbons of dawn that keep turning the darkness to sky. To realise that the ultimate act of creativity is the creation of space. Space that allows the flow of the subtle, as solidified perception gives way to pristine awareness.

The great Longchenpa put it like this, 'Ordinary mind is what happens when you don't know how to relax.' That says it all. Normally, when we relax we grow sleepy. The true way is the very opposite of that. Utterly relaxed in body, speech and mind, yet wide awake with everything tingling. That's it. That's meditation. It's the secret key that you carry away from 'work-it-out' thinking, to unlock the possibility of total perception.

Far below, the first birds of morning were flying the coast in search of a breakfast. Answers from the ordinary mind only lead us to further questions. Like, why should the endless pulses of beings be so plagued by their suffering? Could it be that pain is required to tell us that something is wrong? Without suffering, would we not fall even more soundly asleep? Like the tormented rich, foot-down in Ferraris, racing away from their death who's patiently enjoying the ride in the passenger seat. Without suffering, and awareness of death, would we not just lie, belly-up and bored, in some old garden of a god-realm, sucking mangoes and grinning at the sun?

And then what?

At least the suffering provides an incentive to progress our own release, and the physical relief of those we call 'other'. It wasn't for me to join the front-line heroes, at their tireless endeavour, in the charnel grounds of an African nightmare. Instead, in a vague attempt at intervention, I built a refuge on a cliff in the west. All such efforts are the external and temporary way of sticking a plaster on pain. Complementary to this, the inner way is the leading of a simple life of spiritual practice, dedicated to the benefit of all.

Our situation suggests that we need to stall this habitual racing from thought to thought, in a headlong dash towards death. If we're to loosen the bonds of confusion, we need to learn to be still. It's by allowing the arising of the peace of innate awareness that we can bring peace to the world. The monks of the Skellig Islands knew that. In these times of near-total distraction, it becomes increasingly unacceptable to practise retreat, and increasingly vital to do so. After all, when being still you cause no harm, reduce your use of resources and leave almost no carbon footprint. In the absence of the uproar of continuous thinking, the turbid mind settles and the silent instruction is heard. This is the answer to the fourth question, and I'd truly rejoice if I could begin to live a little like that.

Inspired by Skellig Michael and the Tiger's Nest, I started work on the new building. To pay for it, I sold Lynch's to a friend of Dzogchen Beara. It meant a few more years of lugging blocks and sleeping in workshops, but that was what was, and I loved it.

As a silent retreat, the hassle of the world had to be kept at a distance so, as soon as the building was finished, I'd dig up the road. The Chinese were already driving their own roads over the mountains, into the sacred heart of Tibet. It was robbing the ancient sites of their stillness, violating the last sanctuaries of the earth.

My quest was to promote inspiration by creating an alternative to the noise of the norm. A respite from engines, sirens, media-babble and the chatter-flack of space-threatening mobiles. In doing so, I had to go that bit further. You have to go as far as you dare, then give yourself a shove in the back. I planned to build a few metres from the cliff and then I moved out to the edge. It's like that. You might say that you have to go right to the summit, without going over the top. If you go over the top you come to America and everything turns into Disney. To circumvent such an appearance of a mere facade, I found that one trick was to build with thick walls, and let nature direct their rambling lines. It was an arduous task building along the cliff-edge, bringing foundations up a few metres to floor level, and then back to the parallel cliff behind them.

Sometimes the concrete-trucks would have trouble climbing our track in the rain. Then the driver would reverse his back wheels right up to the edge of the cliff. He'd extend the conveyor into space and spatter a stream of mix onto the site below. The big company refused to deliver saying, once again, that the place was too dangerous. So I found a small firm who had the confidence that comes from needing the business. Again I was grateful for the spirit of those bold Irish drivers, as their near-blind guide waved them back to the uncertain edge of a few hundred foot plunge to the ocean.

And so the work continued. Friends like Neil, Dick and Ann and many visitors from the hostel helped until, on my birthday in November '94, I moved into a half-finished house, as I'd done so many times in the past.

The story goes on but my eyes are becoming less inclined to focus on words. Peering at this page, magnified five-fold on a screen, is stealing what's left of their ability to decipher all this stuff of the world. After this chapter, I have to go back and write the whole book again. I find myself in a race that I may not complete, if my eyesight fails to get me to the final full stop. In that case, the failure of this egotistical attempt to offer a little inspiration might be a relief. Avoiding such an embarrassing expose of my life, I'd simply go back into retreat. How wonderful. And this unfinished work would remain what it already is; just a hopeless attempt to catch, in a net of words, the fleeting shimmer of a shoal of dreams.

As I think about this, I feel such a gratitude for the path that my eyes have led me along, and the way that they've painted my picture. For the experts my eyesight is failing, but for me it's evolving. It may not be so good at objectifying all of this foliage, but apart from that it's inspiring, so I wouldn't change it if they offered me a jet-pilot's eyesight tomorrow. It's not usual to be born without central vision and less usual to be short-sighted at the same time. Forced to look at the world through the side of a lens, I spent a lifetime flicking back and forth, scanning each image to get the best reading. Instant by instant, I sorted alternative displays of phenomena and made up whatever was missing; inventing my reality and reminding myself that I shouldn't believe it.

At the same time, a light-show that emanates from the 'lost' centre illuminated the ordinary world. It dazzled the everyday vision which, when set to 'normal', so bedraggles our version of real. I saw for myself that nothing is solid. I couldn't help but rejoice at the scope of an object's involvement with light; its sparkling, ephemeral nature that denies the delusion of substance. Perhaps that's why I kept grabbing pots of paint, in a futile attempt to cheer up the mundane environment with the rainbow mix of its inner identity. Of course that was fun, but it didn't work because I'd have needed to paint it in light.

And so it was that a career-choice made under threat in a library at school slowly took shape on a rock in the south-west of Ireland. A wind-blasted clifftop transformed itself into a wooded village with gardens. Great teachers were inspired to teach against the backdrop of the vast expanse of the ocean. The Dalai Lama sent a letter of support, while the President of Ireland visited to inaugurate a new Care Centre.

And finally the people came, to assure us that we weren't too remote. They came throughout the year, from all over the world, and often filled local guest houses and farms. They came for seminars and holidays and weekend retreats, and some completed retreats that lasted a year.

Over time, the committee changed and dispersed, and people washed in and out like the cleansing tide on a cluttered strand. And as the early commotion subsided, I saw that each person had made a unique contribution to now. To today, when the Centre is run by the goodwill of many nationalities, inspired by the generosity of its warm Irish heart.

The only outer wish that remains is the one that I came with. To create a small temple here, as an echo from the golden age of Tibet. A container for the precious word that lifts the veils that separate us from our nature. It's thirty years since I planted the trees to provide shelter and permission to build. The trees have grown, permission is granted and, when the cash arrives, if the time is right, we'll build a sanctuary of colour and butter-lamp light, adrift in the fields of splendour. Such a place would indeed make us worthy tenants of this rock, borrowed from time and the seabirds, to create a free-port of the spirit. A clifftop gate to open the minds of all who reach out for the latch.

Now the teachings have been taught, yet still we thrash about in the meniscus. We stare, mesmerised by the allure of its endless display. We've forgotten that, if we're truly still, the quivering surface will settle to reflect the face that no longer belongs to a stranger. The purpose of retreat is to further the quest to become the perfect being that each of us actually is. As a beginner, my own realisation swims in darkness, groping for a glimmer of watery dawn. All that concerns me is the certainty that we can evolve and are evolving, and that is so exciting.

So, in the absence of any possibility of words of wisdom, I'll say a bit about how I live now, in the hope that it might encourage someone who's already sick of competitive consumption.

I live in a small, one-room retreat house, in accordance with my belief that happiness depends on simplicity. I've never used a mobile phone and have no television. I gave up radio whose chatter keeps dragging you back to the terrible playground, to play 'tut-tut' with dreams and nightmares that you fail to recognise as your own. I eat no meat, fish, sugar or dairy products, except if I go out, which is almost never. I rarely touch alcohol and gave up my brief investigation into other mind-altering drugs before I first moved to Ireland. Such substances confuse the natural inspiration of mind and cloud the insights that arise from alert relaxation.

My diet hasn't varied for years. I have cereal for breakfast, a one-course cooked lunch and a handful of raw oats with soya milk for dinner. I drink hot water and occasional tea. It's hard to imagine how delicious water can be, until you've tamed your taste buds and taught them to relax; until they've become de-contaminated from their constant bombardment with chemical sugar. Before long you rejoice at a diet which, for millions, would be an unimaginable feast. When I attempt a meditation retreat, which is conducted alone and in silence, this food is left once a day in my porch. In this way I've passed months at a time without speaking, or seeing a person.

For almost twenty years, I've started my day at two in the morning. It's the best time to practise. You have hours of travelling in a positive curve to the sun, while compassion is readily increased by the thought of a vulnerable world at sleep on its pillow. You cannot help but love us, as we struggle on up with our eyes closed.

If we live alone on a mountain, or in a city, we need this love in our hearts for all that exists. Through spiritual practice in seclusion, this love will steadily grow. On the other hand, should we turn away from the world full of blame and resentment, we'll become a 'loner' whose anger will surely subvert us. We've taken a wrong turning and had better get back to the party. It's all right. That way can lead to an equally radiant path that shrinks our own issues, through the hands-on helping of others.

When Harriet died and the children left, I found that loneliness stalks the planet when the sun goes down. Dusk is when samsara starts to steam up. I found that, if I went to sleep at six, I could by-pass all of that stuff. Loneliness ceased, and I rejoiced in chosen aloneness, which is the elixir from which eventual freedom sips.

Now all of this might sound a bit frugal, but I'm no 'fruge'; not a chance. Frugality implies severity; a tightness of self-denial; the forcing of yourself to give up something you secretly crave. That's no way to overcome self-righteousness; no way to behave; no way to have fun, to be easy and open to joy. The trick is not to give up the object, but to give up desire for the object by seeing it as temporarily illuminated space that you can neither successfully consume nor reject. Otherwise desire is dammed up and you've gained nothing but a dangerous cocktail of grasping and frustration, with judgement like a cherry on a stick. Once you begin to experience the illusory nature of the dance, there comes a natural letting go of all but the most essential. There's no idea of abstinence, nothing heavy going on. You simply cease to want much, and the less that you want, the happier you will become.

It may be a bit tough at first, like giving up sugar in tea, but soon you begin actually to *feel* the freedom. I learnt from Diogenes and the Nymphs of Benitses that this is not frugality, but self-indulgence, through freedom from the chains of indulgence. Indulge your self by wanting less, and what's left becomes more delicious. It's good for you, good for the planet, and it makes you laugh as you tease the doubters that 'Total self-indulgence for the benefit of all' is your personal mantra.

And yet they still call me 'hermit', and even a renunciant. How could I renounce anything, never mind the whole world? What a dualistic concept. Far from renunciation, I've merely lost interest. Lost interest in the dullness. Lost interest in everything but the allowing of awareness and its radiant display. Like the far-away hum of the momentary appearance of an object as it flashes in space. Like this place and this life, that flutter like prayer flags on ribbons of wind. Like this candle that I light in the dark blue stillness of morning, for every mind that wanders time in search of freedom.

And now the sun is rising, dripping pools of liquid light, from a sea that is still shining from the moon. Morning's daughters steal in silence through the dream's remaining traces, to paint silver on the laughing eyes of day. With grace that calms confusion, the velvet curtain rises, and I wake to dream I've woken on the shores of Bantry Bay.

Did we really run through fields of summer lilies in valleys of the mountains that time can find no way across? Did we dance along the banks of the endless streams of meaning, and kneel, terrified and laughing, to drink their diamond waters? Knowing that beyond the opening of the mind, there is nothing to be done, I celebrate the radiance at the heart of everyone.

Alone, attended by the elements, I live in awe of all of this. There's as much self-sacrifice as seagulls feel when they soar the spiral columns of the wind. How could we care for wealth or fame, when our treasuries are stacked with the jewels of infinite potential? So it is with joy that I give up all my dreaming. Except the dream that when this body dies, I'll fly into that vast expanse, from where I'll take whichever turning is of benefit to all of us, as we struggle on our small planets of desire.

Meanwhile, there's nothing left to say. So I spend my time relaxing with the weather, as it rolls in and out of each imagined day.

Glossary

BODHISATTVA: One who is dedicated to working for the benefit of others until all beings are enlightened.

BUDDHA FIELD: Celestial plane on which Buddhas reside.

DAKINI (SKY DANCER): The feminine representation of innate awareness.

DEITIES: Aspects of innate awareness portrayed in statues and paintings and visualised by practitioners as aids to realisation.

DHARMA: The eternal law of the cosmos, inherent in the nature of phenomena. The word of the Buddha.

EMPOWERMENT: A transmission from a realised teacher to authorise a student to engage in a particular practice.

KARMA: The universal law of cause and effect.

LAMA: A teacher of Tibetan Buddhism.

LIBERATION UPON SEEING: The assertion that you can be liberated from the bonds of conceptual mind by the mere sight of a sacred object, script, environment or being.

MALA: A rosary, usually with 108 beads.

MANDALA: Sacred painting or construction that represents the enlightened state.

MANDALA OFFERING: A selection of offerings visualised as the multiverse and all of its contents, offered to the Buddhas for the benefit of all beings.

NIRVANA: Release from the suffering of conditioned existence into enlightenment.

NYINGMA SCHOOL: The oldest school of Tibetan Buddhism focusing on the lineage of Padmasambhava.

NYINGTIK YABSHYI: Core teachings on the practice of Dzogchen, compiled by Longchenpa.

PADMASAMBHAVA: The Vajrayana master who took Buddhist teachings from India to Tibet in the eighth century.

PRAYER FLAGS: Flags of five colours printed with mantras, prayers and images to distribute reminders and blow blessings to all the dimensions of space.

PURE LAND: A location where every object, action and being is imbued with the state of enlightenment.

REALISED MASTER: An adept who has realised and integrated the nature of mind.

RIGDZIN DUPA: A profound practice of the Nyingma school of Tibetan Buddhism.

RINPOCHE: Precious One. An honorific title bestowed on Tibetan lamas.

SADDHANA: A spiritual practice undertaken to achieve eventual enlightenment, i.e. as in Rigdzin Dupa, above.

SAMADHI: A non-dual state of consciousness encountered in deep meditation.

SAMSARA: The relentless cycle of conditioned existence.

TAI SITUPA (AKA SITU RINPOCHE): One of the foremost lamas of the Kagyu school.

THANGKA: A Buddhist scroll depicting a deity, scene or mandala, usually painted on cotton and framed with brocade.

TSOK: Ceremony in which food and drink are consecrated, offered to the embodiments of enlightenment and shared by the participants.

TULKU: An incarnation of a recognised lama.

TWENTY-FOUR SACRED PLACES: Said to exist on various levels of mind/body, and externally as sacred sites in India and the Himalayas.

WISDOM MIND: The innate natural mind released from conceptual bias.

YOGI: An adept who has devoted his or her life to a spiritual practice.

Printed in Great Britain
by Amazon.co.uk, Ltd.,
Marston Gate.